Cory Lebson has been a UX consultant for over two decades. He is the Principal and Owner of a small UX consultancy, a builder of UX community, and a past president of the User Experience Professionals Association (UXPA). Not only a practitioner of UX, Cory teaches and mentors to help professionals grow their UX skills, and conducts regular talks and workshops on topics related to both UX skills and career development.

The UX Careers Handbook

The UX Careers Handbook offers an insider's look at how to be a successful User Experience (UX) professional from comprehensive career pathways to learning, personal branding, networking skills, building of resumes and portfolios, and actually landing a UX job.

This book goes in-depth to explain what it takes to get into and succeed in a UX career, be it as a designer, information architect, strategist, user researcher, or in a variety of other UX career specialities. It presents a wealth of resources designed to help you develop and take control of your UX career success including perspectives and advice from experts in the field.

- **Features insights and personal stories** from a range of industry-leading UX professionals to show you how they broke into the industry and evolved their own careers over time.
- **Accompanied by a companion website** that provides you with featured resources, news, and updated information that will help you stay on top of this fast-paced industry.
- **Provides activities** to help you make decisions and build your own career.

Not only for job seekers! *The UX Careers Handbook* is also a must-have resource for:

- **Employers and recruiters** who want to better understand how to hire and retain UX staff.
- **Undergraduate and graduate students** who are thinking about their future careers.
- **Those in other related (or even unrelated) professions** who are thinking of starting to do UX work.

The UX Careers Handbook

Cory Lebson

Art Center College Library
1700 Lida Street
Pasadena, CA 91103

CRC Press
Taylor & Francis Group
Boca Raton London New York

CRC Press is an imprint of the
Taylor & Francis Group, an **informa** business

A CHAPMAN & HALL BOOK

First published 2016
CRC Press
Taylor & Francis Group
6000 Broken Sound Parkway NW, Suite 300
Boca Raton, FL 33487-2742

CRC Press is an imprint of the Taylor & Francis Group, an informa business

Library of Congress Cataloging-in-Publication Data
Lebson, Cory, author.
  The UX careers handbook / by Cory Lebson.
    pages cm
  1. Human-computer interaction—Vocational guidance.   I. Title.
   QA76.9.H85L45 2016
   004.01'9—dc23
   2015026305

ISBN: 978-1-138-95867-8 (hbk)
ISBN: 978-1-138-90106-3 (pbk)
ISBN: 978-1-315-69772-7 (ebk)

Typeset in Helvetica Neue
by Apex CoVantage, LLC

Printed and bound in India by Replika Press Pvt. Ltd.

Visit the Taylor & Francis Web site at http://www.taylorandfrancis.com,
the CRC Press Web site at http://www.crcpress.com and
the author's Web site at www.uxcareershandbook.com

Contents

Acknowledgments

While you may think that writing a book is an effort of solitude, this effort most certainly was not. Just as this book stresses the value of a professional community for your career, knowing as I wrote that I was surrounded—both virtually and in person—by so many colleagues who helped and supported me is simply an incredible feeling that can never be fully expressed in words.

So my biggest thank you goes to the UX community for the collective support and encouragement. Just a handful of initial social media posts sharing that I was writing this book yielded over 150 offers to help in some way, and I received so much encouragement from so many of my peers through a myriad of conversations.

Thank you to Elizabeth Rosenzweig and Brian Sullivan who connected me with Dave Bevans, who got the process rolling, and to my editors at CRC Press, Mary LaMacchia, Sean Connelly and Katie Hemmings.

Thank you so much to Edie Lee, who I've been lucky enough to work with at Lebsontech since 2008, and who served as a research assistant and editor, and helped me think through so much of this book. And how cool it is that such an amazing co-worker is also my sister.

Thank you also to Ginny Redish who has such knowledge and wisdom about the profession and who has served as a mentor to me for a number of years, initially helping and guiding me as I embarked on a path of UX community leadership through UXPA, and subsequently providing tremendous guidance and advice on this book from before it even had a publisher to contributing content, writing the foreword, and serving as a technical reviewer of the entirety of this work.

Thank you to Amanda Stockwell. From many conversations about resonant philosophies of UX adventure, to co-speaking and co-writing about UX careers, to routine Skype calls to talk about this book, Amanda has been a wonderful sounding board to talk through so many aspects of this effort, and she also authored and co-authored two of the chapters that follow.

Thank you also to Jen Romano Bergstrom, a contributor who has been a consistent presence in so many UX leadership activities over many years—from sharing project work and UX event efforts to co-teaching to working together on the UXPA DC and UXPA International boards. It was a number of early conversations and other UX-related initiatives with Jen that later formed the basis for the philosophies of UX community leadership, which thread their way throughout this book.

Thank you to Rich Woodall for turning my convoluted ideas into the wonderful illustrations that you will find in every chapter and to the additional 25 contributors who provided so much valuable insight through stories and career pathway descriptions and who collectively were so willing to go with the flow and continually tweak their contributions to fit smoothly into the overall story. I won't name them all here because you'll meet them shortly in the text.

Thank you to Josh Tyson at UX Magazine for advice and support, and similarly to Pabini Gabriel-Petit at UXmatters (two wonderful electronic publications, if you didn't know that already).

To the many recruiters of UX positions that I talked to while writing this book—thank you. Your "on-the-ground" insights and validation of the state of hiring was very informative and critical to the integrity of this book. Similarly, to all of those who reviewed various parts of this book to make sure that it was properly reflective of the state of the UX field—thank you as well.

Every UX professional has an origin story. For mine, I thank my undergraduate professor, Kent Norman, for giving me my first taste of this amazing career back in 1992, and for connecting me with my first mentor. And thank you to Dick Horst for my first job in the field in 1994, for being that first mentor, and for continuing to serve as a mentor throughout the years that have followed.

Finally, thank you to my wife, Aviva, and my three daughters, Eliana, Talya, and Nava, who managed to bear with me as I headed back to my home office after many a dinner to keep writing and working on this effort until late in the evening.

So thank you to everyone involved—this book would not be what it is without each and every one of you!

Cory Lebson
Silver Spring, Maryland
May 2016

About the Author

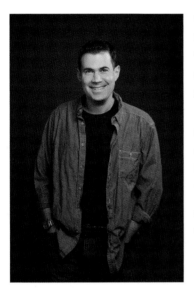

Cory Lebson has been a user experience (UX) consultant for nearly 20 years. He is the principal and owner of Lebsontech LLC (www.lebsontech.com), a successful small UX consulting firm he established in 1997. Through Lebsontech, Cory focuses on user research and evaluation, UX strategy, UX training, and mentoring. He also helps companies better understand the nuances of hiring UX professionals and building effective UX teams.

Cory enjoys teaching, and he regularly gives talks and workshops on a variety of topics related to UX practice, as well as UX careers. He has been featured on the radio and has published a number of articles in a variety of professional publications.

Cory has an MBA in marketing and technology management, as well as an MA in sociology and a BS in psychology. Cory is a past president of the User Experience Professionals Association (UXPA) International and is also a past president of the UXPA DC Chapter. He lives just outside of Washington DC, in Silver Spring Maryland, with his wife, Aviva and three daughters, Eliana, Talya, and Nava.

Connect with Cory on LinkedIn: Cory accepts LinkedIn invitations from all UX professionals and aspiring UX professionals. Connect at linkedin.com/lebson.

Follow Cory on Twitter @corylebson.

Foreword

When Joe Dumas and I wrote the preface to the second edition of our book, *A Practical Guide to Usability Testing*, in 1999, we predicted "continued growth in the community of usability specialists and continued growth in interest in usability from users to CEOs." But I don't think either of us realized just how the field would take off and how it would expand to be the umbrella of pathways and skillsets that Cory describes in this book.

I've watched (and participated with great pleasure) as the field has expanded from **usability** to **user-centered design** to **user experience** (UX) under an ever-widening umbrella. This book covers this wide umbrella and its even newer expansions into customer experience and service design. UX in all its varieties, its domains, its media is an exciting place to be.

And Cory Lebson is the perfect person to take you on your career journey. As he shares with us in this book, he has worked in a wide variety of settings, run his own business, and been a leader in the User Experience Professionals Association on the local and international levels. Helping people get into and grow in their UX careers, as well as helping those who hire UXers, is Cory's passion—and that passion shows throughout the book.

This is the first truly practical and useful book specifically about UX careers. With its detailed and very practical advice and worksheets, *The UX Careers Handbook* can help you decide what type of work you want to do; make a plan to educate yourself for that work; prepare to get that first job or transition from a related career; move up the ladder or move to being your own boss; and become a UX leader—in all the many ways leadership is possible.

I was fortunate when starting my career to have a wonderful mentor who taught me, supported me, and chided me when necessary. Throughout my career, I've tried to pay it forward by mentoring others—in person and through talks, workshops, articles, and books.

A book *is* a kind of mentoring, and Cory Lebson is the mentor you want on this journey—full of knowledge, wisdom, experiences to share, and a large network to connect you to. Through that network, Cory has enticed colleagues to also share their stories—mentoring you even more widely, so you can see UX careers from multiple perspectives.

In addition to 11 chapters of great UX career advice from Cory, you'll find detailed explanations of 16 different UX careers and related fields. Cory wrote two of those sections, and, through his network, had experts in each career and related field write the other 14. If you've not yet thought about all the ways you can work in UX—and how to match your specific interests and strengths to different UX careers, this chapter will amaze you.

Whatever your strengths and interests are, *The UX Careers Handbook* can help you find your place under the UX umbrella. Enjoy the journey with Cory.

Ginny Redish
Redish & Associates, Inc.
Bethesda, Maryland

How to Use this Book

Welcome to your user experience (UX) career journey. You may be just embarking on it, or you may already be deep in the middle of it. Regardless, thank you for letting me be part of it. My hope is to guide you along your path to career success in the UX world.

This book is easy to read from cover to cover; and if you have the time, I highly recommend doing so. However, it's also a handbook. You may want to thumb through to chapters that are most applicable to you now, and then look at other chapters later as your career progresses and they become more relevant. Reading this book non-linearly is certainly fine, and wherever possible, I cross-reference associated information between chapters.

Beyond the Book

The book will periodically refer to a companion website, **UXCareersHandbook.com**, for additional helpful materials and resources. Come back to the site often. I plan to continue to collect resources that tie into the topics of the book and post them to the website.

Book Structure

You'll notice that the title is not about a *career*, but rather *careers*. UX is not a single pathway, but rather an umbrella that encompasses a variety of overlapping careers. Chapter 11 breaks out a number of these career pathways, describing each in detail. If you are specifically interested in investigating individual UX career pathways, by all means, jump right to Chapter 11.

The rest of the book contains a ton of advice, techniques, worksheets, and tips for success across all careers under the umbrella that we call UX. You really have much more control over your own career success in UX than you may realize, and whether you're reading this electronically or in print, prepare to dive into worksheets (or print them from the companion website) or jot down some notes on the many career tips you'll find within the chapters of this book.

While much of the advice in this book could certainly apply to career fields beyond UX, the information and guidance it contains is tailored to tackle the unique challenges of the hot, exciting, and dynamic field of user experience.

Establishing your Foundation (Part 1)

The first four chapters are focused on making sure that you have yourself together before you start looking for a job, whether you are looking for a job right now or want to set yourself up so that it's easy to do so months or years down the road. Do you have the formal educational foundation necessary? Are you continuing to learn informally? If someone looks you up online, will they see a person who is clearly branded as a UX professional? Are you well connected with other UX professionals? **Even if you are mid-way through your UX career, review these foundations, and identify gaps to solidify your career potential.**

Getting a Job (Part 2)

Once your foundations are in place, Part 2 focuses on getting a job—whether a first job or a new job. We'll talk about how to sharpen your resume and work samples and make sure that you can tell your story well. Regardless of where you are now, you'll need to decide whether you want to work as an in-house UX professional, work as a UX consultant with an agency, or perhaps even go independent or start a small UX business. You'll then need to conduct a job search or seek out new contract work, and then you'll need to interview and negotiate. Part 2 guides you through all these steps to getting a job in UX, from start to finish.

Recruiters & Employers (Part 3)

Part 3 focuses on considerations around recruiters and employers.

If you are a job seeker, learn what to consider when working with recruiters (whether in recruiting agencies or company human resources departments), how recruiters can be most helpful to you, and what makes an optimal UX environment with a new employer.

If you are a recruiter or employer, learn what to be aware of as you search for new UX talent and create a work environment that is optimal for UX professionals. *Note that while this part of the book is specifically targeted at your intersection with UX professionals, expect to find valuable insights about UX professionals throughout the book that will aid you in your efforts to best understand and employ them.*

Career Glimpses: What, Specifically, Can You Do? (Part 4)

Part 4 is where we break out the UX umbrella into each of its representative components. You will find yourself described somewhere in here—your particular area(s) of interest and/or your current UX career pathway(s). Learn about these different pathways to understand your options and specifically where you can head within the UX umbrella. You may focus on one of these career pathways, or multiple ones. You can also use this section to get an idea of what your colleagues in other areas of UX do and how they integrate with what you do.

Feedback is encouraged

I've always made sure that anyone who wants to can contact me directly without having to look too hard or use convoluted methods. As such, I continue to be reachable at my one main email address, cory@lebsontech.com. Please feel free to reach out to me:

Have something for the companion website? Please let me know if you are aware of good resources I should add to the website.

Want more content? As you read this book, if you can't find some information that you were hoping to see, let me know. I'll try to blog about it, perhaps find a guest blogger who can address this topic, or remark on it on the companion website.

Bring topics to life! Are you excited about the UX career topics in this book and want me to speak about some of them to a group or at an event? Let me know! I love to speak about UX career topics, help to pull together UX career-oriented events, and get involved in networking opportunities for UX professionals.

We've covered the ins and outs of how to use this book, and you know how to get in touch with me, so now **it's time to dig in!**

Part 1

Establishing Your Foundation

CHAPTER 1

What is User Experience (UX)?

You may have picked up this book because you are a user experience (UX) professional already and want to advance your career, or maybe you've just heard about UX and want to know more, or perhaps you are still in school and trying to figure out what career you should be heading toward. Regardless, it would make sense to start with a single, well-accepted definition of the term and then move on to talk about your UX career. That would make sense—but no such luck.

You see, you've happened on an amazing profession with a phenomenal community, but nobody can agree *exactly* on how to define what it means to have a career in "user experience." That's why the title of this book is plural, a *careers* handbook, because "user experience" is not a single career at all but rather a common name for the umbrella that encompasses a whole range of exciting careers—some of which only came into being within the past few years.

I've watched the umbrella that we now call "UX" change and evolve over the course of my own career. In 1992, I was a sophomore in college at the University of Maryland and discovered an affinity for psychological research, so I enrolled in an advanced research methods class. Within the first month, we were told that we needed to explore the various psychology research efforts that were happening on campus and then pick one for a two-month internship. There were some great options to choose from, but what I got involved in was some research that explored how best to create online restaurant interfaces. I remember this being referred to as "human-computer interaction" or "HCI" research, and soon after I graduated, I became aware of the increasing salience of the Human-Computer Interaction Lab at UMD.

Meanwhile, when I was finishing up my undergraduate work in 1994, I went back to the psychology professor who ran the research lab, told him that I really enjoyed the kinds of research he was doing, and wondered if he knew of any job openings in the field. He referred me to a colleague who offered me my first taste of this kind of work in the real world as a "human factors engineer." This same position today would be called a "user researcher" of screen-based interfaces. And in fact, as you will see when you reach Chapter 11, "user research" and "human factors" are actually separate career pathways today, with only limited overlap in types of work performed.

A few years later in my career, my job title was "usability specialist," still dealing mainly with research of screen-based interfaces. The term "usability" continued to be an umbrella term for many people for a number of years. But then the umbrella gradually shifted through the first decade of the twenty-first century, and "user experience" became more widely accepted as the umbrella term.

Although UX doesn't have a single definition, we can talk about many aspects that all the careers under the umbrella have in common.

User Experience is about Technology

At a high level, UX careers sit at the junction of people and technology. It's the goal—and the ability—to make sure that technology is created in a way that people can use, will appreciate, and will enjoy interacting with it.

> UX professionals strive to assure that technology is created in a way that people can use, will appreciate, and will enjoy interacting with.

While a large number of UX professionals focus on things with screens, be it computers or mobile devices or wearables, many focus on technology without screens and, even more broadly, on aspects of user interactions where technology plays only a small role.

User Experience is People Caring about People

Ultimately, UX is a profession that is centered around people. It's about people who want to help others improve their interactions with a given environment or situation. And whether you are just starting the journey into UX or are already in the midst of it, you have the opportunity to help others. Sometimes very directly and sometimes more indirectly, but ultimately, you get to make a difference.

UX is Exciting

If you want to find a job where you go to work, follow the routine, and go home, day in and day out, well, you might as well put this book down right now. But if you want a job that always offers you something new—new opportunities, new insights, and new pathways—please keep reading. While you don't necessarily need to take your work home with you, you'll find that UX is something that is hard to stop thinking about. UX careers are wrapped in mystery. How do you solve the problem? How do you make things more satisfying for the user? How do you create something that is better than the thing before?

UX is a Melting Pot

As you may notice from the varied contributor backgrounds, my path to UX is downright boring when compared to the wide range of ways that people have connected with UX. We'll talk more later about what pathways might be best, but suffice it to say, you'll find people in UX who came from just about every background imaginable—different majors and different career pathways. Some of those careers, like mine, were grounded in social science. Others might have started in some aspect of technology; some aspect of business or product management; traditional design paths such as print and graphic design; writing; or communication.

In Nielsen Norman survey data, the most common majors of

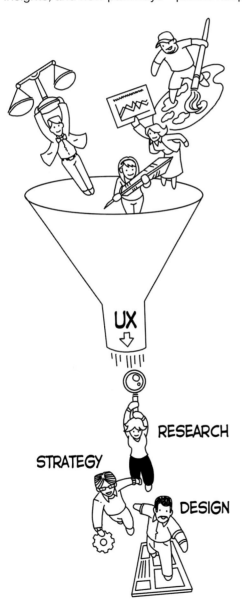

There are many ways to get into UX

UX professionals were reported as design, psychology, communication, English, and computer science,[1] which span a diverse range of academic educational areas. In fact, however, these majors combined accounted for less than half of UX professionals' bachelor's degrees; the survey includes a detailed list of over 100 bachelor's degree topic areas reported by UX professionals. One of the great things about UX (which may also be a challenge) is that there is clearly no one best path to career success.

> UX professionals come from very diverse backgrounds. There are many different paths that can lead to UX career success.

UX is a Community

UX is not just a career—it's a community. While much of my career has been spent doing UX work, another part of my career has been spent doing my best to help that community become stronger and more cohesive. The UX community, a subset of those who do UX work, is a global set of UX practitioners who actively seek opportunities to spend time with other UX professionals. The UX community is an open community that expects every starting point to be different. By the end of this book, my hope is that no matter where you may be in your UX career, you will decide that you want to be part of that community too.

UX is Global

Through my involvement with the User Experience Professionals Association, or UXPA, I have had incredible opportunities to interact with UX professionals from all over the world. I'm consistently amazed by the global continuity of the profession. I can go to any country that has a large UX community and announce my specific UX profession as "user researcher" knowing that those in UX will know what I'm referring to and what techniques and practices I'm likely to employ as part of my daily work. This continuity throughout the larger global community gives me even greater confidence in both the strength and the future of UX careers.

UX is a Big Umbrella

UX has come to be a rather large umbrella and includes a whole host of individual careers. Yet there is conflict in the marketplace. There are those who see the term as beginning and ending with a particular aspect of UX, for example, with interaction design (aka experience design). Any of these elements can also be seen as an umbrella itself, and there is certainly legitimacy in this. For example, doing research could be considered an aspect of the overall UX design process or its own career path that incorporates many other components. Yet, regardless of many potential varied angles of focus, by and large, UX has largely (though certainly not exclusively) become the buzzword of choice to represent the big umbrella.

Curse of the Unicorn

While UX is sometimes confused as representing only one smaller aspect of the profession, UX is also sometimes mistakenly considered to be a single career. You do UX, says the job description, then you must do <include every type of UX career here>. In the UX community, this expectation is known as the mythical UX unicorn. I've seen plenty of resumes that try to appeal to these job descriptions and, in fact, indicate that the resume holder is capable of doing any kind of UX work. Sure, theoretically, anyone can do anything—but everyone can't do everything well.

While a well-rounded set of skills is an asset, it's not reasonable to assume that everyone will be skilled in—or will even want to be skilled in—absolutely every aspect of UX. I'm not saying that these "unicorns" don't exist—and after many, many years and many different kinds of career experiences in UX, there are a few who can successfully balance many skillsets—but **employers, please note that finding the unicorns you seek will be like finding a needle in a haystack.**

While that is enough unicorn talk for now, we'll be coming back to this unicorn discussion again.

UX is Hot

Back in 2007, I was enjoying my UX work—it was my career niche—and I certainly appreciated that it wasn't all that hard to find employment even as the economic recession hit. Yet, I also didn't think all that many people knew what UX was. But then I remember talking to a UX colleague towards the end of the year. He asked if I had heard about the new *US News & World Report* article. They had just published a list of the top careers for 2008,[2] for what they termed a "changing landscape." And "usability/user experience specialist" was one of those careers. I was stunned and excited. And a year later, when *US News & World Report* published their list of the top 30 jobs for 2009,[3] there it was again.

UX continues to be recognized as a hot field[4] across the globe and offers good salaries. Both the User Experience Professionals Association (UXPA) salary survey from November 2014[5] and a Nielsen Norman 2015 Salary Trends for UX Professionals[6] article show great salaries that have remained stable over time (aside from a dip after some unrealistic salaries during the dot-com bubble). Additionally, in conversations with employers who want to hire for UX, a common refrain that I've heard over and over again is the difficulty they have filling positions with qualified UX talent.

UX is Satisfying

UX also comes with a high level of job satisfaction. According to the Nielsen Norman survey report, "most people in UX roles are very satisfied with their careers and compensation, because they enjoy the work and feel well-rewarded and highly valued . . . [UX professionals also] find it challenging and engaging . . . and see their work as being intrinsically good for humanity."[7]

UX Doesn't Just Mean Your Paid UX Work

This is a career book that is not just about what you do at work. Your career is so much more than that, especially in the world of UX. It's everything and everybody and every idea that you surround yourself with.

On the one hand, I could say that I am continually surprised by the serendipity in my own career. One good work-potential connection leads to another connection, which leads to yet another connection. The setting adapts seemingly on its own to set the stage for the next exciting event. A few years ago, I even tried to keep a running sketch of this in Visio. I called it a "serendipity chart" and wanted to use it to remind myself of how each interesting connection and each new project had come about.

But on the other hand, I know that it's not really serendipity that has moved my UX career forward, and it sure isn't luck.

- Your career is propelled forward by how you **envision yourself** and how you frame that vision.
- Your career is dependent upon how much you **put yourself out there**.
- Your career is the **adventure that you create for yourself**.

Be a visionary. Be an adventurer. Don't just think of your career as your interactions in the workplace, and don't let your career stop when you stop doing your UX project work. With this book, my key lesson for you is to keep your eyes and your mind open and always be prepared for the next adventure. Set yourself up to be in the right place whenever the time is right or a new opportunity comes up. Be prepared to follow the strange new path that will open up in front of you because you set the stage for it. In this book, we will cover all the ways that you can set yourself up to succeed in the UX field, regardless of which UX pathway(s) you choose to explore.

Let's get started now and talk about some career foundations.

Get more online at uxcareershandbook.com/what-is-ux

NOTES

1. Farrell, Susan and Jakob Nielsen. *User Experience Careers*, p.46. Nielsen Norman Group. http://www.nngroup.com/reports/user-experience-careers

2. http://money.usnews.com/money/careers/articles/2007/12/19/the-components-of-31-top-careers

3. http://money.usnews.com/money/careers/articles/2008/12/11/the-30-best-careers-for-2009

4. http://www.computerworld.com/article/2496025/enterprise-applications/ux-specialists-are-hot-commodities.html

5. https://uxpa.org/resources/past-salary-surveys

6. http://www.nngroup.com/articles/salary-trends-usability-professionals/

7. Farrell, Susan and Jakob Nielsen. *User Experience Careers*, p.28. Nielsen Norman Group. http://www.nngroup.com/reports/user-experience-careers

CHAPTER 2

Your Career is Grounded in Your Education

If you want to succeed as a user experience (UX) professional, you need to know about UX. But while some fields have clear-cut educational pathways—engineers get an engineering degree, lawyers get a law degree and take the bar exam—there is no one universal UX degree or qualifier, particularly not one that encompasses (or could encompass) all of the careers that fit under the umbrella of UX. Instead, you must create your own educational pathway to UX. But the upside is that it is difficult to go wrong—there are so many ways that you can get into UX.

Understanding the Whole Picture

In the first chapter, we talked about the curse of the unicorn, that is, the mistake job seekers or employers make when they classify UX as a single career, not a set of compatible and often overlapping careers. I caution you that while over time, you are going to gradually and perhaps naturally gain more and more UX skills, perhaps spanning multiple career pathways, you should not initially aspire to be a unicorn—to be the jack of all trades and master of none.

No matter where your area of special interest or expertise in UX lies, you should make sure to have an understanding of the broad framework that is UX, have a general sense of the different UX career pathways, and have a sense of where you and your piece of the UX pie (or burgeoning interest in it) fits into that broad framework.

Learn about the UX pie and then pick your slice

Eventually, if you haven't already, you'll begin to identify your superpowers—those aspects of UX that you are particularly strong in and want to focus on. As a UX professional, you're likely going to be working with people who have other superpowers—other kinds of UX professionals. Understanding the whole UX picture means that you can understand, at least in a general sense, how you will be able to work most effectively together. We'll talk about how to identify your specific superpowers in Chapter 11.

Your UX work and responsibilities are also going to change over time. What you enjoy doing currently or what you may be doing in your first UX job may not be where you find yourself in the next job. So while maintaining a firm focus on what your superpowers are, don't be afraid—and in fact, work hard to—learn about things that are related to what you do, but not exactly what you do.

I've been doing user research work for a long time. While I certainly appreciate books, articles, and blog posts with perspectives on user research specifically, I actually often find articles on other aspects of UX to be even more stimulating as they force me to think outside of the work that I typically do. Similarly, as part of your education and training, make sure that, in addition to learning about your specific chosen focus in UX, you also gain a basic understanding of the full breadth of the UX field.

In this chapter, we'll talk about your formal education options. In the next chapter, we will address the many ways that you can learn outside of the classroom.

> You need to have a general understanding of the broad framework that UX encompasses in order to appreciate how your UX expertise fits into the big picture.

The Value of Your Academic Education

There are many avenues through which you can acquire the UX knowledge you will need (both general UX field knowledge and your specific UX career pathway knowledge). Which way(s) you choose will most likely be affected by your relative starting point.

Not Yet in College

If you are a high school student looking to choose a good college for a UX education, you're pretty atypical (but fortunate!) for finding your interest in UX so soon. Look for a school that has some faculty or departments that encompass aspects of UX. The school should also have majors that match at least some of those listed within the career pathways in Chapter 11. If possible, reach out to the college's UX-oriented faculty to communicate your interest to them; they may be able to advise you about what the program will be like.

Undergraduate Degree

What did you say your major was? Sounds good—you're on a right track for a UX career. The truth is that you can go into UX with almost any major.

Even if you're in your last year of a degree and already locked into a major that is not UX-centered, don't think that a career in UX is out of the question without another degree. You should still be able to enter the UX field with some additional training, either on the job or through more formal training programs. If you still have enough time left, and your college offers it, I recommend that you find some UX-related classes, even as electives, if they are offered. You can also try to find a college professor who is involved in some aspect of UX and ask if you can volunteer to help out on some project or other to get yourself started in the UX field.

If you are early on in your college career, have not yet completely settled on a major, and are at a school where there are "exact match" kinds of majors (perhaps related specifically to design, human-computer interaction, or something else UX-related), consider majoring in one of these fields. If you are at a school that doesn't have a "perfect" UX major for you, check out the list of potential degrees that are suggested as good starting points for the various career pathways described in Chapter 11. Additionally, with plenty of time left in your college career, do your best to see if you can volunteer to work with a UX-oriented faculty member, or perhaps propose an independent research project in your particular area of UX interest.

> There is no single best educational pathway to a career in UX.

College Graduate/Graduate Degree

You can get very far in UX with a bachelor's degree. In fact, for the most part you can stop with a bachelor's degree and you will be just fine for the duration of your career. That said (and speaking as someone with multiple master's degrees, albeit none of which are targeted UX-oriented degrees), a master's degree is never a bad thing in the UX field (and in fact, 52% of respondents of the Nielsen Norman UX careers survey reported having a master's degree[1]).

Sometimes, particularly in certain areas of UX such as user research and human factors, jobs will require, or at least highly prefer, applicants to have a master's degree. Similar to a bachelor's degree, having any master's degree will typically be respected in any UX field. Having a master's degree in a UX field can be even more valuable, not just to show that you're educated, but also to indicate that you have advanced knowledge in one or more areas of UX.

Even better, if you earned your degree recently, you likely have better exposure to some of the most recent literature and theories than your colleagues who either don't have these UX-specific degrees or earned these degrees a long time ago. A master's degree may also increase your earning potential over time. See Chapter 11 to find out the relative importance of a master's degree for the specific UX career(s) you are in or are interested in.

Doctorate Degree

A doctorate degree is a funny thing in UX. In the survey mentioned, only 6% of UX professionals reported having a Ph.D.[2] Occasionally there are certain UX jobs that require a Ph.D. (For example, you may run across some user research or human factors jobs that require this.) But, by and large, you will not need a doctorate in UX. In fact, it can even have certain downsides. For one thing, the time it takes to get the Ph.D. may cause you to put off paid work and valuable real-world work experience for many years. (On the flip side, however, you do gain rigorous academic experience and solid theoretical underpinnings.)

Even more of concern is that in some environments, those with a Ph.D. are sometimes assumed by hiring managers to be more interested in theory than in business, and they may also be assumed to be overly concerned about doing things in a formal and proper way without concern for profitability. If you really do want to pursue a Ph.D., or even already have one, don't let these biases stop you; but keep in mind when you find yourself in conversations with potential employers or co-workers that you may need to offset stereotypes with business savvy.

No Degree

If you don't have a college degree and are already in the work world, in no uncertain terms, do pursue a college degree. While UX is not a profession that hinges on a degree, it is a profession that does respect a formal education. In the survey of UX professionals, over 90% reported having a college degree.[3] So yes, you can make it as a UX professional without a college degree. But without that bachelor's degree, there are going to be more limitations and doors closed to you before you even get a chance to talk with a hiring manager and make the case for how good you really are at what you do.

Academic Degrees in Non-UX Fields

Your academic degree does not need to be specifically in UX to have a successful UX career. As I said, UX professionals have entered the field with a wide variety of degrees. If you are done with university degrees, but want additional learning, you have plenty of options available besides going back for another degree. The rest of this chapter talks about how you can have classroom experience outside of a formal degree and the next chapter reviews ways you can learn about and gain UX knowledge outside of the classroom entirely.

- You should have at least a bachelor's degree for most UX jobs.

- A UX-related degree is very helpful but is definitely not required to become a UX professional.

How useful were these subjects?[4]

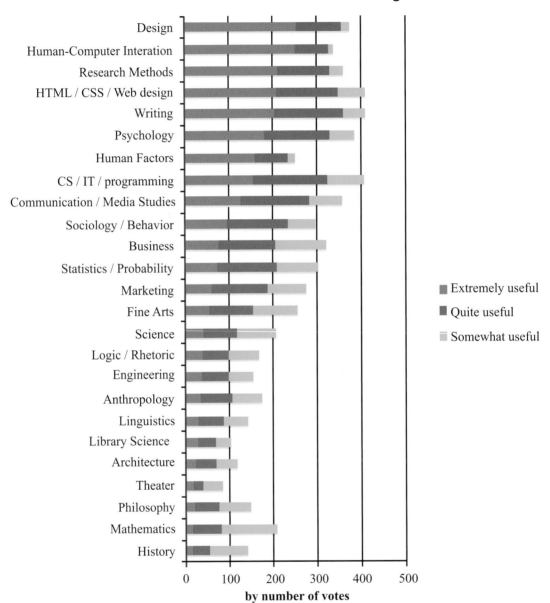

by number of votes

CORPORATE LAWYER TO UX PROFESSIONAL

By Nick Gould, Chief Operating Officer, Cooper

A career in UX can begin anywhere. I'm living proof of that fact. Twenty years ago I was a corporate lawyer. Today, I'm a leader at a respected UX design, research, and strategy consultancy and president of a global association of interaction designers. It was an unlikely path, for sure, and I wouldn't necessarily suggest law school as a stepping stone to a design career. But one of the most interesting aspects of the UX profession is how many different occupations and fields of study can, unpredictably, provide a strong foundation for success in UX.

Mine is just one example of the many unusual courses that people have charted on their way to a successful UX career. For me, the journey was mostly about discovering the kind of job I really wanted and finding it in the burgeoning field of UX design. Being a good candidate for a career in UX is less about whether your current career or training has prepared you for UX, but rather whether the kind of person you are—what interests and excites you, and what you're good at—makes you suited for UX work.

So, what do law and UX have in common? More than you might think. For example, a contract lawyer's job is to think of ways that relationships between two parties can possibly go wrong and to minimize the damage to clients if bad things happen. This requires imagination (and a certain paranoia) that is also very useful for conceiving of interaction scenarios between people and products or services. Also, in litigation a lawyer's job is to frame a set of facts in a persuasive way—to tell a story that makes sense. Storytelling is also a crucial skill for a number of UX career pathways.

Of course I didn't jump directly from practicing law into managing UX design projects. The actual progression was more gradual. The first change was a movement, as a lawyer, into the technology space. I was involved with business development and strategy for online products. These roles were a logical connection between the technology business I wanted to be in and the legal and business skills I had developed in my initial career. These jobs brought me closer to the product development and marketing process and helped me to discover a new set of interests and capabilities. So, when an opportunity to join a new design consultancy arose, I was able to see how working in this new field would be an enjoyable and fulfilling career direction to take—and one in which I could be successful. It was still a hard decision to make this leap—and the journey hasn't been without bumpy patches. But I certainly have never wished I was still a lawyer!

Nick Gould is a digital business and product development leader with strong ties to the global UX and interaction design community. An accomplished sense-maker and storyteller, he is adept at finding signals in the noise of customer input, stakeholder priorities, and competitor actions. Nick specializes in developing concise and inspiring narratives that illuminate a product's performance, envision new scenarios, and align project teams around experience strategies. Nick was President of the Interaction Design Association (IxDA) from 2014 to 2016 and has served on the IxDA Board of Directors since 2009. Prior to Cooper, Nick was CEO and owner of Catalyst Group, a pioneering user experience design, research, and strategy consultancy in New York. Before that he was a corporate lawyer.

The Value of Professional Programs

To be in UX, you *must* be a person who desires to learn continually, even beyond your academic degree. Professional programs are particularly helpful for those who are entering UX with a non-UX-oriented degree and/or from a career outside of UX. But even for those with UX-oriented degrees, your learning should never stop. You need to learn on the job, and you need to find other ways to stay on top of this ever-evolving field as well. Don't worry—you have many options and opportunities—both formal and less formal.

Certificate Programs

Regardless of your level of formal education, if you are seeking UX training that does not lead to a degree, one additional academic option to consider is a certificate program. Several schools have certificate programs specifically related to UX or specific career pathways within UX.

A certificate is neither an academic degree nor is it "certification" in UX. Rather, a certificate is something that you can include on your resume and mention when applying for a job. It represents a supplemental education that is specifically geared to UX, even when your actual college degree or degrees are not.

These programs are sometimes available as distance learning programs with minimal or no need to be onsite. A UX-specific certificate program can really be helpful if you are planning to break into the field. A certificate program will also often be structured so that you can simultaneously hold a full-time job—perhaps even a job that can concurrently give you some on-the-job insights into a new UX-related career.

Professional Training Programs

In addition to certificate programs through academic institutions, you have many opportunities to learn through UX-oriented professional training programs. Sometimes even more so than academic options, these training programs will be exclusively focused on what you need to know about UX to succeed in business. These programs may be intensive "boot camps" that take place over several days or weeks. They may have after-work options, perhaps meeting once or twice per week.

There are also professional training programs that meet partially or entirely online. However, there is a lot to be said for in-person interaction opportunities as a source of both learning and effectively normalizing your UX interests and background with your peers. So, if at all possible, see if in-person options exist where you live.

"Certification" Programs

Some professional training programs go one step further: They offer "certification" to those that complete the course. This may be called "UX certification" or "Usability certification" or something similar.

The idea of certification is a remarkably sensitive topic in the UX community, and you should be aware that there is no fully (or even mostly) accepted UX certification. In the United States, while there are a handful of reputable training programs that offer "certification" upon completion, there is no national standard of any kind for UX certification to go by.

In Europe, there is now an International Usability and UX Qualification Board (UXQB), which started in Germany and has made headway in Switzerland and the UK. Unlike the United States-based certification programs, where the certifier and the trainer are one and the same, the UXQB is a consortium of individuals that promotes a public standard for certification but that farms out the training to other organizations. Although there is a very respectable level of credibility to the UXQB and to the way that they are approaching the certification model (and it will be interesting to see how this model succeeds in the marketplace) my advice to you remains the same:

You do not need UX certification to get a UX job or succeed at your job.

While those who are deeply embedded in UX tend to be both cautious and somewhat cynical about the idea of UX certification, those who are not embedded—particularly recruiters and employers who are not in UX but are looking to hire UX professionals—sometimes look to certification as a quick marker of background knowledge. To that end, my advice to you is as follows:

- **If you see a job posting that requests or requires certification**: If appropriate, let them know what I said about certification, and feel free to quote me. It's on the record—I even published an article about certification and UX professional organizations.[5]
- **If you are an employer or recruiter:** Do not request or require certification in your job posting. It's not going to be a marker of anything aside from knowing that the job candidates you receive took one pathway to professional education instead of another. And it may even turn away valuable highly qualified applicants.
- **If you have completed a training program that offers you certification of some kind:** That's totally fine and certainly a positive that you completed a reputable program of study. I'd advise you, however, to treat the certification as you would any other formal or informal program of study or coursework: describe it as training and input to your knowledge as opposed to framing this certification as your end goal. Be cautious that if you proclaim certification as equivalent to a degree or as letters after your name, while this may look like a positive to an employer or recruiter who is not particularly embedded in the UX field, highly knowledgeable UX practitioners might bristle or scoff at your overemphasis on this certification.

Finding and Choosing a Program

Whatever educational or training option you are considering, you need to look carefully at each program's goals to see how they match with your own.

Learning Doesn't End with Formal Training

Okay, you're done! You've learned all you needed to at a university and/or through other formal training, and now all you need to do is perform your UX work, right? Wrong—it's not so easy! Outside of your paid work, you need to keep learning, keep reading, and keep attending talks and events.

We're going to conclude this book in Chapter 13 with a discussion of how our field will continue to evolve and change—both the types of technology we deal with and the methods that we use. You can—and must—continue to learn from the moment you finish your formal training through to, well, forever, in order to succeed in your career as a UX professional.

Get more online: uxcareershandbook.com/education

NOTES

1. Farrell, Susan and Jakob Nielsen. *User Experience Careers*, p. 11. Nielsen Norman Group. http://www.nngroup.com/reports/user-experience-careers

2. Farrell, Susan and Jakob Nielsen. *User Experience Careers*, p. 11. Nielsen Norman Group. http://www.nngroup.com/reports/user-experience-careers

3. Farrell, Susan and Jakob Nielsen. *User Experience Careers*, p. 11. Nielsen Norman Group. http://www.nngroup.com/reports/user-experience-careers

4. Farrell, Susan and Jakob Nielsen. *User Experience Careers*, p. 51. Nielsen Norman Group. http://www.nngroup.com/reports/user-experience-careers

5. http://www.uxmatters.com/mt/archives/2014/05/certification-by-ux-organizations-is-there-a-business-case-for-this.php

CHAPTER 3

Never Stop Learning

In the last chapter, we talked about the user experience (UX) education that you get from formal training, be it from a college or university or professional training program. But as we concluded there, that's only the beginning of your education in UX, and whether you are just starting your career or you've been doing UX for the last 20 years like I have, you can never—ever—stop learning. Don't worry, that's good news! Why? Because UX is not a static field. There is nothing stagnant about any part of UX: methods continue to improve, technology advances by leaps and bounds, and the people you really work for, the users, evolve over time. The only way to keep pace with those changes is to continue to learn.

Learn On Your Own

LEARN FROM BOOKS

There are so many good UX methods books out there, and new books come out regularly. Most books are associated with a particular career pathway or perhaps even two or three of the pathways that fall under the umbrella of UX. Each contributor for the career pathways in Chapter 11 recommends one or more books (and in fact sometimes they wrote one of those good books!). These books and others can be found on the companion website.

LEARN FROM THE WEB

You might think of books as slower-moving luxury cruise liners and articles and blogs as speedboats—perhaps less formal and less rich in all the details, but a way to get lots of new and exciting knowledge, ideas, and perspectives out to

Never stop learning to stay on top of new information and trends

a wide audience of readers quickly and efficiently. The companion website will continually be updated with lists of good blogs.

Although you can bookmark good sites and then flip from website to website periodically looking for new and interesting content, not only is this tedious, but it is perhaps less likely something that you're going to do on a regular basis. Therefore, I recommend using RSS feeds to stay current.

I've been an avid reader of RSS feeds for many years and use a number of RSS feeds to stay on top of things in the UX world. If you're not familiar with RSS (Really Simple Syndication), it's a way of getting data fed to you. Through RSS, you subscribe to a news or other information source so that whenever new stories are published, those stories are immediately listed in your chosen RSS reader. I use Feedly.com as my RSS feed aggregator and then use the Reeder app on my iPhone to pull my RSS feed directly from Feedly. (Although Feedly has an iPhone app too, the Reeder interface just works better with my own reading habits.)

If you are already using RSS feeds or are willing to use RSS feeds, consider creating your own custom UX news feed. My feed includes a number of sources of UX-related articles and blogs as well as feeds for articles and blogs that are related more generally to technology trends outside of UX. Since UX and technology are so intimately tied together, also keeping apprised of what is happening with technology can only help frame and better well round your UX lens.

In addition, there are several tools for creating regular alerts of new content that gets indexed in Google or other search engines. My tool of choice (mainly for its simplicity) is Talkwalker (http://www.talkwalker.com/alerts) in which you can enter whatever search criteria you want and then create an RSS feed to have that feed run constantly. Alert terms could be as simple as "User Experience" or could represent some of the specific UX pathways we'll discuss in Chapter 11 or even particular areas of interest within those pathways. You'll have a choice of seeing all results or just the best ones (as defined by Talkwalker). I'd suggest that you just look at the best to catch the highlights and trends you don't want to miss—otherwise you can be flooded by results that are less worthy of your reading time. Even then, you may have to play around a bit with your alert terms to get the results that you want.

While you're at it, consider an alert for your own name (as long as your name is not super-common) to monitor your brand, as we will discuss in the next chapter.

Finally, you can also use a crowdsourced approach to see new and trending stories. Assuming that you follow or are connected with a core of UX professionals on various social media (which we will discuss more in the next chapter), applications, such as Nuzzel.com, will review your connections and aggregate stories based on how many of your connections are talking about those stories. In the case of Nuzzel, you don't even have to be connected to read news stories because user feeds are public. All that you need to do is use someone's public nuzzle feed to see an aggregation of their connections, such as http://nuzzel.com/CoryLebson.

Learn From Podcasts and Webinars

Although I admit to being much more of a reader than a podcast listener, I've spoken with UX professionals who download a variety of UX-related podcasts and listen to them when they have time, for example during a long commute.

Webinars, while often not as convenient as podcasts that you can listen to anytime you want (although some webinars are recorded), sometimes offer a greater degree of interactivity. You often get to see slides or other elements on

- Stay on top of current UX and technology trends by reading books, articles, and blog posts.

- Take advantage of available UX-related podcasts and webinars.

your screen while you listen, and sometimes you have the opportunity to do exercises or ask questions of the speakers.

Learn From UX Organizations

Adapted with permission from Cory Lebson, "These Are My People: The Value in UX Organizations," *UX Magazine*, Article no. 1075 (2013).[1]

In addition to the formal learning opportunities that we talked about in the last chapter and the kinds of learning that you can do on your own that we just discussed, one of the other key ways you can learn and stay current is to join a UX-related organization. Whether it's a national/international organization, one of the organization's chapters, or a local Meetup (*meetup.com*), these groups provide a phenomenal opportunity for you to learn from both selected speakers and from your peers. I found professional organizations to be so valuable that I dedicated nearly a decade of volunteerism to supporting one of them.

While my own experiences have been centered with the User Experience Professionals Association (UXPA), many UX professionals (including contributors to this book) have found great value through extensive involvement in not only UXPA (uxpa.org), but other organizations as well, including:

- Interaction Design Association (IxDA) — ixda.org
- Information Architecture Institute (IAI) — iainstitute.org
- Customer Experience Professionals Association — (CXPA) — cxpa.org
- Human Factors and Ergonomics Society (HFES) — hfes.org
- Qualitative Research Consultants Association (QRCA) — qrca.org
- Society for Technical Communication (STC) — stc.org
- ACM Special Interest Group on Computer-Human Interaction (SIGCHI) — sigchi.org
- American Institute of Graphic Arts (AIGA) — aiga.org
- All sorts of local Meetups via meetup.com and elsewhere

TYPES OF ORGANIZATIONS TO CONSIDER
Chapter-based Organizations

Chapter-based organizations can be national or even international. While an international organization provides resources that can quite literally span the globe, the chapters each provide a more narrowly targeted geographic scope. If you are in a metropolitan area, it's likely that one or more chapter-based organizations has a strong presence.

Local Organizations and Meetups

Although chapter-based organizations certainly provide a variety of UX events, activities, and resources, there are also many other independent, local UX organizations. Some can be found on Meetup.com, while others only distribute information via a separate website, mailing list, or in social media. Do a quick web search, and you're likely to find several different local UX organizations around you.

Guidelines to Identify an Organization that is Right for You

- **Location:** Are organizational events based at where you work or live? Are there virtual events?
- **Target audience of organization:** Do the goals of the organization align with your career interests?
- **Benefits of affiliation/services provided:** What kinds of opportunities appear on their events calendar? What other benefits does affiliating with the organization offer?
- **Recommendations by or knowledge of current members:** Have you heard positive things about this group from others, in person or through social network channels?
- **Size:** Is the group big enough that you will be exposed to everything you are looking for in an organization? Is it small enough that you can find your niche?

What UX Organizations Provide

UX organizations present great opportunities for learning, often providing an event infrastructure with monthly or periodic events. I find that the in-person communication and opportunity to ask questions of a speaker, as well as subsequent discussion with fellow attendees, adds a lot of learning value beyond what you can get by simply reading online.

UX organizations also provide the opportunity to discuss UX with your colleagues and to sync up and essentially normalize your UX jargon, ideas, and methods with your peers. In short, the very nature of these organizations and the networking that they often promote is fertile ground for peer-to-peer learning. You can learn new things without even realizing that's what you're doing.

> UX organizations and meetups provide a phenomenal opportunity to learn from both speakers and your peers.

You can find lists of organizations on the companion website, on both the webpages associated with this chapter and on the webpages associated with the individual career pathways in Chapter 11.

Learn From Conferences

In addition to local events, there are an ever increasing number of UX-oriented conferences, some of which are associated with the UX organizations I've already mentioned and others that are independent efforts. To decide if a conference is right for you, look at the topics. See if those topics match the Chapter 11 career pathway(s) you are most interested in. From the conference description, see if you can get a sense of the kinds of people who go to the conference. That can let you know if those going have careers that are reasonably harmonious with your own job aspirations.

PROFESSIONAL DEVELOPMENT: FIVE QUESTIONS TO ASK A PROSPECTIVE EMPLOYER

By Dan Brown, Principal & Founder, EightShapes

Your UX career development is not a solo effort. While it is ultimately up to you to manage your own career growth, there should be other people at your workplace actively helping you to further your career. It is up to you to facilitate that process—to make sure the right people are involved.

To support your growth, your employer should provide a robust infrastructure, including processes for assessing performance, help with setting goals and creating a plan to achieve those goals, and a way of executing that plan, including getting iterative feedback.

Many employers go above and beyond these basics. Employers may pay for classes, books, and conference attendance. At my UX design firm, we give every employee the opportunity to attend a yearly conference of their choosing anywhere in the world. We strongly support attending local events and will buy pretty much any book someone wants. We've paid for online learning classes too. While these are nice perks, though, they won't drive growth the way feedback and a development plan can. Genuine growth comes from opportunities to work on projects alongside colleagues and peers who can bolster and challenge your efforts.

FINDING A WORKPLACE THAT SUPPORTS PROFESSIONAL GROWTH

There are several essential elements to professional development programs. Before taking a job, make sure you know what your new employer offers. Here's what you can ask:

1. *"Who is responsible for my professional development?"*

What to look for: There is someone (a manager or senior person) also in UX who is responsible for facilitating your professional development.

Besides you, the best person to help you is someone who's going to care as much about meeting your goals as you do. At a small company like mine made entirely of designers, an employee's manager (also a designer) is responsible for shepherding their professional development. At some places I've worked, however, this was the domain of Human Resources. Beware that while HR may get the mechanics of professional development better than anybody, they don't necessarily get the nuts and bolts of being a UX professional.

2. *"How does my manager facilitate my professional development?"*

What to look for: Your manager should provide at least annual reviews, or even better quarterly reviews. During these conversations, you and your manager should review your portfolio relative to your goals. Collaboratively evaluate whether your work supports growth in the right direction, and what you can be doing to further improve. The essence of this evaluation is a discussion of your portfolio—whether that's design work, research work, or something else—in the context of goals.

Your manager should be well versed in what makes a good goal. At my company, our first professional development endeavor was a disaster. People came up with 8–10 goals, including developing skills and writing blog posts and working on specific projects. The following year, it was clear that having too many goals not directly related to project work leads to a feeling of failure. You get to the end of your year and you think, "I worked really hard, but I didn't accomplish any of my goals!" It wasn't for lack of trying; it was for lack of alignment. Good goals are not only aligned with corporate objectives but are also expressed in a way that makes them realistic for project work, regardless of what kind rolls in.

We now have two main guidelines for goals:

- You can only have 2–3 goals per year.
- Your goals have to make sense within project work.

When goals don't align with project work—work that makes money for the company—it's difficult to dedicate time to them. Goals that align with projects, however, give you a sense of direction during your everyday work. A great goal says you want to learn a new skill (like JavaScript) or expand your knowledge (on typography, say) and comes with a plan to work on that as a part of a project.

3. *"How is professional growth built into the company culture?"*

What to look for: The ideal corporate culture for UX professionals supports taking on challenges and encourages continual feedback and review, particularly from peers and colleagues.

Growth is fueled in large part by exposure to new challenges and by having access to frequent and honest feedback. Make sure to ask about the potential for increasing responsibilities and challenges over time and about how you can expect to get feedback on your work.

The people you work with every day are perhaps the most qualified to give you feedback. A great company culture will have colleagues sending "virtual high-fives" to each other, forwarding praise from clients and customers and copying managers or project leads.

4. *"What does my career development plan consist of?"*

What to look for: Managers should be able to set out examples of a clear plan—a set of objectives supported by specific project-based activities and mechanisms to measure progress.

In a previous job, I'd fill out a self-evaluation form and drop in a few goals. There wasn't much to the process beyond that. This became the "anti-pattern" when we were designing the review process at EightShapes. My partner and I wanted employees to create two artifacts: one assessing their performance and one that set their goals along with a plan for achieving them.

5. *"What criteria do you use to assess my performance?"*

What to look for: Every organization should have a list of skills and expectations specific to your discipline or field.

Job descriptions are helpful, but they don't have the whole story. In our early days, our company developed a long list of skills and expectations. Some of these are behaviors like "Seeks out ad hoc feedback," and others are specific skills like "Develops novel ways to document UX." Because everyone at our company is a designer, these expectations fit across the board. Some organizations may have generic expectations, however, regardless of role or position. At one job, I was evaluated for my appearance. Did I start to tuck in my shirt? Definitely. Did it make me better at my job? No.

GREAT JOB; MINIMAL PROFESSIONAL DEVELOPMENT AVAILABLE

Not every employer will have a robust development infrastructure. A corporate system for UX professional growth is, no doubt, valuable, but it is not essential for development. You can set your goals and you can have a plan, regardless of where you work and what they offer. You are, after all, a UX professional. For this project (your professional development) you are the user. Figure out what you need, validate those needs, and create a plan for getting there.

In 2006, **Dan Brown** co-founded EightShapes, a design firm based in Washington, DC. EightShapes designs responsive websites and establishes design standards for Fortune 500 clients. In his role as "HR guy" at EightShapes, Dan monitors, tweaks, and reflects on the professional development process, which serves a dozen designers at any given time. Dan has written two books, *Communicating Design* and *Designing Together*, which deal with communications and collaboration on design teams. Follow him on Twitter @brownorama.

Learn From a Mentor

While you can learn so much about UX from your formal education, professional programs, independent learning, and resources provided by UX organizations, there is a special and unique value in finding a mentor. A mentor can guide you along your journey and push you toward being a better UX professional—perhaps even simply through a series of periodic small conversations. If you have the opportunity to work with a mentor, you'll even have someone to watch what you do as you do it and correct you when you don't do it as well as you can.

Currency in Mentorship

You don't hire a mentor, pay them a bit of money, and then say "teach me all you know." Instead, be aware that there is a currency to finding a mentor. While it is true that someone may want to mentor you simply to give back or pay it forward, you should never consider this a default condition.

In fact, ideal relationships in any case, be they for work, friendship, or romance, all have something in common—reciprocity, such that you and the other person both gain from the relationship. In the same way, the ideal mentorship is really one that allows for a reciprocal relationship of added value. If you find a mentor, you should be helping that person in exchange for the help you receive. If you have the opportunity, you can help with your mentor's UX work—you can provide insights from your own experiences, and you can help them to brainstorm or think creatively about things which could, in fact, be easier for you without as much career-history baggage. When you do identify a mentor, while you don't necessarily need to figure out all the ways that you can add value immediately, you should continue to think about how you can reciprocate.

Find a Mentor at Work

If you're lucky, you may have a natural mentor at a job. Perhaps a more senior co-worker or someone to whom you report, who naturally wants to help you do your work as part of their responsibilities. If you don't have this natural relationship immediately but have identified someone that you'd like to help guide you (and assuming you have permission from your job), take the initiative and ask to help them on one or more projects.

Find a Local Mentor Outside of Work

Although some are fortunate to have great mentors at work, many are not so lucky. Consider contacting local professional organizations and Meetups. Sometimes the organizers may be aware of people who have the time and the desire to help those newer to the field.

Even beyond formal connections, simply going to local UX events and talking with a variety of UX professionals may help you identify someone you click with and who would be willing to help you grow in your career. You can volunteer to help with a project as your time permits in order to learn from someone who might have something to teach you. Or on a smaller scale, you can ask to take a potential mentor out for coffee or a drink or maybe lunch. Chat with the person as an informational interview about what you're trying to figure out about your own career—but do not do all the talking. In the name of both reciprocity and learning, ask them about themselves and let them share with you, not just answer your questions. If you both have a good time, perhaps arrange a subsequent conversation a month later.

Find a Mentor Who is Not Geographically Local

If you cannot find a local mentor available to you, or you need someone to guide you in some very specialized aspects of your career, consider a mentor who is not geographically local to you. You may be able to identify someone through professional organizations, or perhaps through mutual connections. If your relationship is totally remote, consider video calls via Skype or Hangouts. Take advantage of any way you can to build a relationship with this person, and seeing each other, even through a screen, brings you one step closer together.

- Find a mentor at work, through a professional organization, or through mutual contacts.

- Mentors are more likely to take you on if you are clearly enthusiastic about UX.

- Try to reciprocate, helping your mentor in any way you can.

Mentors Like Future Rock Stars

I have mentored professionals throughout the years, some of whom I've worked directly with and others through a series of conversations or non-workplace interactions over time.

Sometimes, it was expected as a part of my job to help more junior staff. In other cases, as part of my consulting offerings, I have been hired by companies explicitly to mentor their staff while I was "on the clock." I will say that I have certainly preferred to see elements of future UX rock stars in those I was mentoring—that is, those who seem to have the interest, the inclination, and the ability to do really well with the appropriate guidance. Because this mentoring was part of my paid responsibilities, however, their ability to be successful was not a decision factor in my taking on the responsibility.

When not mentoring in a paid work capacity, however, the rock star value becomes more salient. Junior UX professionals have asked me for guidance with their careers or with specific UX research/evaluation skills; and given a finite amount of available time, my preference definitely is to help those who have the energy and enthusiasm for the work. Perhaps not all that differently than a hiring manager, I want to use my time to help those who can to show me that if I give them some guidance they will become very successful and valuable to the UX profession. **So when seeking a mentor, be sure to express your true enthusiasm and desire to learn and to make a difference in UX.**

Mentor-aggregates for Those at Any Point in Their Career

Even if you have been in the field for a long time, don't think that you can't have or wouldn't benefit from a mentor. In fact, being willing and able to learn from your colleagues will help you continue to have a successful career.

Instead of a single mentor, both those new to the field and those who have been doing UX for longer can create what I call a mentor-aggregate. Essentially, you focus on building a solid network of other professionals so everyone can constantly help each other and provide knowledge and career advancement. When we encounter work things that frighten us (I still do!) we

Mentoring: How It Happens[2]

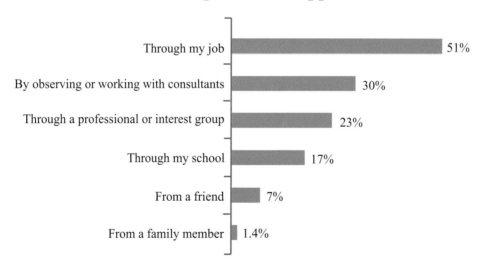

then have others to turn to, so that we can learn from their knowledge and experiences.

Learning Does Not Stop

It can be easy to become complacent when your job security is good. You may feel like you know everything there is to know about your field and can take a break from learning. I caution you to remember that this field is constantly evolving, in methods, technology, and users' needs. If you don't stay on top of trends, methods, and jargon, you will eventually be left behind—and it's much easier to stay current than to try to catch up later when you are flagged for not being on top of things.

We've covered how you can (and should always continue to) learn about UX, so now it's time to think about how others learn about *you*, starting with your personal brand.

Get more online at uxcareershandbook.com/learning

NOTES

1. http://uxmag.com/articles/these-are-my-people.

2. Farrell, Susan and Jakob Nielsen. *User Experience Careers*, p.57 Nielsen Norman Group. http://www.nngroup.com/reports/user-experience-careers

CHAPTER 4

Personal Branding and Networking for Career Success

Your career image means a lot. So much so, in fact, that even before looking for a job, you should be working on building your user experience (UX) brand and network. Your goal is to create a clear and articulate story of who you are and how you can add value with your UX skills. Then you need to take that story and make sure that it can be broadcast far and wide.

Build Your Brand

Very often you'll find yourself choosing familiar brands. You choose these brands because you know what the product is and you know that you'll likely have a positive experience with the product.

As a frequent business traveler, one of my travel rituals upon arriving in a new city is to find a grocery store and stock up on some food for my hotel room. If asked, I would say that of course I believe in supporting local businesses over chains whenever possible—and the local stores are likely going to be a more interesting experience. Yet, when I arrive in that new city, I look for familiar chains and will drive further to get to them. I'm usually short on time and want that familiarity and consistent experience to start my business travel.

Build Internal Coherence into Your Brand

Similarly, this coherence of brand is just as important for you as it is for a grocery chain. You need to be—you are—a UX professional, and no matter where someone looks or what someone hears, they need to see and hear consistency in your UX identity: what aspects of UX you specialize in, and how you fit into the overall UX process. If someone talks with you, what you say needs to be in sync with what that person would find online. This consistency of brand is not something that just happens; rather, it's something that you have to work at—that you build.

Internal coherence: Someone searching for you will see a singular brand.

External consistency: You match a specific type of UX profession.

Your brand must include internal coherence + external consistency.

Make Your Brand Externally Consistent With Typical UX Careers

It's important to point out, however, that while internal coherence is critical to success, so is external consistency. If you want a UX job, employers and recruiters need to be able to match you with a type of UX professional. Are you a researcher? A designer? An information architect? Or are you claiming skills in multiple areas of UX?

Picture Your Brand: Believing is Seeing

In my teen years, and immortalized as my senior quotation in my high school yearbook, my mantra was "Some things must be believed to be seen." I remember printing this out across three attached dot-matrix pages in those years and pasting the message above the door to my bedroom so that I would never forget. In subsequent years, I came to see that this could be more efficiently stated: believing is seeing. This short and simple phrase, an inversion of the typical "Seeing is believing" means in this instance that you need to know in your mind what you want your brand to be. If you can't picture it in your mind first, you are going to have a lot of difficulty with both internal coherence and external consistency.

Include Internal Coherence + External Consistency

I have a unique name. If someone Googles "Cory Lebson" with or without quotes, everything they see is related to me. Clicking through the first few pages of hits shows a very consistent brand. It's me, and I do UX. Of course, I've been doing this stuff for 20 years; there must be 20 years of content out there to Google, right? Not actually true. The web as a useful tool to learn about people hasn't existed for that long. And search engines like Google like to show fresh and relevant material anyhow, whenever possible. So in fact, pretty much everything that is in the first few pages of hits is less than 5 years old.

Now, put this book down or flip away from your e-reader for a moment. Google yourself. If you have a common name, think like an employer and add some additional keywords to your search string that represent job skills that you claim to have. I'll wait.

. . . I really will wait . . . give it a shot.

Okay, now what did you find? Did you find a brand that an employer will love? Did you find link after link about yourself that paints a consistent UX picture? Did you find links that fit well into a mold that employers or recruiters might be looking for? Do you clearly seem to have expertise in specific UX career pathways that are described later in Chapter 11? Is it obvious you have the skills and experience to take on a new career in these areas?

You found some family pictures? That's fine. There are some family pictures out there for me too, and I'll explain shortly why that is a good thing. By and large, though, you want the job-related matters to be the most salient.

Did you find something negative in the first few pages? Shows your partying nature? Uh oh. One bad link in the first few pages can spoil the bunch. But you can often do something about it. First, see if you can get the offending content removed. Track your way to the site owner. If the negative information is on some form of social media, see if you can get the poster to remove it.

SEARCH ENGINE FINDINGS WORKSHEET

Let's keep track of what you found today from a first page of hits on Google or your search engine of choice.

My brand as of (date) _____

Common themes that run through the search results

- _____
- _____
- _____
- _____
- _____

Looking at the search results, an employer would think that I have experience with

- _____
- _____
- _____
- _____

Specific skills that an employer would think that I'm very good at

- _____
- _____
- _____
- _____
- _____

Bad news for my personal brand that I need to clean up

- _____
- _____
- _____
- _____

Build Up Your Google-ability: Create Your Brand

Even if you can't remove offending content, working to get the important things about yourself out there could help crowd out what you don't want to be found. When is the last time you went through say ten pages of search listings? Five pages? Two pages?

What else can you do? A lot! You just need to commit to taking the time. We'll talk about all of this more in the pages that follow, but here are some starters:

CONTENT WITHIN YOUR DIRECT CONTROL

Create social media profiles on popular social media platforms: You have a lot of control in making sure your UX side is well represented on social media profiles. We'll be talking about LinkedIn and Twitter the most, although I'll explain why Facebook has value too.

Post your resume, yes as a PDF: There are plenty of places to upload a PDF document and you'll have a link that you can reference from elsewhere. You'll pretty much have ultimate control in painting a picture of who you are. Your resume needs to be fully compatible with your LinkedIn profile. And please don't tell me that you actually have multiple versions of your resume to support your multiple types of jobs that you look for (and even worse, that you've created multiple social media profiles for this reason). As a UX professional you know (or should learn quickly) that often what is being developed needs to simultaneously meet the needs of multiple specific audience groups; treat your resume the same way. We'll talk more about the specifics of your resume in Chapter 5.

Consider your own website—with your own domain name—and let that domain name be your name. The cost is quite nominal these days. You've got those UX skills, so use them to show who you are. Create a website that would make your college professor or mentor proud. Don't end up like the cobbler whose children have no shoes with a sub-par website. (It's amazing how easy it is to fall into this trap!)

- Be **searchable on the web.**

- **Create social media profiles** on LinkedIn and Twitter and use these to your work advantage.

- Consider a **UX blog.**

- Be **visible and salient in person and virtually**—sometimes this will trickle to the web (and has lots of other advantages).

- **Network, network, network!**

Create a UX blog: This is really easy to do. I use WordPress for my website/
blog mapped to my own domain name, and I highly recommend this approach.
Of course the harder part is that you need to come up with relevant UX content
to post. I'll say more about blogging shortly.

Avoid typos and errors: When I teach UX classes, I include a slide of all
the crazy errors I've found on public-facing websites—spelling errors like
the website that said that they are supportive of new pogroms, and content
errors like the website that pushed their users to call with questions, yet the

Create a strong, professional UX presence online

phone number was missing a digit. **Don't let this be you!** Double-check, triple-check, get a friend or pay a proofreader to review your stuff—website, resume, and blog—as well as your social media profiles that we'll discuss momentarily. Even though your errors are honest mistakes, they still reflect on your commitment to professionalism.

Get a professional headshot: If you want to give your brand a professional looking boost, you should strongly consider a professional headshot to use for anything associated with your professional image online. It doesn't have to cost a lot. Whatever you do—no selfies, even ones that you think seem "professional," and don't let it look like you chopped someone else out of the picture.

NOT DIRECTLY CONTROLLED CONTENT

Be visible: Simply put, you should show up at places where you can be seen doing UX work or talking with others in a UX context. Work is sometimes limited by privacy agreements, but not always. Figure out how your presence at your workplace can be made more visible and more tightly associate you with your UX skills. Can you represent your workplace somewhere—even if it's on your own time?

Be salient (in person): Figure out how to associate your name with a UX event—whether because of your job or because of what you offer to do. You could be a speaker or a panelist. You could offer to blog about the event or volunteer in some other way. You could chair or be the point of contact for an event committee. These sorts of name mentions in particular are going to start to bubble up as hits in Google and replace things that don't as solidly supply the brand details you are looking for. When those in the field or who are hiring for UX are thinking about someone with your UX skills, you want them to immediately think of you!

Be salient (virtually): You can offer to do webinars for others or provide guest posts on others' UX blogs. If you don't have ideas, let them know what you consider your expertise, and ask if there is any content that they might be missing or looking for others to write about.

Watch Your Privacy Settings

As my kids begin to join the various social media, I tell them that, as best practice, they should adjust their privacy settings appropriately and I help them do this. That advice is certainly true for you too. But in this electronic world, particularly

> Your personal life online can affect your career image.
>
> Be vigilant about your privacy settings.
>
> Don't assume anything online is truly private.

as we as UX professionals are to a large extent fully enmeshed in that electronic world, even things that you hide with your privacy settings should never be considered private. Assume that they will become public at some point. That's just the way it is: real privacy doesn't exist in the electronic age. **For the good of your career, do not trust privacy settings to protect any content that would harm your career image or brand should it become public.**

Network Now!

Adapted with permission from Lebson, Cory. "Care About Your UX Career? Network Now!" *UXPA User Experience Magazine*, Volume 13, Issue 1 (First Quarter 2013).[1]

Creating your brand is not enough. You also need to advertise your UX brand. How? Through networking. Even if you have the best UX job in the world, you need to be networking now. Why? Because no matter how happy you are now where you are, you can never assume it's going to stay that way forever. UX as a career burns brightly. As I've said before, you're pretty lucky to have ended up here. Yet the downside of burning brightly is that your job comes with some built-in instability and volatility. That's just the way it is—you may have a wonderful job right now where you will stay for many years. But don't ever let anyone convince you that you are completely safe in your job. That is why you need to network. But I'll tell you a secret—it can be a lot of fun to learn from others in the field, to share about yourself in the name of networking, and to open yourself up to new possibilities (paid work or otherwise) that you may not yet be aware of.

By definition, UX is centered on understanding people: the people we design for, the people that participate in our research studies, and the people that ultimately use our products. Give your UX peers the opportunity to get to know you, and at the same time, take the opportunity to get to know your peers. How do you do this? By networking both electronically and in person. A wider network means more job opportunities and support from those in your profession, as well as the ability to help further the UX field. You may not realize until long after the fact that the 5-minute conversation and business card exchange you had with another event attendee one day turned into the opportunity that came to you several years later.

Who You Should Network With

As a UX professional, you should focus on networking with other UX professionals, as well as those who understand the value of UX. I once made this statement when I was speaking, and someone in the audience tweeted the quote. Shortly after, I saw an unhappy tweet from someone not at the event who basically told me that I was being short sighted—that everyone is worth knowing. Of course it is wonderful to have a wide range of relationships with a wide and diverse range of people. And while knowing a wide range of people and having a large set of loose social ties is important, when you have to put effort into networking for business purposes, stick with those who will understand what you do. Don't be like the real estate agent who once showed up at one of my talks. She approached me afterwards to basically reveal that she had no interest whatsoever in UX or in my topic but she shows up at talks—any talks—because you never know who is going to want some real estate!

Networking Online

LINKEDIN FOR UX PROFESSIONALS

There is no question that if you only had access to one social network to further your UX career, it's LinkedIn. LinkedIn is chock-full of UX: UX people, jobs, groups, and articles.

Here's how UX professionals should use LinkedIn:

Make your LinkedIn profile usable: Everything that you might include in the design or recommendation for a website is also true for your LinkedIn profile. Make it easy to skim, and make sure that key information pops out.

Create an accurate profile: Your profile should reflect who you are professionally but focus on your UX skills and experiences. This doesn't have to be a resume and doesn't have to be all inclusive.

Create a meaningful LinkedIn URL: Consider using your first and last name. Mine is simply linkedin.com/in/lebson. If you share a name with others, perhaps use your name + "UX," which could be beneficial for SEO purposes too.

Structure your profile so that the UX experience stands out, and remember how your brand is derived: If you've done work outside of UX, de-emphasize it. Someone who wants to hire you may appreciate your diverse background but will still look for your core UX focus first.

A single profile MUST do the job: Never create two profiles. Your UX work often means creating a single website or app for multiple audience groups, and your LinkedIn profile needs to function the same way.

Get recommendations: Don't be embarrassed to explain to your recommenders how you think their recommendation can best align with your profile and thus the brand you're trying to project. While a generic "great to work with" recommendation is fine to sprinkle in, for the most part, recommendations should highlight your UX skills and experiences. Be ready to give a recommendation back for anyone from whom you requested a recommendation. (That means if you don't like them, don't ask them for a recommendation even if they like you.)

Give unsolicited recommendations: When you think someone has done a great job, let them know. It is a great way to "pay it forward," and it feels really good to get these.

Connect on LinkedIn to anyone you meet in a UX context: My experience has been that UX people are very apt to connect to other UX people. And in addition, those with careers that are tangential to UX will be your next best group to connect with.

Consider that many weak ties are often more valuable than a few strong ties: Your network is just that much stronger for it. If you are looking for a UX job and the hiring manager is also a UX person, having a large network of other UX professionals will often mean that you are connected to the hiring manager several times over as a second-degree connection. I connect readily with other UX professionals myself, and I bet that if you're connected to other UX professionals, you and I are likely no further away than second-degree connections.

Look up other UX professionals: Use the web or LinkedIn mobile app to learn about others in your world. Don't be afraid to let them know—you're not spying. This is information they are putting out there to let you know who they are. Referencing something you saw on LinkedIn can also potentially be a good conversation starter.

Be helpful: Even if not for yourself, don't hesitate to leverage your connections to help others who may need it. Make sure your network is visible to your connections. If someone sends you a request for an introduction to one of your connections, by all means make the connection. Perhaps it's another "pay it forward" strategy; but at a minimum, it just feels good to help colleagues in this way.

Join UX groups: There are many good UX groups on LinkedIn with interesting posts and where you can contribute based on your background. Do a search for "user experience" or specific job titles or job skills and you'll find thousands of groups. To identify the groups that are likely going to be the most valuable to you, consider looking at how many group members are in your network according to LinkedIn (e.g., first-, second- and third-degree connections).

Also consider LinkedIn groups that represent UX within your local geography as these are likely going to be the most useful in connecting you to the UX community around you. You can join up to 50 groups—so go ahead and join 50 UX-related groups that are of interest. By default, group members from all 50 groups will be able to contact you directly, so choose wisely. You have the option of receiving regular emails from your groups. In order to not be overwhelmed by LinkedIn emails, I select my top few (which change periodically) for emails. When I have time, I go to the other groups that are set not to send me emails, just to see what's happening.

LinkedIn Pulse: LinkedIn Pulse is essentially a blogging tool that directly links to your LinkedIn profile. Of course you need to generate some quality UX content. You'll get quick feedback on content success with real-time data on the number of reads and number of likes from your UX peers.

Reach out, catch up, and strengthen: LinkedIn is wonderful for making connections **and** periodically reminding contacts that you exist. To add to that, when you have some time, pick a few contacts who you have interacted with in the past but have lost touch with and send them a note saying hi and asking them to a morning coffee or maybe an after-work drink.

Should you be a LION? A LION is a LinkedIn open networker who basically connects with everyone. I don't recommend that you be a LION. A large network of random individuals has the potential to be overwhelming. I will say, however, that I average getting one LinkedIn invite a day from someone I don't know. As long as I can look at their profile and see that they are a UX-er or have a career that is at least tangential to UX, I'll connect with them. (So if you're reading this book, feel free to connect with me!) **Don't be one of those people who says "I only accept connections from people I have deep**

personal relationships with." You're not pledging your undying loyalty as long as you both shall live; you're building your UX network!

Twitter for UX Professionals

I keep my Twitter posts almost exclusively within a UX framework. Here are recommendations, based on my experience:

WHO TO FOLLOW

Professionals in your specific UX discipline: I'm clearly centered as a UX research, evaluation, and training professional, and I follow other UX professionals whom I know personally or who tweet about these usability-related topics.

Related UX professionals: I also follow some UX professionals who are in careers with specialties other than my own. I follow those whom I either know personally or who tweet about things generally related to UX.

Following back: You are not required to follow people back just because they follow you; but if they have an interesting profile or interesting tweets, certainly consider it.

WHAT TO TWEET

Consider a mix of tweets that will intrigue those who are in your field professionally. In terms of UX, my tweets center around events, places, professional items, and personal items. And throughout all your tweets, remember to involve your @colleagues. UX careers is not a zero-sum cut-throat situation. Rather, you promote them, they promote you, and you all rise together.

Tweets of place:

- **Meet locally:** Do you have some free time? Tweet that you're around at a particular place and time for a drink.
- **Meet while traveling:** Have some free time during some business travel? Again, that spontaneous coffee or drinks with colleagues has business value.
- **UX events and conferences:** Maybe you're going to be present at a particular UX event or conference, or maybe you're a speaker—either way, let your network know you'll be there.
- **UX volunteerism:** Are you volunteering your time somewhere in a UX context?

- **Good events you can't get to:** Are there other interesting talks and events that you heard about, even if you can't make it?

Tweets of thought:

- **Your blog posts**
- **Others' blog posts** that you find interesting, perhaps with a personal note of what you consider particularly meaningful
- **Useful content on Twitter** that someone else has tweeted, ideally as a modified tweet where you can add value with a comment or endorsement of an idea
- **Broadcasting of professional needs** as long as those needs can be seen by your boss and your colleagues

Personal tweets:

- **Your human side:** I occasionally tweet something that shows my human side (like running a 5K with my father and my daughters) so that others can get to know me as a person (with good character traits) in addition to the UX professional I am.

What not to tweet

- **Sensitive issues:** In short, don't tweet anything that will be particularly sensitive. You don't want to be that person whose work-related tweets are avoided because you can't stop spewing your political views, your religious views, or because you appear oblivious to socially acceptable standards of appropriateness.
- **Whining:** Please don't complain publically about your job, your boss, or your current life situation. Nobody wants to engage with a grump.
- **Too much self-promotion:** Of course, you tweet about yourself. That's okay. But avoid continual tweets that are overly self-promotional or focused on the sale. You don't want to turn into an advertisement and end up the victim of ad-blindness.

Facebook for UX Professionals?

While Twitter and LinkedIn provide the best opportunity for professional social networking, I'd be remiss to suggest that Facebook has no value in business. Facebook posts tend to be focused more on the personal than the professional, but that is not necessarily a bad thing. Giving people the opportunity to know you a bit more personally—and getting to know them more personally—will help to strengthen your business connections too. So I will connect with other UX professionals on Facebook as long as I know them, am pretty sure they know me, and I'm interested in getting to know them better.

A number of my Facebook posts are personal in nature, but I would like other UX professionals to know me just as I would like to know them through their personal posts. I do post business items as well, including locations, activities, and UX ideas.

A much greater portion of my connections actually read and respond to my Facebook posts than respond to me through other social networks. That's the nature of Facebook. If you are one of those people who say that "Facebook is just for personal connections," please reconsider.

Writing a Blog

Sure you can share good content that you find on the web with LinkedIn and Twitter, and there is certainly great value in this. But you get extra credibility bonus points for being the producer of that content as a way to add your value to the greater UX community. While I'd encourage you to consider trying to publish your thoughts and experiences through UX publications, it is certainly very easy and quick to set up a blog.

Consider starting your own blog related to whatever area of UX you are in, or more generally in your particular career track.

- **Don't try to sell your services** explicitly.

- **Demonstrate your wisdom** in your field and **show your passions.**

- **Reuse your favorite blog entries** for talks, publications, or in other creative ways.

It has been over four years since, on a whim, I started blogging. This was the first time that I had ever tried to maintain a regular stream of entries. While sometimes it has been relatively easy to both come up with topics and write them up, other times, billable work has been rather intense, and my blogging effort was put on the back burner. Since starting, I've managed to generate an average of one or two posts per month (in recent years, cross-posted to both my own WordPress site and LinkedIn Pulse) and get a collective average of 6,000 article reads per year. I've also gotten contract research work specifically because clients read my blog posts and liked what they saw. When, in December of 2014, I posted that I was about

Announcing this book generated 92 likes and 50 comments as well as another 50 or so messages through other channels and helped identify contributors

to write this book on UX careers, I not only found the positive feedback on the post reassuring, but in reviewing the comments + another set of separate email messages from people who read the post, I was able to identify several of the contributors for this book.

As long as you're within the general UX framework, it's up to you what you want to write about—that is, as long as it is generalizable enough that readers are interested in it, and as long as you don't become too sales-oriented. I'm always happy to promote the blogs of others when I find a particular post interesting, but I will avoid blogs that start with some great stuff and then use it as a lead-in for their bold sales pitches. Sure you want to let people know about your knowledge and perhaps skills through your blog, but do it quietly and gently. You don't want your readers to feel betrayed by your reasons for generating the content.

As a starter, these are the tags that I often use in my WordPress blog on Lebsontech.com:

Accessibility; Advocating for UX; Consulting; Disaster UX; Heuristic Expert Review; Networking; Project Management; Speaking; Training; User Research; UX Adventure; UX Career; UX Leadership; UXPA; Writing

Know that the value of your blog entries is more than just the reads that they garner. Rather, they can be repurposed and reused in a variety of contexts. I've found that blog entries provide me with a way to get feedback from my peers that later convinces me to turn these into publications, conference presentations, talks, webinars, and even guest appearances on radio shows. Blogs have provided me with ready source materials that have helped me to appear extra knowledgeable in conversations with my peers since I'd already thought through particular topics. I even use one blog entry to quickly tell the recruiters who email me daily what kinds of work I do (as a contractor through my company) and what kind of work I don't do.

From my experience, I can also tell you that putting your blogs on social media can lead to additional followers, as well as retweets, likes, and @mentions from other UX professionals.

Search Engine Optimization (SEO)

While SEO isn't quite as solidly associated with UX as perhaps it should be (which we'll discuss more in Chapter 11), a good UX professional should be at least somewhat knowledgeable about good SEO principles—one of the top points being that websites should be using keywords that users would be keying into search engines. Similarly, you should be making sure that the keywords that you use to refer to yourself in your social media profiles, blog entries, and anything else that you have control over, are optimal. Think about your external consistency. How well do you synch up with positions that people may be looking for? Even if you aren't looking for a job at the moment, do a keyword review. There are a myriad of tools that you can easily uncover with a Google search. These tools will look at your content or perhaps your LinkedIn profile and do a keyword analysis or tag cloud. Did you find your UX job skills? Do your skills match up with a certain type of UX?

Networking in Person

Networking electronically is important and will give you national and international reach. That said, the greater the effort you put into networking, the more you will get out of it. Get out there and talk with people. Go to conferences and events both locally and nationally, and if you are up for it, internationally as well.

Genuine interest = engagement.

Truly engage with the people you meet. Show interest in them—not fake interest—find the things about that person that are of most interest to you, and talk about them.

First Conversations: Prepare Your Elevator Pitch

Just like a good social media profile, your elevator pitch is your real-world profile. Craft an elevator pitch—**30 seconds for you to explain what you do and why you are worth talking to**. Then practice it, tweak it, iterate it, and commit it to memory. When you do then meet someone new, while you don't necessarily need to use your elevator pitch, you'll have it in your back pocket.

As I noted with Twitter, please don't use your first conversation to complain about your boss, your job, or anything else. Its fine to say that you're looking for something new, but avoid the specifics or those you're talking to won't want to talk with you for all that long. (And of course that's not to say that you should bottle in your feelings, just save them for those closest to you.)

Deeper Conversations: Radiate Your Passion

I recall a time when I was in graduate school and was talking with a faculty member about having to make the case for something. He was making some suggestions, when suddenly he hit on something that I really liked and I became very enthusiastic. I wasn't aware that my body language had changed, but all of a sudden his eyes lit up and he said, "Show that passion and you'll make your case!" Since then, I've become much more aware of how people react when they feel genuine passion about an idea (and know how I may—or may not—be solidly engaging with enthusiasm). But even being aware of this myself, when I'm in a conversation with someone else who is successfully radiating their enthusiasm about a plan or idea, I can feel myself getting drawn along, too.

It may sound silly, but try it out in a mirror. Express your passion to yourself. Watch how your body language changes, and gain control. Are you leaning forward? Gesturing with your hands? Smiling? Showing wide-eyed excitement? Then watch what happens when you can genuinely and appropriately express yourself in public in the same way.

Use Business Cards

I was at a conference a number of years ago and met a woman who told me that she didn't believe in business cards. When I ran into her a few years later, she handed me her business card. Paper business cards are a basic, primary method of exchanging initial contact information. While technology makes it possible to exchange our information electronically, paper business cards remain an essential element of connecting.

If you have business cards from your place of work and are comfortable with this representing your brand, then by all means keep using these cards. But I'd encourage you to get your own business cards printed if you:

- can better reflect your brand on a card with information of your own choosing
- prefer to have your contact information be your own, not that of your employer
- want to encourage people to connect with you on your preferred social media channels (this one is important)
- are looking for a job

If you have both company business cards and personal business cards, make sure to still use your company cards when appropriate, particularly if you're "on the clock" or at some function where you are representing your company. When you are on your own time, however, for example if you attend a UX organization's evening event on your own volition, you can use your personal cards.

Carry your business cards with you—I keep a core set in my wallet and a backup stash in my laptop case. You don't have to throw them at people; but when someone hands you a business card, it is ideal to reciprocate with a card of your own. Also, sometimes people will explicitly ask you for a business card.

If you want someone to remember something specific about the conversation, feel free to write it on the card as you hand it over. If you want to remember something about the other person, make a note of it on their business card. (And this means that even as we all have our preferred mobile devices—and apps that will absorb business card contact info after the fact—it's still worthwhile to carry around a plain old fashioned pen!)

Work Through Shyness or Introversion

I've lost count of the number of times I've heard UX professionals say that they are introverts. I've heard it in individual conversations, group conversations, and even from speakers at conferences. Is it true? Are introverts attracted to UX? I believe that many UX professionals are probably self-classifying as introverted when in fact they may be shy or just feel under-confident. An introvert[2] is more reserved and may not be as comfortable in groups. A shy person[3] may still want to be around people but may just feel awkward or uncomfortable about doing so and may want to avoid these situations for that reason. An under-confident person may feel like they don't have anything valuable to add even when they do.

While I lean towards extroversion and am relatively outgoing, there have certainly been instances where I found myself somewhere surrounded by people whom I didn't know, and without a defined role in the situation, I have felt shy. So, regardless of how you classify yourself, how do you overcome shyness, introversion, or other potential barriers to networking when doing your UX work or surrounded by other UX professionals?

- **Have a purpose.** I've sometimes taken a "mall intercept" approach when doing user research—placing myself in the right place where I could find the right people to conduct my research. They were strangers, but I had a strong purpose and I had a nice incentive for them for participating. It was easier that way to approach the strangers than it would have been if I didn't have a well-defined mission. Similarly, when you end up in a situation where you have an opportunity to do some UX networking, make a plan. Consider volunteering to sign people in or help in some way. You'll have a defined purpose that way and feel more confident in being there.
- **Make a goal.** Even if you don't want to volunteer, create an achievable and quantifiable goal: decide that your job is to meet X new people, or collect X business cards, or perhaps make X new LinkedIn connections.
- **Find an ally.** Whether you are in the field, at a conference, in a meeting, or at an event, find one person to initially talk to. Make some small talk, warm up. If someone else is nearby, it becomes easier to loop them into the conversation and gather people around you.
- **Know your brand and be clear on who you are.** Be ready with that elevator pitch that you've committed to memory. Know your brand and articulate it smoothly!

UX Adventures: Volunteer Your Time and Improve Your Career Potential

Adapted with permission from Lebson, Cory. "UX Adventure: Enhance your resume, improve your career potential, and feel the excitement!" *UX Magazine*, Article No. 983. (March 22, 2013).[4]

UX work can bring about exciting challenges and interesting interactions with people. But exciting work will always wax and wane as UX projects come and go. While your salary may be constant, you may not always enjoy the projects that you are working on. The good news is that invigorating UX-oriented projects don't always have to come from work; in fact, they don't have to be paid efforts at all.

Value in Unpaid Work

There are many reasons why you may want to get involved in unpaid UX work: maybe you want to enhance your resume. Maybe you want to meet other UX professionals who can help you find new jobs and new opportunities. Maybe you want to learn by increasing your exposure to various areas of UX. Or, as in my case after having been in the field for nearly 20 years, maybe you want to generate some additional excitement and challenge in your UX life.

"UX Adventure" Defined

I wrote a blog post about a year of exciting UX volunteer leadership activities and was stunned by the level of positive feedback that I received from my colleagues. In response to the post, I also got a number of ideas and proposals for ways to have UX adventures the following year, including a request to do a radio show about professional adventure, which was an adventure in itself. This then led to an article on UX adventure in *UX Magazine* and a subsequent blog post on how to teach others to have these adventures.

When I told a colleague that if one Googles "UX adventure" in quotes, I have the first two hits, she responded, "But nobody else talks about UX adventure—of course you'd come up first!" Over time, I've been so excited to see others now using this phrase to refer to both their paid and unpaid UX-related activities.

Value of a UX Adventure

A non-work adventure may be simply for the thrill of the adventure. A work adventure, however, whether or not it's actually paid, is not just about making existing employment more thrilling. A work adventure is also about ways to enhance current and future employment, project marketability, and overall career potential. A work adventure increases exposure to those in your chosen profession. A work adventure increases your visibility and allows you to be noticed professionally, beyond just by your employer.

I often find that I don't know which adventure is going to lead to professional gain but as we discussed in Chapter 1, one thing often leads to another. For me, a random 5-minute conversation at the lunch table of a small conference led to a UX evaluation project six months later. An event organizer that I had intrigued by volunteering my time referred another client almost a year later. A UX networking event I organized led to some job interviews for attendees. While I didn't get any professional gain from the latter, it felt really good to contribute to those in the UX field in this way!

Finding the Time

We are very lucky that the UX field has continued to grow, that work is plentiful, and that companies seem to struggle to keep up with the growing demand for UX professionals. But plentiful work and busy practitioners might mean that there isn't all that much time for volunteer work or business-type activities outside of work hours.

However, as it turns out, time is not a zero-sum game. In response to my original UX adventure blog post, one of my colleagues suggested that the Yerkes-Dodson model was an important frame. The Yerkes-Dodson model, originally developed in the early twentieth century, says that performance increases with what they termed "arousal." In terms of UX adventure, perhaps as we get more excited about our professional activities as a whole (including both paid but mundane and unpaid but exciting activities), we can become more efficient at the paid work, leaving more time for the unpaid work. We can run more efficiently, and seemingly get much more done than otherwise would seem possible.

Embarking on Your Own UX Adventure

STEP 1: IDENTIFY YOUR STRENGTHS

Are you ready for your own UX adventure? The first step is to identify your strengths.

What are your skills? Reference strengths outside of UX. Are you a good writer, event planner, photographer, musician, or fitness guru? Do you enjoy socializing in person or virtually? Really anything can be tied into a UX adventure. The key is to tie in something (outside of UX) that you enjoy doing.

Who are you? The first and most critical portion of this work adventure curriculum would be a visioning of who you are now and who you want to be. This involves a certain amount of self-reflection and perhaps a verbal or written acknowledgement of who you are as an individual and what hats you may wear in life. Yet this adventure, while tangentially related to general self-reflection and goal-directed self-actualization, at its core is about how you can find the most meaning through work—work that perhaps doesn't mean obediently following a standard definition of what it means to work.

What are you passionate about? In addition to who you are, to have an adventure you need to be doing things that you love. Those things do not have to be rooted in your work per se, but you would need to have the opportunity to creatively come up with things that can tie together who you are with what you love and simultaneously provide work value.

I very much enjoy public speaking, teaching, writing, and in-person networking, so many of the adventures that I've had revolve around those types of activities, often tied into things I am passionate about. But I also enjoy running and hiking on nature trails, so one summer, I created a local event where I arranged to have the park service lead me and a number of other like-minded UX professionals on a hike.

STEP 2: IDENTIFY THE ADVENTURES TO PURSUE

You know what you like, but what kind of adventure do you want to pursue?

Volunteer for an established group. Maybe you want something with a lot of direction where you can be told what needs to be done. You can volunteer with a local meet-up or a local chapter of a larger organization that covers particular aspects of UX that you are interested in. Different regions have different active organizations. (Refer back to Chapter 3 for more on the value of UX organizations.)

Consider being a free agent. Organizational affiliation is not the only way to have a UX adventure. Initiate or assist in creating events, workshops, seminars, Meetups, or gatherings to help promote or define UX. You can create an event or workshop yourself and promote it via social media and possibly word of mouth. While you may not be able to generate the numbers that you could through a larger organizational affiliation, you aren't likely reporting attendance numbers on your resume. The act of proposing a workshop and following through on it is what matters.

Traveling? As we talked about in what to tweet, consider just tweeting where you'll be next and see what happens. On a recent business trip, I called the hotel where I was going to stay and asked them to recommend a nice bar. I tweeted that I'd be at the bar, got seven likely affirmatives, and ended up being joined by three other UX professionals. I enjoyed this networking supplement to what otherwise would have been a trip involving only paid work. Will anything come of these types of conversations? You never know!

You can have a UX adventure without leaving your desk. For me, simply promoting the idea of UX adventure is an adventure all its own, and I've done a lot of that without even leaving my office. Consider a topic and pitch it to the various UX-oriented publications as a possible article. Your blog can be an adventure too, as could your use of social media.

Try public speaking (you can do it!) While a work adventure does not require public speaking skills per se, gaining exposure from doing talks certainly opens up doors to other things as well (and in my framework, those talks themselves can be adventures). While for some people public speaking may be more natural than for others, assessing what topics you can speak about within your chosen career pathways and learning how to create effective slides with optimal use of graphics and a targeted message could be quite valuable. In addition, simply having the opportunity to practice and talk about anything, work or otherwise, in front of people who are interested in listening could be a great confidence booster.

Your turn. I've mentioned ideas that fit in my personal UX adventure framework; but for yourself, think outside my framework and make it your own. Take your personality, skills, and passions and do a little brainstorming: how could you combine these into your own UX adventure?

Optimize Your Brand

Even if you are not looking for a job or career move right now, you will thank yourself years down the road when you are exploring job opportunities that you took the time to improve your brand over the prior years and can now reap the benefits. Start now! Figure out what you should do immediately, and what you want to try to do in the future—in a month or even in a year. Once you have established a plan to improve your brand and started acting on this plan, it's time to figure out how you're going to illustrate your value with a solid resume and impressive portfolio samples.

 Get more online at uxcareershandbook.com/brand-network

IMPROVING MY BRAND WORKSHEET AND CHECKLIST

My plan as of (date) _____

Include date goals and/or details for any ideas you want to explore in the future

Social media platforms

- _____ **LinkedIn:** Make sure my profile is updated and represents my UX skills well.
- _____ **Twitter:** My goal is to tweet (UX related) ___ times/month.
- _____ **Facebook:** My personal posts will help my work colleagues to know me better.

Personal web presence

- _____ **My own website** _____
- _____ **Post my resume** (PDF) _____
- _____ **Start a UX Blog** _____
- _____ **Come up with a system for proofreaders** to check my work for typos _____

Opportunities to increase my salience

- _____ **Increase my visibility** with my existing employer _____
- _____ **Volunteer** or take on a role at a UX event _____
- _____ **Offer to speak** for a local organization or propose a talk at a conference
- _____ **Propose an article** for a UX-related publication
- What I'm passionate about (and which could feed into my UX adventures): _____
  _____

Networking

- _____ Prepare and rehearse my elevator pitch
- _____ Arrange to catch up with at least _____ colleagues per month
- _____ Make sure that I network with or reach out to ____ new people per month
- _____ Join a UX organization and attend at least _____ events/year _____
- What I'll do to overcome shyness _____
  _____

NOTES

1. http://uxpamagazine.org/care-about-your-ux-career/

2. http://www.myersbriggs.org/my-mbti-personality-type/mbti-basics/extraversion-or-introversion.htm

3. http://apa.org/topics/shyness/index.aspx

4. https://uxmag.com/articles/ux-adventure-enhance-your-resume-improve-your-career-potential-and-feel-the-excitement

Part 2

Getting a Job

CHAPTER 5

Resumes and Portfolios to Illustrate Your Value

With Amanda Stockwell, Vice President of UX, 352 Inc.

Some of the text in this chapter is adapted with permission from: Stockwell, Amanda. "Never Trust a Skinny Chef" *UXmatters* (February 11, 2014).[1]

While as a user experience (UX) professional you have (or will have) the benefit of a great number of job opportunities, you also have some unique challenges when it comes to describing yourself and your work clearly. As we discussed at the beginning of this book, UX is not a tightly defined career and there is no one set of ideal experiences or single path into UX. These variations and ambiguities can make the normal challenge of capturing your expertise in a few bullet points or sample artifacts even more difficult.

The good news is that if you are someone who is inclined towards UX from the outset, you are lucky to also likely have a valuable set of skills to draw on when crafting your resume and portfolio: user-centered design. The same UX principles that give users a positive experience can guide you in creating a resume and portfolio that lets you showcase your UX value.

Use user-centered design principles to guide you when creating your resume and portfolio.

- Research your audience and their needs and goals.

- Make content understandable for all possible audience groups.

- Make information easy to skim.

- Include visuals to illustrate information presented.

- Get feedback and iteratively improve.

Know Your Audience

IDENTIFY YOUR USERS

The key to designing a great UX is to gain a thorough understanding of the people for whom a product is being designed. Not only do we, as UX professionals, need to identify who those people are, we also need to consider the context in which they will use a product. This knowledge helps us make informed decisions about whatever we're building.

Designing a resume and portfolio is no different. In this case, the primary users are prospective employers, whether that is a recruiter, a hiring manager, or a client soliciting your services. Understanding the context in which they'll be viewing you and your deliverables can help you set expectations appropriately and deliver key information in the best way.

Understand Your Typical User's Situation

Let's go ahead and posit that the following two statements about the target users are true:

- **They are pressed for time**, often under pressure to find the right person for a job as soon as possible for some urgent UX needs—they probably have a bunch of candidates to review and may have multiple positions to fill simultaneously. So you'll need to make your resume easy to skim, and make sure it's easy for your users to quickly understand who you are, what skills you have, and what kind of work you are looking for.
- **Those who are seeking talent are not intimately familiar with the nuances of UX roles.** (They have not yet read this book!) When you're applying directly to a company, often a human resources staffer or a recruiter sees your work first, and neither is likely to have a background in UX. Therefore, you need to make what you can do super-clear, spelling it out in terms that these non-UX professionals will understand.

Learn as Much as Possible About Your Users

Web Research: Find out whatever you can about your audience from any reputable information source you can access. Use the power of the web to better understand your audience and get some context around them.

When considering working with a specific company, go to their website and to job review sites to find out about their company culture, products, and projects.

LinkedIn Power: As we discussed in Chapter 4, LinkedIn is a powerful tool not only for your own branding, but also in how it lets you find out about other people. Between search engine and LinkedIn queries, see if you can find the names of UX staff at some interesting companies or names of those who do the kind of work that you want to do. Take a look at their profiles and see how they describe their work. You can learn a lot this way.

Use Content Strategy Skills

KEEP TRACK OF WORK

Once you've carefully considered your audience, it's time to start creating or updating your core hiring deliverables: your resume and portfolio. Just as many web content projects begin with a content audit to document and analyze all the existing parts on a site, consider using a similar process to assess your career experience content. Starting with a comprehensive list of everything you have done makes it easier to analyze your work, identify the most important pieces, and spot and remove the ROT—redundant, outdated, or trivial content.

Develop a method to document your work. For example, consider keeping an ongoing log of projects in a spreadsheet with high-level descriptions of tasks and work samples that you have available, using a structure that would be typical of a content audit. Customize this to your specific needs. Make the listing as comprehensive as possible, and note whether you've already included something similar in your portfolio. When it's time to update your resume or portfolio, scan the document to see what new items you might want to highlight. While record keeping like this may seem difficult to keep up, it will help you always be prepared when you realize a need to update your materials or find a specific example for a unique effort to which you are applying.

Your documentation does not need to include only projects that you were paid for. If you are just starting out in your UX career and don't have a lot of work to show, you're still going to want something to demonstrate your UX skills. Consider using projects that you pulled together as part of course assignments, or possibly things that you did on your own for practice. You can also convey your soft skills and key personality attributes.

Consider including in your spreadsheet:

- **Employer** or contract
- **Specific project**
- **Project start date** (month and year) and/or project end date
- **Deliverable types as columns** for deliverables where you had significant input (put an "x" in those columns as appropriate. You can also add notes to cells with supplemental information)
- **Currently included on resume**: Yes/No
- **Portfolio-ready**: Yes/No

For example, your columns could look like this:

Employer/ Client	Project	Date	Persona Creation	Ethnographic Research	Low-fidelity mockups	Currently included on Resume	Portfolio-ready	File location
Acme, Inc.	Public facing website redesign	July, 2016	X	X		Y	N	

Apply Content Strategy to Your Resume

Include your top skills: Your resume should highlight the UX skills that you're best at and most want to continue doing, rather than a laundry list of every kind of work you've ever done.

Sync your resume with your LinkedIn profile: While your resume and LinkedIn profile don't have to say exactly the same thing, if someone were to look at one and then the other, they should clearly see the same person with the same backgrounds and interests.

Succinctly introduce yourself: An employer needs to know who they're getting a resume from and how to get in touch with that person. Make sure that your resume clearly states your name and a title of some kind, either an actual title or else a conceptual tag line of something as simple as "Interaction Designer."

Include a picture: Make it as professional as you can get. I encourage you to pay a professional to give you an official headshot. This takes time and has a cost but helps cement your professional image.

Header from Cory's resume

Summarize your UX career pathways and most valuable attributes: (In Chapter 11 you will see a number of common pathways and associated descriptions.)

Clearly state what you are looking for: Be aware that your resume will make its way into many databases. Therefore, you need to come up with a reasonably generalizable statement about what you're looking for that will work for a specific job or for future jobs that may come along. You will be better off if you can come up with a single objective statement (or set of statements) that can define the complete universe of jobs that you are looking for.

Articulate your brand: Think back to Chapter 4, where we discussed your UX brand. As you think about your resume, if you haven't already, consider how your brand mirrors the career pathways/skill sets in Chapter 11.

- **External consistency:** Does your resume show skills that fit nicely into a UX career pathway or even support that you are skilled in multiple pathways? You want your resume to tell a crisp and clear story about how you fit incredibly well into one or more of these pathways.
- **Appropriate strengths:** Does your resume articulate your key strengths? If it's not clearly apparent on your resume that you have these specific strengths, consider including a personal profile section that highlights your personal strengths.

What can I help you with?
- **Strategy meetings and design workshops** as well as informal design discussions
- **Design critique workshops and expert (heuristic) reviews:** usability, information architecture, mobile/responsive display, content analysis, search engine optimization (SEO), web analytics
- **Preliminary research and requirements gathering:** interviews, documentation reviews, competitive analyses
- **Exploratory research** such as ethnographic studies, contextual inquiries, cognitive walkthroughs
- **Usability testing** anywhere (in-person or remote) at any point in the development process
- **Accessibility** (W3C WCAG 2.0 and Section 508) reviews and training (DHS Trusted Tester Certification)
- **Focus groups** related to websites and technology
- **Card sorts** including both online and offline efforts, creation and analysis of dendrograms
  Details on Lebsontech Research & Evaluation

Skill summary from Cory's resume

Provide your relevant skills in context: To ensure full understanding of your skills, be sure to specify the activities where you used those skills. For example, instead of writing "Led project X from conception to launch," *elaborate*. Explain exactly what the job entailed, as in the following example:

User Researcher, **Staples,** November 2011-September 2014
- Designed, moderated, and analyzed goal-directed usability tests and presented recommendations to a variety of audiences
- Planned, wrote, analyzed, and presented customer goal and usage surveys
- Collaborated with internal teams to develop, launch, and synthesize associate-facing surveys
- Performed in-store shopping intercepts to gather customer feedback on retail programs and processes
- Planned, administered, analyzed, and presented internal stakeholder interviews
- Applied usability heuristics to identify the strengths and shortcomings of multiple interactions and websites
- Planned, facilitated, analyzed, and presented customer and potential-customer focus groups
- Contributed to requirements gathering and project planning processes
- Planned, wrote, analyzed, and presented taxonomy and hierarchy research
- Worked with various business-unit decision-makers to unify project goals and approaches
- Analyzed and compared feature and interaction strengths of competitors
- Provided expert reviews and opinions on the best user experience for a variety of cross-channel projects

Position from Amanda's resume with skills identified in line

Your resume should highlight your personal strengths and be clear about where your UX expertise lies.

Even if you are just starting out and don't have paid work to show, apply the same treatment to your sample work and indicate what specifically you did, how you decided to do it, and in what context you can imagine it being helpful. You need to tell your story and you need to illustrate that story.

Include Non-paid Work

In Chapter 4, we talked about UX adventures—those exciting experiences that are related to UX but that aren't necessarily related to your paid job. Consider also including some UX adventures on your resume. You could provide some intriguing basics and then a link to additional information. Perhaps you've given a talk or spoken at a conference or for a local meetup. Maybe you've volunteered your time in some UX-related way. Let this be known—it shows that UX permeates other aspects of your life and illustrates your passion.

Make Sure Your Resume Looks Good and is Easy to Read

With good user-centered design, the audience should be able to read information on a page quickly and efficiently. Likewise, make sure your resume is easy to skim.

- **Feature and highlight only the most important information**. Make sure your text is easy to skim and understand. **Choose concise, quality content** over quantity.
- **Best practices for search engine optimization (SEO) apply to your resume, too.** Over time, your resume will find its way into a myriad of databases. Therefore, keywords in the resume need to match the keywords that you think recruitment teams are likely to search for.

Validate Your Content

Once you pull together your resume, use any of the job posting sites that we discuss in Chapter 8 to see what skills they are looking for and what UX skills are clustered together. Don't be intimidated by the requests for UX unicorns, as we discuss in Chapter 1. Rather, find the jobs that are really a good fit with your existing skillset. Make sure that all the skills that you have, and, hopefully, the skills that multiple job postings are looking for, are clearly visible in your resume.

If you find there is a skillset that is consistently requested in job postings for your UX focus area but that you can't honestly claim to have, do as much research as you can to learn more, and consider pursuing some training on that skillset. That way, you will still be able to explain to a potential employer that you understand a skillset and that performing the actions required will not be a big leap from the skillsets that you do clearly possess.

Get Feedback

As with any UX project, getting representative user feedback is absolutely critical to your success. Ask friends, family, and trusted colleagues to provide honest feedback. Each will have a different perspective and suggest tweaks that you wouldn't have considered on your own. Because your target audience might not fully understand the nuances of UX, it can be especially helpful to get that feedback from your connections outside the UX industry. Still, if you can, do your best to also involve a few more experienced colleagues who are knowledgeable about UX and the kinds of jobs that you're looking for. Ask them if you've done the job that you set out to do.

Also identify someone who is good at those nitpicky grammar elements that you are likely not to see when looking at your own work. If your resume has an error—whether a simple spelling error or a major gaffe, a hiring staff member may not pass on your resume, no matter how good your work is or how impressive your experience.

> Never submit a resume without having at least one person proofread it first.

After your resume has been thoroughly proofed, it's time to put it out there. As we discussed in Chapter 2, post your resume on the web publically as a PDF document. Plenty of places could host a PDF document, but the key is to end up with a simple URL link that includes your name and the word "resume" in the URL as a best practice for SEO. Post this link to your LinkedIn profile, and have it ready when someone asks you for your resume. Also consider putting a date stamp on this resume, as well as the link where the resume can be found, so that if it finds its way to a recruitment or employment database, the recruiter or employer will know how old your resume is and where they can go to find the most recent copy. Of course if you do this, regardless of whether you are

> Extensive portfolio that illustrates work efforts is available for presentation.
> See recommendations on LinkedIn (http://linkedin.com/in/lebson).
>
> This resume was last updated on January 15, 2016. (Most recent version at www.lebsontech.com)

Cory's resume footer with a last updated date so if it is pulled from a database, recruiters can see how old it is and can find a new copy looking for a job or not, give yourself a reminder to post a new version with a new date every few months, even if nothing has changed, so that your resume is not tossed aside as "old news."

You certainly can feel free to post your resume to the various career sites that we discuss, and it can't hurt from an exposure perspective. That said, be prepared for a lot of junk emails from recruiters and recruitment organizations that use these services to send information about jobs that may have nothing to do with your UX experience.

Illustrate Your Expertise with Work Samples

While there may not be one set of deliverables that will prove your UX abilities, a portfolio, or curated set of past work samples, is the best way to tell your story and thus demonstrate your skills and expertise to new clients or potential employers. A visual representation of your work that demonstrates what specifically you've created, what process you followed, how your work fits into the context of other's work, and the impact that your work had can help employers immediately understand your value.

One good way to summarize a lengthy project is to create a case study: a single but detailed story around your work. Provide supporting visuals, perhaps a photograph of the initial brainstorming whiteboard, an image of you conducting an interview, an annotated screenshot of the prototype, and a snapshot of the final test report. Images are easier to digest and help recruiters and employers to quickly understand what types of work you do.

Keep in mind that your audience does *not* understand the context of your projects. Even if the hiring manager knows how to create wireframes, that person might struggle in trying to interpret a specific set of wireframes. To ensure that your audience has the context they need, overlay annotations, provide explanations, and describe how you and the team made your final design decisions. What did you learn along the way, and how did you come to your final conclusions? Recruiters and hiring managers want to understand what

> Your portfolio should illustrate the impact your work has had to help employers immediately understand your value.

Tell your UX story through your portfolio

you did, how you did it, and why, and even the most beautiful wireframe or prototype isn't going to tell that story without some additional context.

Navigate Confidentiality and Non-Disclosure Agreements

While classroom projects or publically available work can likely be shared without any problem, eventually you'll likely arrive at a conundrum that many professionals have: you have some great work but you are not supposed to share it. So what do you do?

Consider whether it is possible to strip out anything confidential. While you don't want to render your deliverables so sterile that they lose all meaning, you may be able to strip out just enough to eliminate confidential elements while still maintaining the integrity of the project. You can also replace confidential words with generic words, or if you have to remove something like an image, you could replace it with a wireframe-type box that simply says "Image removed for confidentiality purposes."

Quantify Your Value

It is also important to highlight your role in project successes to clarify your value to non-UX-minded hiring staff. Teamwork is important, but what did *you* add? Perhaps your suggestion helped streamline the design process and allowed the company to get a product to market faster than expected. Maybe a research study that you initiated was able to highlight a key problem that was easily fixed and increased user satisfaction.

Clearly defining business challenges and how you were able to make things better is speaking a language that those who are making the hiring decision can understand, and simultaneously illustrates your communication skills. You can convey this kind of information to others without them needing any in-depth technical or UX knowledge. It also demonstrates that you can work within constraints and that you understand the business side of UX.

One simple framework to demonstrate your work samples in your portfolio is the PAR format: Problem, Action, Result (note that "Problem" is sometimes broken into two pieces, called the STAR format: Situation, Task Action, Result). You can use this simple PAR (or STAR) breakdown to set the context for the project and why it was important, specify your role and actions throughout the process, and explain your value by quantifying the outcomes.

EXAMPLE PAR

Problem	Action	Result
Staples, Inc. wanted to expand their delivery options and provide users with the ability to reserve an item online and go to a local store to pick it up. **The goal was to make for an easier purchasing experience for users, and therefore drive more overall sales**, including in-store add on sales. There were challenges with the existing order management system and with integrating the website and mobile application into well-established store employee roles.	I served as the **usability project manager** for this project, which meant that I was responsible for **representing the usability for all aspects of this project**, including planning and execution of: – **Discovery research** – **Competitive analysis** – **Initial requirements discussions** – **Brainstorming sessions** – **Iterative usability testing** – **Validation testing** – **Launch analysis and tracking** – **Customer satisfaction ratings** I worked with a project manager, an interaction designer, and business decision makers.	The initial phase of the project launched almost exactly one year after kick-off, which is staggering considering the size of the undertaking and numerous systems and employee processes that needed to be integrated. Progress continues to be monitored as the program is updated, but initial results included; – **More than 50% higher dollars per transaction** – **38% product attachment rate in store** – **Approximately $1 million/week in sales**

PAR WORKSHEET

1. Problem

    a. Issue & its importance _____

    _____

    b. End goal _____

    c. Challenges _____

    _____

2. Action

    a. My role _____

    b. My responsibilities _____

    _____

    c. Who I worked with and how I worked with them _____

    _____

3. Result

    a. How long it took _____

    b. Immediate results _____

    c. Long term outlook _____

Design Your Materials

Once you have all of your content identified, keep in mind that appearance matters in resumes and portfolios, even for those who are not involved in the visual design end of things.

Besides being sure to include visual representations of your work, consider other ways to make your resume and portfolio visually appealing. Be aware that the pallet of colors, fonts, and the distance between lines of text can greatly affect readability and visual aesthetics. When in doubt, keep things simple and lean towards pared down colors and simple fonts.

Consider Using the T-Shape or Broken Comb Visual

To quickly and visually display your skillset, consider using the T-shaped or "broken comb" model. In both cases, you plot your various skills along one axis and your level of expertise along the other axis. If you have a broad set of experiences but one or two areas of deep expertise, the chart will end

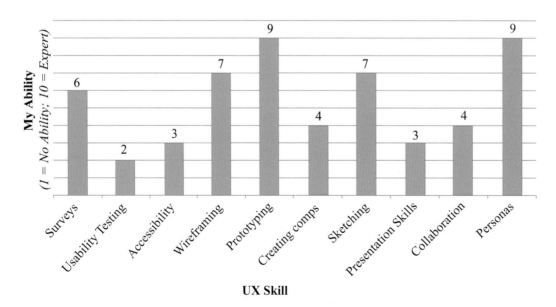

Example Broken Comb Chart

BROKEN COMB WORKSHEET

To create your own broken comb chart, first choose the 10 UX skills/activities that best capture your knowledge. You could also include a few things that you are not as strong in to provide a comparison point to your strengths. Then, honestly assess how strong you are in each area in relation to your other skills, and plot on the y-axis. Using a 10 point scale is easy to grasp and makes it easy to compare levels. There is no strict science to this, but be honest and keep in mind that you are trying to communicate a quick snapshot of your strengths.

Top 10 UX Skills *(X axis)*   **My Ability (scale of 1–10)** *(y axis)*

1. _____   _____
2. _____   _____
3. _____   _____
4. _____   _____
5. _____   _____
6. _____   _____
7. _____   _____
8. _____   _____
9. _____   _____
10. _____   _____

up looking something like an upside-down T. If you have varying levels of expertise in a wide array of UX skills, the result ends up resembling a comb with tines of various lengths. This simple graph is an effective way to quickly summarize your skillset.

Decide where to apply

As with your resume, make sure to have others review your portfolio materials for clarity and typos. Once you have all of your materials ready to share, it's time to think about which type of UX job situation might be the best fit for you at this point in your career.

Get more online: uxcareershandbook.com/resume-portfolio

Amanda Stockwell is the Vice President of UX at 352 Inc. where she leads a team that provides user research, usability testing, and UX strategy services. Amanda's expertise has helped companies new to UX assimilate user-centered design into their existing processes. Additionally, Amanda has unique career advancement insight from her tenure working with a top recruiting company, where she evaluated client needs and associated job descriptions, reviewed and interviewed scads of UX professionals, assessed those candidates for particular roles, and helped individuals shape and advance their UX careers. Amanda has a human factors background and an engineering degree from Tufts University. Follow Amanda on Twitter at @MandaLaceyS.

NOTE

1. http://www.uxmatters.com/mt/archives/2014/02/never-trust-a-skinny-chef.php

CHAPTER 6

Work In-house or be an External Consultant

You can practice your user experience (UX) skills by working in-house or by being an external consultant. There are different ways to practice within each option:

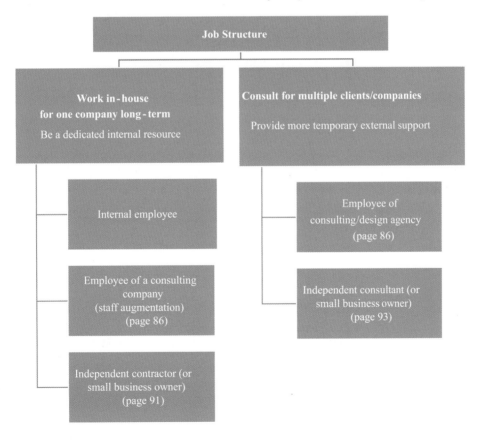

While the UX methods that you might use across both job structures may be similar, and many UX professionals spend some time working in-house and some time as a consultant over the course of their careers, UX professionals often show a preference for one of these two job structures over the other. Personally, while I did spend one year working in-house at a distance learning company, I found that I have gravitated towards being an external consultant and have spent by far the majority of my UX career that way.

In the pages that follow we will first discuss the advantages and disadvantages of being an in-house dedicated resource for one company. Then we will talk about being an external consultant for a consulting firm or agency. Finally, we will discuss the convergence of in-house with consulting—working as an internal consultant.

While this chapter focuses on working for an employer (whether as an employee of the company that needs your services or as an employee of a consulting firm/agency), Chapter 7 will focus on considerations when working for yourself as a freelancer or small business owner.

In-house Employment: Dedicated Resource

As an in-house resource, you focus your energy on a single company, you'll likely work within a single product line, or perhaps focus within a single corporate division. You may do this one of two ways: as an in-house employee or by working for another company and being placed as a full-time contractor for the client.

Share with Colleagues

As in-house staff, you cater to the needs of one company. You are likely to go to an office at least several days per week although this is not always the case. There are certainly many in-house UX professionals that work mainly out of their homes or shared co-working spaces nearby.

You are often going to have a consistent set of colleagues, which means opportunities to work with people who perform many different functions for your employer. In companies with large UX departments, you will likely have other UX-oriented colleagues to collaborate with on a regular basis and perhaps you will even feel that you have a workplace family of sorts.

Expect a Good Place to Start

There is a lot to be said for starting your UX career in-house. You become deeply embedded in a company and learn the company-specific ins and outs of UX. Conversations with your co-workers will likely provide a wealth of opportunities for on-the-job learning. The company will hopefully want to invest in your future with them by helping you continue to grow in your UX career with training and other activities that will help you stay current.

Experience the Entire Project Lifecycle

As an in-house employee, while your specific role on any given project will likely vary over time, you will often get to be a part of the entire project from the time you join until the product, or a new version of the product, is launched. Not only can this be immensely satisfying and easy to see how you've made a difference, but you have the chance to gain deep experience, which you can use on other projects in the future.

Really Understand the Users

In my one year in-house at a distance learning company, I gained exceptional perspective on their three primary user groups—parents, students, and teachers. Not only did I learn from qualitative and quantitative user research that was exclusively related to these three groups, but I also learned from talking about these user groups multiple times and in multiple capacities with product developers and those who were creating the necessary interactive curriculum.

Similarly, in whatever environment you find yourself, know that you're likely going to end up being very expert about a particular user type—so try to find a job with a user audience that you look forward to learning more about.

Create a Culture of UX

Another great thing about having this single-company focus is that you have an opportunity to make a difference and perhaps influence the salience of good UX practice over time in your company. I suggest that even if you are enjoying a stable, comfortable job, you can find subtle ways to continue to demonstrate the value of UX to those who are not involved in UX. You could even ask for permission to do some UX-oriented lunch and learn sessions for those in your company who aren't yet familiar with UX.

If you have the opportunity, you could create some kind of internal white papers describing how good UX techniques have been implemented. Take the opportunity not only to feature what you've done to make UX better, but also, what others have done as well. Even those who do not have particular UX roles would certainly appreciate being called out for helping to shape a positive user experience.

Most importantly, when people in your company have questions, you should spend time with them to explain the value of good UX in providing corporate products. You really can make a difference as an in-house corporate UX resource in more ways than you might have originally considered!

Be Aware of Potential Negatives

While there are many advantages of working as an in-house corporate resource, there can be drawbacks for some people. If you prefer to have frequent new and different experiences in your work, there is a chance that in-house work may feel too predictable for you. In addition, over time, while you are being exposed to an entire product lifecycle and other aspects of UX through coworkers, you may be missing out on exposure to different ways of approaching UX and completely different types of challenges that just don't exist at the company you work for.

Do you want to be a dedicated in-house resource or consultant?

Working for a Consulting Firm/Agency

As I said earlier, I spent one year working in-house; but for the remainder of my UX career, I have been a consultant. For a number of years, I worked for consulting agencies—both large and small. Eventually, however, I went off on my own as an independent consultant. We'll talk more about being an independent consultant in the next chapter.

Long-term, Full-time Placement

Working in a consulting agency could involve long-term, full-time placement as a contractor for a specific company—helping them meet their UX needs. Aside from the technicalities of who your employer is, what is often termed as "staff augmentation" means that you may be functioning more as an in-house UX professional.

As a consultant working long-term in-house, the corporate culture may see no difference between you and an employee. Alternatively, actual in-house employees may not see you exactly as their peer: they may respect your ideas more because you represent an outside perspective or they may respect your ideas less because you're still somewhat of an outsider.

Consult for Multiple Companies

The kind of consulting I talk about in the remainder of this section is being an outside consultant to clients—working on specific projects either short-term (full-time or part-time) or long-term but part-time. When you work for a consulting company (often called a design or UX agency), your company will likely bid you on projects where they think your skillset will be a good match. If the client agrees and your company gets the project, you'll be helping the client with your UX expertise.

MORE EXPOSURE BUT LESS DEPTH

A big advantage to consulting is exposure to more diversity in UX practice, to different corporate work structures around UX, and to a wider variety of people. You will temporarily be involved in a variety of companies over the course of your time as a consultant. You will see how UX is treated differently from company to company. You will be exposed to a vast array of UX challenges. You will learn about a wide variety of products and audience groups as they relate to UX.

On the other hand, what you gain in exposure and stimulation from all these different environments, you lose in depth. You'll likely interact with co-workers at your primary employer's office; but, depending on your setup, you might not end up doing all your project work with them. The projects you work on will often be temporary engagements, and you may not see products through their entire development lifecycle or learn important UX skills as deeply as if you were working in-house.

MORE UNKNOWNS

As a consultant, you will find that you won't always know what is around the corner. Your projects may be repetitive or may each need a different aspect of your skillset. Either way, if you don't like a lot of variability in your life, then consulting may not be for you. However, if you find the unknown to be exciting, and if you enjoy variety over depth, you may find consulting to be a great fit.

MORE BALANCING REQUIRED

While your boss will hopefully do his or her best to manage your workflow, if you're working on two projects for two disconnected companies simultaneously, you may have to manage competing demands without any communication between your two sources of work. If both projects urgently require your assistance during the same time, you could end up doing a lot of juggling. You could work more hours in a short period than you prefer.

Of course, this can also happen within a single company, and there are deadlines wherever you are; but as a consultant, you lose a layer of protection. While some may find this too stressful, others may find that they enjoy the challenge and thrive in this type of situation.

POSSIBLE BENCH TIME

Being on the bench means that you work for a consulting company (or as an independent consultant) and there is simply not enough work. You end up with minimal—or no—billable work.

Your job in a consulting company is often only as secure as their ability to find work for you (or you to find work for yourself). Companies may keep you on the bench for a while; but, eventually, they will have to let you go if they are unable to put you on new projects.

As a consultant, be prepared for those times on the bench. (Even if you work in-house, you may find times when you are less busy—so what follows may be useful ideas to keep in mind even for in-house employees.)

You may like in-house work

if you are inclined towards:

- Predictability and stability

- Co-workers that you can learn from and get to know well over time

- Experiencing the entire project lifecycle

- Getting to understand a specific set of users very well

- Less variation in responsibilities over time

- Only dealing with UX from one company's perspective

You may like consulting work

if you are inclined towards:

- Varied work locations over time

- Exposure to different approaches to UX

- Exposure to a wider range of audience groups

- More surprises in what your next UX projects may be

- Responsibilities that vary more over time

- Balancing or juggling multiple projects

If you figure out ways that you can add value for your company, your company may keep you longer than others. Here are some suggestions:

- Even when you're busy, **as you think of new ideas, start building yourself a list of non-billable projects** that would help the company. At one company where I worked, when work was light, an employee used his skills to demonstrate how the interaction design of the corporate website could be improved. Meanwhile, I offered to use my database skills to query, analyze, and clean up a master database of participants for the company's usability tests.

- **Ask what you can do to help.** Remind the appropriate people about the skills you have, even if those skills aren't those that you normally use on the job. Ask how you can use those skills to help the company.

- You may not be directly responsible for business development, but try to **brainstorm ways that you can use your existing contacts or new contacts to get more work** for yourself and for the company. Employees who can generate their own work can be very impressive to a company. Some companies may even give you a percentage bonus on billable work that you generate yourself (particularly if this is not part of your core job requirements).

On the bench and nothing to do: Particularly if the consulting firm you work for is a very large business, they may tell you that you're on the paid bench, but they don't require anything of you for the time being. If you've already tried to use your skills in other ways for the company and are out of ideas, consider, and perhaps talk with your company, about ways to use your time for self-improvement activities so you are ready to do more on projects for the company in the future.

- **Spend time learning.** Online learning opportunities for UX abound.
- **Create or locate practice activities** in areas where you feel you need more experience, perhaps in areas where you have some level of skills or knowledge but not expert skills.
- **Consider whether your side projects can become examples** of your skills. We talked about portfolios in the last chapter and possible issues of privacy and confidentiality. If, while "on the bench," you do a side project for your company that has nothing to do with client work, you may have less of an issue with corporate privacy concerns for your portfolio.
- **Iterate and improve your brand; figure out ways to network or renew relationships with your colleagues**. As we talked about in Chapter 4, this is always important, and certainly even more relevant when you are "on the bench," just in case they can't find more work for you and have to let you go.
- **Take a look at what jobs are out there.** You don't have to apply, but it's always good to be prepared, just in case.
- **Don't lose hope.** Take comfort in the fact that UX is hot, and you will find work soon one way or another!

In-house Consulting

At some large companies you may also find internal UX consulting groups. These job opportunities may include both benefits of being in-house (such as a potential for deeper relationships and a finite set of clients) and benefits of working for a consulting organization (such as exposure to a wider variety of projects).

INTERNAL CONSULTING: BEST OF BOTH WORLDS

By Jen Romano Bergstrom, User Experience Researcher, Facebook

During the last year of my PhD work in Applied/Experimental Psychology, my funding to work with my advisor was up, and I found myself with two potential routes for income while

I finished my dissertation: bartend more or try to find a job related to my field. When a posting for an internship with the US Census Bureau Human Factors and Usability Research Group circulated around our department, I had no idea what usability was, but I seemed to have the skills that they were looking for, so I applied and was hired.

IN-HOUSE CONSULTING IN GOVERNMENT

At the US Census Bureau Usability Lab, I worked on lots of different products—websites, web-based surveys, and paper surveys. My team was largely an internal resource for any Census Bureau group who needed or wanted user feedback. Teams approached us, and we worked with them to design studies to understand how people interacted with and thought about their product. There was generally little urgency—things often moved slowly—and you got out of it what you put in. I clocked in and out, and I was able to sometimes work from home. I really liked this internal consulting role—I was involved with many projects at any given time. Relationships with teams flourished because I worked with them over many iterative tests.

CONSULTING AT A RESEARCH AGENCY

In my time at the Census Bureau, I realized that a UX career would be a great fit for my skills and interests. I learned and grew a lot, but ultimately, I felt that I needed something that moved faster. I was also interested in learning about and testing other types of products, and a social science research consulting firm, Fors Marsh Group (FMG), gave me just what I was looking for. There I led projects and started a UX team. The projects were fun—they moved fast, and there was less red tape than in government work. It felt like a win for me! While this experience at a true consulting agency was fun and a great learning experience, there were times when I just wanted to do UX work and not simultaneously manage so many people and projects.

INTERNAL CONSULTING AT A LARGE CORPORATION

After a few years at FMG, I bumped into a former colleague at a conference who was doing UX work at Facebook. One thing led to another, and I ended up with my next career leap—back to an in-house consulting role—but instead of for a government agency, this time it was for a large corporation.

In my role as a User Experience Researcher at Facebook, I design and conduct UX studies, analyze data, and present to teams. I don't manage people, but I still manage research projects—from planning, to implementing, to providing findings and suggestions for future research. Where I used to go broad and shallow in my projects, now I go narrow and deep. My main responsibility is to one specific product team, but I get to work with others, too. This allows me to strengthen my relationship with one product team but also get to know others in the company and work on a variety of projects.

In my previous roles, I felt that my team would do the research and pass over the findings. At Facebook, I work alongside the product managers, designers, marketers, etc. towards a common goal. Everyone moves fast. We do not clock in or out, and we work whenever and wherever it is most productive for us. It is a very flexible environment that enables me to be creative and efficient and make an impact on big products.

THE CONSULTING TO IN-HOUSE SPECTRUM

UX professionals have lots of options. While some jobs really are pure consulting agency jobs and some are purely in-house work, many UX jobs really fall somewhere in the spectrum between in-house and consulting. I am happy that I have tried out different environments. Who knows what the future holds, but for now, things at Facebook are going well, and it works for me!

Jen Romano Bergstrom is a User Experience Researcher at Facebook, where she works to understand the UX of Facebook in emerging markets. She specializes in eye tracking, usability testing, survey design, and UX for older adults. Jen is the co-author of *Eye Tracking in User Experience Design* (2014) and *Usability Testing for Survey Research* (forthcoming, 2016). Jen is actively involved in the User Experience Professionals Association (UXPA) and American Association for Public Opinion Research (AAPOR) organizations—she has served on both boards and assists in UX event planning for other organizations as well.

Employee or Independent Contractor

In the United States, you can work with a company one of two ways as classified by the tax form on which your earnings are reported to you and to the Federal government. While what I'm describing here is specific to the United States, many other countries have similar structures.

You can be a "W-2" employee, meaning that the company considers you an actual employee of the company: They withhold taxes on your behalf, and you generally receive "benefits" such as a subsidy on your health insurance, paid time off, funding of a retirement account, and other perks.

You can work for a company on a "1099" basis. This means that you are considered an independent contractor of the company, not an employee. You do not generally receive benefits, and you are generally responsible for paying your own taxes.

You need to be careful when considering independent contacting for full-time work. For one thing, the 1099 approach for long-term, full-time workers is often frowned upon by the US Internal Revenue Service[1] (IRS). Also, while you may find that your hourly or day rate is better than an employee's salary, you'll forfeit any opportunity for benefits from the company, and your job security is generally somewhat lower. Another risk of independent contracting for full-time work is that you may have less opportunity to do business development to try to find more work when the project finishes up.

That said, sometimes this opportunity may be the only thing that is available for work that you really want to do or you might just enjoy a little more feeling of freedom in not being so tightly tied to a company as an employee.

If you are considering working on a contract basis, whether full-time or part time, this might mean that being an independent UX consultant is a good next career move. In the next chapter, we'll explore the pros and cons of doing just that.

Get more online at uxcareershandbook.com/job-structure

NOTE
1. http://www.irs.gov/Businesses/Small-Businesses-&-Self-Employed/Independent-Contractor-Self-Employed-or-Employee

CHAPTER 7

Independent Contracting or Starting a Small UX Business

Adapted with permission from Lebson, Cory. "Are you Ready to Be an Independent UX Consultant?" *UXmatters*. (January 27, 2014).[1]

For much of my career as a user experience (UX) consultant, I supported client companies while working full time on a consulting firm's payroll. A number of years back, one very large consulting organization hired me for a 6-month, full-time gig working on-site for a client. When, at the appointed time, the project concluded successfully, the consulting firm didn't immediately have any other UX work for which I was suited. No problem; they were large, had deep pockets, and were optimistic. They told me they were putting me on the bench as we talked about in the last chapter. What did that mean? It meant that I'd continue to be employed, but there was really nothing that needed doing. "Relax," they said, "and stay nearby in case we need you on short notice." So I went home and did just that. I went to the beach for a few days with the family and caught up on household chores.

At the time, this made me feel safe. Here was a company that cared about their consultants enough to pay me to do absolutely nothing when they couldn't find any project to put me on. But now after being an independent consultant for a number of years, when I look back on that time, I see things a little differently. Yes, they were certainly worthy of respect for keeping me on the payroll even when I was on the bench. However, knowing what I know now about billing rates for companies like that, I figure that their profit from my working for them for six months was greater than my pay for one year. Certainly my being on the bench for a month or so wasn't all that big a deal for them financially.

As we have just discussed, you may find yourself wondering whether it makes more sense to work in-house, focusing on the needs of one company, or to work across multiple companies as a consultant. But within consulting there lies yet another important decision: should you continue to work as an employee of a consulting company or go out on your own and hang up your own shingle as an independent consultant?

As an interesting and valuable aside, know that **the considerations that go into going off on your own as an individual independent consultant and starting a small business with employees are actually very similar.** While this chapter is focused primarily on individuals, if you are interested in taking it one step further, you'll still want to read on.

Consider the Pros and Cons of Working for Yourself

There are a number of typical pros and cons when working for yourself. Of course, it's worth recognizing that while none of these attributes are absolutely unique to independent consulting, they are often much more frequent for independents.

PROS

- **Money**: The profit is yours—all yours.
- **Benefits**: You have more flexibility in choosing what benefits you want (particularly in countries like the United States where these are often connected tightly with your employment). In some ways, this is the ultimate in cafeteria plans.
- **Flexibility**: You can set your own hours, as long as you can make them work within your clients' needs.
- **Commute**: Your office can be in your home—although it doesn't have to be. There are often co-working spaces available, offering you some co-workers and forcing you to get dressed up, or at least dressed, to go to work. And you can choose a co-working space at a location close to home.
- **Control**: You are your own boss. You can try to win projects that you will enjoy and also have the option to turn down any projects that don't interest you.
- **Satisfaction**: Achieving success in your own business can be emotionally rewarding.

CONS

- **Lack of stability**: Your workload may ebb and flow over time, meaning your income won't be regular.
- **No safety net**: You have to create your own safety net, disciplining yourself to save up enough of your profits during busy times so you'll still be able to pay your bills when work slows.
- **Obtain your own benefits**: While (again particularly in places like the United States) it's easier to get individual insurance than in the past, you still need to do the legwork to find your own coverage. And this insurance can be expensive when you are footing 100% of the bill.
- **Less water-cooler talk**: You might have colleagues on a project, but not necessarily over the long term and not as often.
- **No office space**: You need to carve out a dedicated space for work at home or find a co-working space in a convenient location.
- **Sales**: If you don't constantly sell your services, you might not always be working. Selling takes time, energy, and courage.
- **Negotiating**: You're responsible for all discussions about your rate, your hours, and your deliverables.
- **Office supplies and equipment**: You are often responsible for your own equipment—not only purchasing but also troubleshooting your technology (or hiring someone to troubleshoot) when there are problems.
- **Business travel**: Nobody will likely be covering your travel to speak at or attend a conference, or travel to a neighboring city to meet a potential new client.

SMALL BUSINESS CONSIDERATIONS

What about starting a small business?

This pro and con list is just as accurate, but now you have some additional pros and cons.

Pros:

- **More work.** You can potentially take on larger projects and have the ability to juggle more projects simultaneously.
- **More profit.** You stand to make more money since you'll likely be charging more for employees' billable hours than what you compensate your employees.

Cons:

- **More responsibility.** You need to make sure you have enough work for your employees or you lose money or have to consider letting them go.
- **Less flexibility.** You may have less opportunity to "go with the flow" and may have to work harder to maintain a robust pipeline of project revenue.
- **HR issues.** You need to deal with payroll and employment benefits.

- **Non-billable time**: You will need to work outside of billable hours to make necessary connections and bid for potential work, and also to deal with other general business-related needs such as contacts, billing, administering your own benefits, paying your self-employment taxes, etc.

BE WILLING TO TAKE RISKS AND MAKE SALES

Some independent UX consultants are not successful, while others are wildly successful. I have observed two important things that lead to success in independent UX consulting: a willingness to take risks and a willingness to sell.

- **What kind of risks are you taking?** You risk not having work or not having enough work. You risk underselling your services and earning less money than you should by filling your schedule with lower-paid work just to know that your schedule is full. Or you risk overbidding and losing a project entirely. You have nobody at your company to back you up if things go wrong with a client—and at some point or other, you will experience the disappointment of an unhappy client. You need to be willing to take those risks, learn from your mistakes, and always keep moving forward.

- **What does it mean to sell?** There is always going to be some aspect of bidding. You might respond directly to a request for proposal (RFP). A company might ask you to be part of a team that responds to an RFP, and you'll need to contribute your part of the proposal and do some negotiating with the company that is leading the proposal. But selling doesn't just mean being reactive; you need to be proactive as well. You've got to get yourself out there—beyond just doing your work—and market yourself.

SMALL BUSINESS CONSIDERATIONS

Risks and selling are largely the same if you are starting a small business. While you could hire a dedicated person for business development, this would likely come a little later once you have grown big enough to support someone exclusively on overhead dollars.

POSSESS ENOUGH UX EXPERIENCE AND EXPERTISE

An important thing that you'll need to assess before you make the jump to independent consulting is whether you're an expert in some particular area of UX. This does not mean you must have absolutely comprehensive knowledge of that area—that's hard to prove anyway. Rather, have you done a variety of work in the right UX career paths, and can you describe it to potential clients in a way that lets you justifiably argue that you have expert-level skills in one or more areas? Do you have enough projects under your belt to comprehensively

Independent contracting involves some risks but can also be very rewarding

back up those claims? I personally declare my expertise to be in UX research and evaluation, UX training, and UX strategy, and when I started as an independent consultant, I had 14 years of project experience focused in those areas in my resume and portfolio.

You can certainly grow this expertise by working in-house to meet one company's UX needs, but it is often better for your independent credentials to have done project work for a variety of different companies/clients over the course of your career. If you've been employed as a consultant with a consulting firm, you may find that the leap to independent consulting is not as great.

> Acquire a broad variety of experiences in your areas of expertise before going out on your own.

SMALL BUSINESS CONSIDERATIONS

Your own experiences will be of the utmost importance, although by hiring other UX professionals you can gain credibility from their experiences, too. When you hire employees, do not only think of your immediate needs but also how their skillsets and backgrounds could impress potential clients in a way that complements what you personally bring to the table.

HAVE EXPERIENCE WITH THE LINGO

Sometimes it's the little things that make a difference in how you come across to potential clients. One thing I've noticed over the years is that different companies and industries use different vocabularies in conversations about UX. I've seen some cases where the lingo tends to be more techie, while in other cases, it has its basis in marketing terminology.

What kind of language you should use also depends on who you're working with. I sometimes work with developers or designers or project managers or stakeholders with other backgrounds—and sometimes with all of them at once. The greater the variety of the situations in which you've worked before making the jump to independent consulting, the better you'll be able to sell your services to whomever inquires about them, and the more you'll come across as knowledgeable.

Manage Your Own Benefits

For the most part, this section is based on a United States-based structure. Expect to find significant differences here by country.

One hesitation you may have about independent consulting (particularly in countries like the United States where more types of benefits are tied to your employer) is taking care of your own benefits, and this is a reasonable concern. While I am not a lawyer or any kind of tax, benefits, or HR professional, I will try to give you enough information here to explain that you probably don't need to take an employee position instead of being a freelancer simply because of the benefits.

For the most part, you can replicate the benefits of any employee position, and it may actually cost you less than it would cost the company to provide those to you.

Good **individual health insurance** coverage in the United States is relatively easy to buy online since the Affordable Care Act went into effect, and you no longer have to worry about pre-existing conditions affecting your coverage.

Life insurance is easy to find on your own, as long as you don't have serious health issues from the outset.

The same can be said for **long-term disability insurance**, although it can be a little bit of a pain to have to document your freelance income instead of employee income, using tax returns + copies of all the checks that you have received.

Short-term disability insurance is not usually all that well priced for individuals, so here is where you have to make sure you have your own short-term safety net fund built up to cover your bills before long-term disability would kick in.

Saving for retirement is possible with several options, including individual retirement plans, which can give you tax savings opportunities to match your own contributions in tax deductible ways.

Clients may require you to have **general liability insurance**, but this is relatively cheap when compared with other types of insurance, especially if you don't have any other employees.

> Managing your own benefits is often quite feasible, and you can match most aspects of typical employee benefits packages yourself.

What may seem like a downside is that you have to pay for all of these insurance coverages yourself, and you have no paid holiday or vacation time. However, like your self-provided benefits, this all would need to be taken into account and baked into your rate. Psychologically, you will need to remember that it's okay to take vacations. (It's very important to accept this!)

SMALL BUSINESS CONSIDERATIONS

Small business benefits for employees present an increased level of complexity. You may want to contact an employee benefits agency to help you find and administer benefits that are best for your business.

WORKSHEET: DECIDING TO BE
AN INDEPENDENT CONSULTANT

Is independent consulting right for me?

- _____ I am comfortable taking risks to achieve my goals.

- _____ I am a good communicator and networker.

- _____ I can confidently sell my services.

- _____ I have UX expertise that I can demonstrate on a resume and in a portfolio.

- _____ I have experienced UX work in a variety of different organizational environments.

- _____ I have built up a reasonably strong network of UX professionals (and if I haven't I'll take every opportunity now).

- _____ I am comfortable working more than 40 hours a week at times to juggle multiple contracts and non-billable business-related activities.

- _____ I have the discipline to create a financial safety net for times when I do not have enough billable work.

- _____ I know that the buck stops with me, and I can handle setbacks emotionally.

Get Ready to Become an Independent Consultant

REV YOUR ENGINE

Say you've weighed the pros and cons of being an independent consultant that we've talked about, and you feel that you have the necessary experience and character traits to go for it. Is it time to quit your job? Probably not.

Becoming an independent consultant doesn't usually mean that you just wake up one day and declare: "I'm tired of my old job. I quit. Now, I just need to find some freelance work to take on." At least that would not be the *recommended* approach.

Rather, you need to start revving your engine long before you reach that break-away point. In fact, the truth is that you should be revving your engine all the time anyway for the good of your UX brand and career, as we talked about.

CREATE YOUR BUSINESS ENTITY

It can be exciting to form a real business, give it a name and basic legal structure. In the United States, you would typically structure your business as a sole-proprietorship, a Limited Liability Company (LLC), or a corporation. You may be able to do this all online, but you may also want to consider consulting a lawyer and/or tax advisor to learn about what is right for you.

> **SMALL BUSINESS CONSIDERATIONS**
>
> If you are thinking about including employees in your business, this will likely figure into what type of business entity would be best for you to create.

Identify Your Breakaway Point

In my own case, I was working full time at a company but had decided that enough was enough. I was ready. The only problem was that I had no work, so I put out some feelers. Within about six weeks, I found a project that matched my skillset, was nearly a full-time gig, and would last for about three months. That was just long enough to enable me to cement my new identity as an independent consultant, but still allow me a little time to start simultaneously searching for other work.

By the time my first project ended, I had found another nearly full-time gig that lasted for a long time. As time progressed, my hours on that contract gradually diminished, and I replaced that single project with a number of smaller projects.

I may have been lucky that things transitioned as smoothly as they did for me. However, even if your break-away point and transition time does not go as perfectly as you envision, take comfort in the fact that UX is a hot field. If you have done your prep work and can be patient enough, you have a decent chance of things working out for you as a freelancer in the long run. And if for some reason they don't, your resume and portfolio should now be even better-primed to put yourself back on the regular job market.

How will you know when you've reached your breakaway point? Most importantly, you should *feel* ready—or at least nearly ready. Here are some questions that you may want to ask yourself:

- Do I have a project that will let me break away?
- Is that break-away project going to let me spend some time on business development, so I can lock in my next project?
- If I don't immediately find another project after the first one, can I manage financially? Emotionally?

Set Your Rate

Setting your hourly or daily rate is one of the hardest things that you are going to do as a consultant and business owner, and rates will vary tremendously. You don't want to be too low and be underpaid, but you don't want to be so high that you don't get work. So many variables go into your rate that you may have to experiment, at least when companies don't already have a "take it or leave it" number. If you have employees, the minimum rate that you can bill them out at will be impacted by what their salaries are.

What Should You Do to Determine Rates?

- **Talk to others who do what you do**: Share what you're thinking about your rate range, and ask UX peers with whom you feel comfortable talking about rates.

- **Consider starting high**: Your goal is to come up with a rate that is near the top of the range that people will be willing to pay you. But let clients know that you are willing to negotiate. If you had started low, you'll never know how much they were willing to pay.

- **Consider flash sales**: If you're really hungry for work, consider letting potential clients know that you're significantly discounting your rates for a short period of time to fill gaps in your schedule.

In addition, remember that a contractor's rate has to take into account many factors such as covering benefits and overhead time. While we are not going to go into the specifics of rate calculations here, the book's companion website provides links to calculators that can help you in this process.

Be Honest

I work from home, and I have had many conversations about image with colleagues who also work out of their houses—whether alone or with employees. Many say that they want to look professional, so they keep the fact that they primarily work out of their house hush-hush. Their website is designed to make them appear bigger. They may have a P.O. box. Or they use their real address and add a "suite" to it. Or they use a virtual address.

How my company shows up on Google Maps: What were you expecting?
A corporate office building?

Nobody is supposed to know that they work out of their house because they believe that if potential clients found out, they wouldn't want to hire this company to do their work.

Is this true? If I tell my clients exactly what my business is and that my business office is in my home, will they not give me business? I certainly have not found this to be the case.

The benefits of being honest about who you are, as an individual and as a business, outweigh the benefits that might be gained by trying to inflate one's business or personal image. And it can be risky to create a misleading image. In fact, if someone types "Lebsontech" into Google maps, guess what comes up?

You're Going to Slip

You shouldn't pretend or inflate your business credentials because you will very likely get caught. I can think of one small business owner who inflated credentials to include usability testing. When I asked a question—not as a test, just because I was interested—and the answer I got back showed a serious lack of knowledge, it potentially discredited this person's entire skillset—if the truth about this was so stretched, what else is this person exaggerating or not telling me?

It's harder to appear confident. Sure, you can try to appear confident in everything you do, but it's a lot easier to be truthful and have a practice of being open than it is to always worry that someone will find out the truth and your business will go down the tubes in a tangle of lies.

Being confident in what you say is a much bigger turn-on to potential clients than any kind of big office ego might be. So my advice is to accept your business for what it is for now. Being honest about it doesn't mean you have to be shy about letting people know what you are hoping your business will become a few years down the road.

> Inflating your business image is risky: You put your integrity on the line.

Have Colleagues, Not Competitors

Depending on your business model and long-term plans for your company, you may see yourself as competing with other freelance UX consultants or small consulting firms. But it doesn't have to be that way. In fact, if you are like me, you may find that there is an advantage to being non-threatening and dealing with freelance consultants and other UX consulting firms as colleagues, not competitors.

When another UX professional and I first spoke on the phone, we found that we had a lot in common: we both run small user research firms and both enjoy doing similar kinds of user research. It was great connecting and comparing stories. We had a brief awkward moment, however, when the other UX professional said that their company was interested in getting involved with a particular large organization, and I responded that I, in fact, was doing a small project for that same organization. There was then a brief pause, perhaps suggesting a moment of concern that we had been going after the same work. While it turned out it that we were actually talking about entirely separate departments, this experience reminded me that the line between colleagues and competitors can sometimes be very thin.

If you are worried about how your company stacks up against possible competitors in general or for a particular potential project, you might consider doing a SWOT analysis—strengths, weaknesses, opportunities, and threats of a business venture. Specifically, strengths = what gives the business an edge over other businesses; weaknesses = what disadvantages a firm has compared to other businesses; opportunities = what external prospects exist for the business; threats = what external hazards can cause trouble for the business.

I personally have never done a formal SWOT analysis of my company, however, and I don't think much about other UX professionals or companies as competitors. I prefer to think of them as colleagues because others have been a source of opportunity for me; and I rarely, if ever, find myself competing with anyone I know for work.

Think About Alternative Business Strategies

My advice is this: consider the value of being seen as non-threatening versus being seen as a competitive threat. Consider the value of being available for other UX consultants

> Bidding directly on contracts is not the only way to get work as an independent consultant. You can also focus on filling in the gaps for contract work that other companies bid for.

1. **Assess yourself honestly**: Are you at a good place in your career to consider such a career move?

2. **Rev your engine**: Prepare with good networking and personal branding (see Chapter 4).

3. **Create your business entity**.

4. **Work towards your breakaway point**: Look for a first contract that would allow you to break away.

5. **Set your rate**: Take into account your own needs and business expenses (equipment, insurance, vacation time) and get a feel for what is reasonable to charge in your field.

6. **Project your image**: Put your best foot forward, but don't try to concoct a fake front that would be hard to sustain.

7. **Consider your business model**: Do you want to compete for contracts on your own, or would you rather fill in on contracts that someone else has already won?

8. **Go for it!** It's worth a shot, and remember, it doesn't have to be the way you work for the rest of your life. If you have all your ducks in a row, don't be afraid to take the plunge!

who need you instead of blazing a trail entirely separate from, and perhaps in competition to, your peers. Then adapt your business strategy to support what you believe will really help you and satisfy you in the long run.

My strategy is to be a colleague whom others want on their projects. While I do sometimes work directly for companies if they come to me, I often work as a sub-contractor for other consulting companies who already have or are bidding for work. Sometimes I even white-label my services. By white-labeling I mean that I am willing to represent other companies, even using their branded email addresses or business cards with their clients if they request it for a particular project. Unlike some who are against white-labeling, I don't turn away from representing a different company for a particular project. If you're considering white-labeling your services, I wrote an article on benefits of this approach for UX Magazine.[2]

Go For It

Going off on your own as a freelancer or starting a small business with other employees is certainly not for everyone. But for some, it is an exciting opportunity to be your own boss, to set your own tone, and to be fully responsible for your own successes and failures.

The decision to go independent or start a business is not something to take lightly. There is risk involved, and a lot to think about, including your goals and your business strategy. But if you do go independent and start your own small business venture, you may find a lot of enjoyment and personal satisfaction.

Get more online at uxcareershandbook.com/independent

NOTES

1. http://www.uxmatters.com/mt/archives/2014/01/are-you-ready-to-be-an-independent-ux-consultant.php

2. http://uxmag.com/articles/go-ahead-white-label-your-services

CHAPTER 8

Landing a Job (or New Contract Work)

In this book, we've discussed many ways to improve your potential to land a user experience (UX) job before you even start to look for specific opportunities. We've covered building your brand and online identity, creating a resume and identifying ideal work samples, and considering whether you should be looking for in-house or consulting work or should consider becoming an independent contractor.

Now that the foundations are in place, and you know—or at least are starting to identify—where you want to go within the broad scope of UX, it's time to start the job search.

Staying Aware

Situational awareness is critical in all aspects of your life. When you walk down the street, you wouldn't be all that wise to stare at your mobile device and lose sight of the world around you. Crash—splat.

Similarly, while there are UX jobs aplenty, we also all live in a fairly volatile job world. Even as you enjoy the job you are in—and you certainly do not have to be in any rush to leave a good job—make sure to keep yourself updated.

Do not let your online identity go stale. Keep your resume and portfolio current. Just as important, stay aware of the current state of the job market. Keep an eye on what jobs are being posted. Keep a sense of how many jobs seem to be cropping up year to year.

Do you see jobs that are a great fit? Are jobs starting to look for an emerging new skill or asking job seekers to apply a new method? Not only are these insights helpful for that time in the future when you do begin to look for a new job, they also point out to you what skills you should be working on strengthening in your current job.

Getting the Word Out

Your strategy for looking for a job will depend on how public you are willing to make your search. The more publicity for your job search you're willing to have, the more you will be able to let others know that you're available for work, increasing the probability of a job finding you instead of the other way around.

If you are looking for contract work: Looking for a job and looking for UX contract projects are actually fairly similar processes, so much of the same advice applies to both situations.

Reach Out to Your Network

Getting a job in UX can sometimes be more about who you know than what you know. Some jobs don't get posted publicly; rather, they are spread by word of mouth. Reach out to your existing network, and let them know that you're on the market. Review your contacts to remind yourself of who may be useful to alert to your availability. Also, consider reviewing your contacts on LinkedIn or other social media platforms where you are apt to know many of your connections personally.

Post About Your Job Search

If you're willing and able to be very open about your job search, consider posting it publically as your status with LinkedIn, Twitter, and other social media. If you are looking for contract work, it is often easier to be open about this since you won't necessarily have to worry about upsetting an existing employer. As a contractor who usually takes on smallish projects, I both tweet and post to LinkedIn whenever I see a light month coming up. I find that I often get a retweet or two from those who are interested in helping me spread the word.

Go to UX Events

Go local. Get on local UX event mailing lists and show up at the events. While it is great to combine UX learning with networking, put most of your efforts on

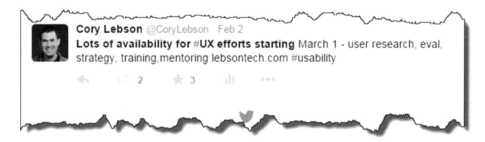

Cory's use of Twitter to alert his network of availability

meetups and specific events that might give you opportunities to meet other UX professionals in your area. Ideally, events will note that there is dedicated networking time either as the event itself or before/after a speaker.

Go larger. If you're okay with considering a larger geographic scope, consider attending an international, national, or regional UX conference, even if you need to pay your own way. Talk with both attendees and exhibitors (who will often have a booth specifically to look for UX talent).

Let people know. Whether at a local event or something larger, consider an eye catching "Job seeker" on your name badge. Also, consider making business cards that say that you are looking for a job, list key skills that you think can add value to a company, and provide links to a resume, portfolio, and social media profile.

> **HOW TO LOOK FOR A JOB**
>
> - Tell your network you are looking: contacts, personal connections, and trusted colleagues
>
> - Post your job search on social media
>
> - Go to UX events and network
>
> - Check out online job boards
>
> - Create a custom job board feed

Looking at Job Postings

You can look for UX job postings in many places. You will find both sites that are very UX-specific and those that are more general but include many UX listings.

However, be aware that job postings are often just best guesses at what a team may need. You could completely qualify on paper, but not be a good fit at all; or you could have just a few of the supposedly required experiences but be a great fit. So don't be afraid to apply to a variety of roles.

Should you end up moving forward with an opportunity that doesn't fit your goals or skills, you can always take yourself out of the running. Also keep in mind that a company doesn't need to be advertising a particular role to be willing to consider you. If you show a great amount of passion and have pronounced skills, sometimes a company can find a way to bring you on board or will contact you the next time they are hiring someone with your skillset.

UX-specific Job Boards

Job boards that are UX specific are generally not particularly comprehensive. Also, while in theory all jobs that are posted to these boards are UX oriented, in fact, UX orientation is often determined by the company posting the job, and so it may or may not represent what a UX professional would consider a UX skillset job. Still, these boards are often a good place to start your job search as they already include one level of directed vetting by companies.

Boards include:

- uxjobsboard.com
- uxjobs247.com
- uxswitch.com
- justuxjobs.com
- uxdesignjobs.net
- uxmag.com/uxjobs
- uxpa.org/job-bank
- ixda.org/page/job-board

General Job Boards

While general job boards are likely to have longer lists of jobs available, you'll likely have to work a little harder to limit your search to UX jobs. Try using the list of potential job titles associated with your designed career pathway(s) in Chapter 11. You can start on job boards that seem to have the heftiest listings of UX jobs:

- Indeed.com
- Simplyhired.com
- Careerbuilder.com
- Dice.com
- Monster.com

Also consider using LinkedIn: https://www.linkedin.com/job/home.

Custom UX Job Board Feeds

In Chapter 3, I described how I use RSS feeds to stay on top of things in the UX world. I'll give the same advice for job boards. With not too much effort, you can create your own custom RSS job board.

Particularly with the larger non-UX-specific job boards, you often can have your search auto-run repeatedly, and every new item that is listed can be sent to you via an email message or put into your RSS feed. I prefer the RSS feed route because potential jobs are piped into a running list, and you get to choose your RSS reader of choice in which to view them. Ultimately, this provides a more consistent job posting review across all job boards.

After setting up an RSS reader if you don't already have one, the next step is to create the URL of your custom job feed. To do so, in most cases, simply do your search as you normally would on the job board and then copy and paste the resulting web address with your embedded search strings into your RSS reader.

For example:

Do a search on Indeed for user experience jobs in San Francisco and copy the URL.
http://www.indeed.com/jobs?q=user+experience+design&l=San+Francisco%2C+CA

Paste the web address into your RSS Reader. Feedly shown here

Your feed is created!

Once your feed is created, all you need to do is to review the listing in your Reader on a regular basis as your feeds will be updated at least several times per day. You can create a search for each of the specific job types that you might expect.

While you're likely to find a higher percentage of relevant jobs in your search results by using job titles, given that there is so much inconsistency in UX about which titles are associated with which skillsets, you can consider searching for specific skillsets as well. If a simple search isn't doing the trick, you could also use advanced search forms that exist on the various job boards to narrow your search in other ways, for example if you're looking specifically for full-time or contract efforts.

Advanced job search from Indeed.com

WORKSHEET: JOB SEARCH STRATEGY

UX professionals and recruiters that I would be comfortable reaching out to:

- _____
- _____
- _____

Upcoming UX events where I could network:

- _____
- _____
- _____

Places where I could tell others that I'm looking for a job (social media, job boards, etc.)

- _____
- _____
- _____

Creating a Cover Letter to Apply for Jobs

Once you find a job you want to apply to, it's time to send your materials. Your resume, which we discussed in Chapter 5, details your experiences and, at a high level, explains what kind of job you are looking for. Your cover letter, on the other hand, needs to very concretely explain how the experiences and background you detail in your resume tie directly to the company to which you are applying. Let's think about the cover letter a bit.

Do Your Research and Try to Understand the Needs of the Company

Why are they hiring? What exactly are they looking for with this position? In what ways are you a really good fit? Ultimately, what can you do for them to make them stronger as an organization? Spell out how you can help them; don't expect them to figure it all out on their own.

Match the Job Posting to Your Cover Letter

In the job posting they've likely already told you some things that are important. Match those things line by line with your cover letter. Make sure that for every point that is mentioned in the job posting, you've explained to them how the job posting describes you. While you shouldn't necessarily detail all the experiences you don't have, if you don't have an exact match to what they asked for in the job posting but have something pretty close, use your cover letter to explain the near-fit in a way that shows that you know what they are looking for and think that it is manageable given some of your experiences.

Provide Bonuses Even if They Haven't Asked

Don't hesitate to surprise the company with bonuses if there are ways that you think they haven't even imagined that you can provide value. For example, they may not need someone who understands the particularities of whatever industry they are in, but if you've done work with similar companies before, letting them know this can be useful. The cover letter is not, however, the place for including any activities or interests that are not intimately tied to the job that you are seeking.

Proof Your Cover Letter

Because you customize your cover letter for each company, it will probably have some new writing that hasn't been looked over. Make sure that you have someone proofread the cover letter before you send it. Companies get many resumes. A typo in your cover letter can eliminate you before anyone even looks at your resume.

Save a Copy of Your Cover Letter

It's very likely that your cover letter will be submitted electronically, either by email or pasted into a web form. Particularly in the latter case, make sure that you save a copy. Then if they do reach out to you, a week or even months later, it will be much easier to remember how you initially framed your experiences.

Give Options to Contact You

The more ways that they can contact you, the better. Give options to contact you by email, phone, Skype, Hangouts, or any method they can use to find you. There is no harm in suggesting that you are open to both voice and video calls, even if they don't take you up on the latter.

COVER LETTER TIPS

- Research the company's needs and say how you can meet those needs

- Match job posting skill and experience requests to your own situation

- Offer any extra value you can provide beyond requested skills

- Proof and save your letter

- Provide multiple ways that you can be contacted

Following Up

Do one round of follow-up over two separate communication channels in case one method has a technical snafu. You have at your disposal the telephone, an email, or perhaps a message through LinkedIn. If you try to follow up over two separate channels and still hear nothing, then consider it a dead end and move on.

The interview is your chance to connect with and impress your audience

Interviewing

Making it past the initial screening process to an interview at a company often means that someone has determined that you probably have the proper skillset and qualifications to succeed in a position. Congratulations! The flip side is that you're now being judged against other candidates for culture fit and for skills that can't really be determined from reviewing a resume and portfolio. Such skills could include your ability to think on your feet, or give a great presentation, or just fit in with the rest of the team.

Research the People who will Interview You

As best you can, identify in advance the individual or individuals who you'll be talking to during an interview. Look them up on the web and on LinkedIn—just like you can be sure they'll be doing for you! What are their titles and roles (and, therefore, what type of questions and qualifications are they most likely to be interested in)? What of their past experience or personal interests may intersect with yours? Doing your research and tying what you learned into the conversation demonstrates your attention to detail, understanding of context, enthusiasm for a role, and ability to personally connect—all of which are important.

Research the Company and its Projects

You'll also want to research the company and its projects before your interview—again by spending time on the web. With this knowledge in hand, you can demonstrate that you took the time to learn about them, show your interest, and identify areas of your background that are natural fits for their needs. Doing your research can also help you identify the things that you would like to learn about the company while you're there. Interviewers appreciate when a candidate comes ready with their own set of questions.

After you do your research about the company, consider adapting these starter questions and adding questions where you find additional gaps in the things you need to know.

- UX specific questions

  - Is there a UX team? Product development team?
  - How are these teams structured? Who is in charge?
  - How does your role fit into the existing teams?
  - What specific UX skills already exist on the team? (Ask specifically if others on the team or whom you would likely be collaborating with have skillsets that overlap with yours.)

- General culture fit questions

  - What is the management structure?
  - Who would you report to?
  - What's the work environment like? (Perhaps ask if you can have a tour.)
  - How does the company feel about working from home? Flexible schedules?

Come Prepared

Ideally, come prepared with a laptop or tablet that has electronic copies of your portfolio items. Consider paper copies of the most relevant deliverables that can best illustrate your value. Interviewers can take notes on the paper versions as you tell your story.

Bring paper copies of your resume. While the likelihood is that they'll have a copy already, do bring a few paper copies of your resume with you as a backup.

Consider showing up with tools of the trade. These might include pens, markers, sticky notes, or a mini white board. Also bring some paper for yourself to take notes. While you may have one (or more) devices with you, consider that these may be tied up with illustrating your background.

Throughout the interview you want to be telling a story with the specific goal of being hired. Recreating pieces of your story within the interview can help demonstrate your credibility and keep the interviewer truly engaged.

Look the Part

Remember that appearances matter. The way you present yourself also tells a story of who you are.

Arrive early. Ensure that you have clear directions about where to go, show up slightly early, and present yourself as you'd like to be seen.

Do your best to figure out how people dress where you're going. You don't necessarily have to wear a suit. Also, if you're looking for a job outside of your current geography, consider culture. In the United States, you are apt to find more suits in New York City than San Francisco.

This should be a no brainer, but of course don't look like you haven't gotten a haircut in way too long, or neglected a recent shower. You want to make a positive impression on as many fronts as possible.

If you go to lunch, pick the right food. If they take you to the cafeteria for lunch, enjoy the opportunity to see corporate culture through a different lens. But be beware that they are still observing you, so pick food that you can eat neatly and without too much fuss while carrying on a conversation between morsels.

Be a People Person

Hiring managers will expect a UX professional to be a people person, at least at some basic level—and perhaps more than at a basic level. You don't have to appear excessively gregarious, but you do need to demonstrate that you can relate to people.

Show that you can go with the flow. The path of each interview will be different, so show your flexibility by going with the flow of whatever they have planned. You may be initially asked to tell a little bit about your background and then show items from your portfolio. You may be presented with a challenge to solve, based on UX skills that they expect you to have. You may have a series of additional one-on-one interviews with different staff members or sit in a room with more than one person from the company who interview you together. Be prepared for all these experiences.

Be aware of your body language. After I gave a talk once, someone told me that it was such a gift that my body language matched the message that I was trying to deliver. I remember thinking to myself that it wasn't a "gift"—rather, I'm constantly evaluating the body language that I'm projecting.

As we discussed in Chapter 4, you can do this, too. Are you smiling? Projecting excitement? Leaning forward? Are your arms open as you explain with your hands how you made a difference or are they crossed and appear defensive? Positive body language doesn't have to be something that just happens; it's something you can control.

Be positive. No matter how unhappy you are at your current job, do your best to avoid saying negative things about your current employer, or anyone else for that matter. No one likes a complainer, so don't let this be you.

Be gentle if their frame doesn't match yours. UX is a profession of competing frameworks. Would you call yourself a user researcher but the company is calling you a human factors engineer? Do you consider yourself a UX designer where the company is calling you an information architect? That's okay, but it's up to you to do the translation. Explain gently to them in an interview (whether or not you've explained this before the interview) that you're framing your experiences one way but fully understand how they are framing them another way. Be careful not to imply a level of arrogance by insisting that your way is the right way, even if you find yourself thinking it.

Consider what you tell them about your salary. You are likely going to be asked either before the interview or at your interview about your salary expectations—how much you currently make and how much you expect to make. Be honest about how much you currently make, but if you have phenomenal benefits in some ways, it's certainly fine to comment that your salary was also supplemented by these valuable benefits.

When asked how much you expect to make, think carefully. You don't want to go so high that they consider you too expensive or totally mismatched with

---

INTERVIEWING TIPS

- Research the company and your interviewers.

- Bring copies of your resume and portfolio (paper and/or electronic).

- Bring tools of your everyday trade.

- Arrive slightly early.

- Ask about the position and team you would be joining.

- Present yourself professionally.

- Be friendly and positive with your body language.

- Plan what you want to say about salary if it comes up.

---

what you have been making, but you don't want to go so low that you don't get what you deserve. Try to put off this discussion until you at least know that they want you. That will give you a bit more bargaining power and will also allow you to scale back what you are asking if they seem very interested in you but tell you that they can't afford you.

Dealing with Rejection

It's inevitable that not every candidate will be hired for every role. Know that there are any number of reasons you may not get an offer, even if you are really well qualified: a project or team could lose funding, there could be internal politics at play, or there could have just been another even better-qualified candidate or someone who fits the internal culture better.

It's entirely appropriate to ask either the recruiter or the hiring manager for specific feedback about what could improve your chances of being hired in the future. If you're truly passionate about a specific role or project, keep in touch and maybe a similar role will come up later. Above all else, maintain positive interactions; the UX community is a small one and word about reputation spreads quickly. If you handle a rejection gracefully, it could even lead to your next job.

Accepting an Offer!

When you get the offer you want and accept it, don't forget to thank the people involved (such as recruiters, hiring managers, and people who interviewed you) and let it be known that you appreciate all that went into it. Next step—celebrate! It's exciting to take on a new role, whether it's a two-day project or a full-time, permanent position.

Set yourself up to succeed in the first few weeks on a new job by learning as much as you can about the company and culture before you start. Check if there are reviews on culture sites like Glassdoor or blogs written by people on the team. If possible, meet the team you'll be working with.

Getting Your First UX Job

If you are looking for a UX job but your current position is not in UX, much of the information presented in this chapter is still applicable to you. However, while you certainly have the benefit of frequent UX job openings, you will need to strategize about how to break in to the field.

Demonstrate Your UX Skills

Sometimes the first job can be the hardest to land. Being flexible can help—being willing to try a role in an industry you haven't considered or in a location that you've never been to can lead to more possibilities and potentially fantastic experiences.

You need to demonstrate in some way that you have not only the interest in the job, but also the skills necessary to do what needs to get done. If potential employers are advertising a job that lists years of experience, they are not looking for you to waltz in and tell them that you want to work there without demonstrating in some way that you can handle the job and add value to the company.

While you may not have on-the-job experience, if you studied certain aspects of UX in college, it's certainly possible to use this to your advantage. Don't be afraid to show your school or side work to demonstrate your expertise, and play up the fact that a company can help mold you into the kind of practitioner they need to flesh out their team.

Ultimately, your ability to get a job depends on your ability to accurately and succinctly frame your academic and professional experiences towards your UX goals.

Start with an Internship

Look for posted UX internships. If a position is designated as an internship, you certainly need to demonstrate that you have an inclination to do the work—showing your excitement and enthusiasm, as well as at least some basic semblance of the necessary background—but you don't need to have the level of experience necessary for a regular job. The experience you get in an internship for a few years can be just what you need to really break into the UX field as a true UX professional.

Create your own internship. As long as you can show that interest and inclination, and that you are not too concerned with a robust salary for the moment, you can target companies that you are most interested in. Do web research and look on jobs boards and on LinkedIn. If you find a job posting that asks for only a year or two of experience, you may have a reasonable shot suggesting that they hire you in an internship role in exchange for a lower salary.

Through your research, try to find contacts that you can email directly about your interest in an internship. You will likely have a sense of needs from the job posting; think about how you can help meet those needs as an intern. Consider asking if you can set up a time to talk by phone or perhaps have a video conversation to start. If at any point you think it makes sense, offer to take someone out for coffee or a drink to talk further. Ask questions, find out more about their UX needs, and explain that in exchange for learning on the job, you think that you can add lots of value as an intern.

BE AN INDISPENSABLE INTERN

By Jessica Ivins, Facilitator / Instructor, Center Centre and Leslie Jensen-Inman, Co-Founder and Institutional Director, Center Centre

An internship is an excellent opportunity to learn and grow professionally. As an intern, you get to experience—first-hand—what it's like to work within an organization. You get to know—personally—the people who work in that organization. And the people you work with get the opportunity to know you. They learn if you're a good fit for their company culture and potentially, whether you can be an effective member of their team long-term.

DEMONSTRATE YOUR VALUE

Think of your internship as an extended job interview or a project in your portfolio. Hiring managers look for interns who can produce great work. They also look for interns who have the soft skills needed to build meaningful professional relationships. These are the basic requirements to meet.

What separates a good intern from a truly awesome intern—the one who gets hired for a full-time position once the internship is completed—is demonstrating initiative and showing a strong desire to learn.

BE EAGER TO WORK AND LEARN

As an intern, make sure you're never without work. Ask for back burner projects to work on if you finish higher priority work assignments. When I, Jessica, was a junior UX designer at an agency, I sometimes ran out of work to do, and so I contacted my boss to let him know that I was finished and would work on a back burner project in the meantime. My boss appreciated my initiative, and thanked me for keeping him up to date.

Years later, when the tables were turned and I mentored a UX intern, she went out of her way to make herself useful and was always excited to learn new things. She offered to help me when I seemed overwhelmed and she told me she wanted to learn everything she could before her six-month internship ended. Her actions demonstrated an incredible initiative that I greatly appreciated.

Be receptive to feedback, and be open to learning. This field changes quickly, and everyone continues to learn with it; even senior-level practitioners and managers are continually learning. Also, when people notice that you're eager to learn, they're more willing to help you and mentor you. You'll build relationships with people who can become strong references.

MAKE EVERY MINUTE COUNT

An internship is a gift that lasts for a limited time. It's up to you to take initiative, to be proactive, and to get the most out of your experience. So do everything you can to be an indispensable intern and you will be adding incredible value to both your workplace and to your own career journey.

Jessica Ivins is a UX designer and educator who volunteers much of her time to the UX community. She's a faculty member at Center Centre, a UX design school in Chattanooga, Tennessee, that prepares students to be industry-ready UX designers. Jessica has spoken internationally at large conferences, volunteered for educational initiatives in her community, and served on the board of PhillyCHI, Philadelphia's UX community. Prior to joining Center Centre, she was a senior experience designer at Happy Cog and lead UX designer at AWeber. Follow Jessica on Twitter @jessicaivins.

Co-founder of Center Centre, **Dr. Leslie Jensen-Inman** is a designer, speaker, author, and educator. She combines nearly 20 years of design practice and eight years of instructional background—including five years as an assistant professor at the university level—to make Center Centre an extraordinary learning environment. Leslie shares her research and thoughts on design, learning, and leadership, through writing for publications and speaking at events. She is creative director and co-author of the book, *Inter-ACT with Web Standards: A holistic approach to web design*. Follow Leslie on Twitter @jenseninman.

BREAKING INTO THE UX FIELD

- Be flexible—consider roles in various industries and locations.

- Use school or personal side work to demonstrate your expertise.

- Look for posted UX internships.

- Create your own internship.

- Offer to get involved with UX work at a non-UX job.

- Show your excitement and enthusiasm!

Switching Careers

If you have already established yourself in a non-UX-related career and want to transition into UX, you may find that you have some additional options.

Learn New Skills at Your Current Job

It's often easier to learn new skills and then transition roles within a company than to look for a completely new position. If what you're already doing is close enough to the UX team at your company, try to see whether you can start taking on some UX-related roles. Express your interest and see if you can help out by making the case that with this additional versatility you can be even more valuable to your company.

Create an Internship within Your Industry Vertical

If you can't make it work at your current job, consider reaching out to others within your industry. While UX work is often fairly industry agnostic, you may be able to make the case that your domain knowledge can make you a valuable asset even though you haven't done much within a UX framework as yet.

LESSONS LEARNED FROM A CAREER SWITCHER

By Chelsey Glasson, User Experience Researcher, Google

I started out my professional life as a public policy analyst. As a side project for this role, I was once charged with designing a promotional website for a special program that I led. I was surprised to feel an immense amount of satisfaction from the process of creating something that I knew would be consumed by and helpful to a larger audience. Unfortunately this also meant a realization of how dissatisfied I was with my primary job responsibilities. In response to this epiphany, I quickly enrolled in graduate school in order to make a career transition, but at the time, I was not at all aware of the UX field.

Leaving a secure government job to go to graduate school was terrifying. Even more terrifying was when I discovered I had enrolled in the wrong graduate program halfway through it! At one point in my pursuit of a Master of Arts in Communication, I randomly took an elective course in design, which forever changed my life: I learned what interaction designers and user researchers were, that there was a shortage of such professionals, and that my university offered a master's program for aspiring UX professionals. After completing the course I knew without a doubt that I wanted to transfer into the UX program. And while I received pushback from my advisors, family, and friends, I nevertheless stood the course and eventually made the transition.

My new graduate program was wonderful in that it quickly opened the doors to networking opportunities within the UX community that helped me land a UX internship early on in the program. Looking back, though, I'm not confident the student debt I took on was worth the return. If I were doing it all again today, I'd probably explore a UX boot camp. Fortunately, more and more companies are becoming accepting of alternative forms of education and training in UX—what seems to matter most these days are one's skills and experience as opposed to academic credentials.

During my second year of graduate school, my UX internship turned into a full-time job offer! Once hired I made my first career mistake in not putting enough emphasis on building relationships with UX folks within and outside the company I worked for. I thought that what mattered most was working hard, and that my hard work would speak for itself and provide job security and opportunities. Eventually I learned that many UX job opportunities come about through a referral from someone in the UX community. I've also found that to be an impactful UX professional, your colleagues need to trust you, and trust is built off relationships.

When it finally dawned on me how important networking was, I admit I was intimidated and nervous in initially engaging with the larger UX community. What I found though is that the more I forced myself to network, the easier networking became. I'm happy to report that I now look forward to networking and attending UX events and am highly active in the UX community.

For a few years after finishing graduate school, I carried around a fear that job opportunities would be hard to come by without more experience, so I didn't hesitate to accept the first job offer presented when I was looking. I also assumed that UX professionals basically did the same thing across different environments, so why would I need to be picky? This faulty thinking led me to accepting a job I should have passed on, a situation that led to difficult circumstances that took me years to get out of.

Eventually I learned that there's a wide diversity in what UX professionals do across different environments and companies. For example, in some environments interaction designers and user researchers take on narrow responsibilities. At such companies, a user researcher might solely conduct rapid iterative testing and evaluation, and a designer might solely work on icons. At other companies, UX professionals take on much broader roles and responsibilities.

It also became apparent that work environment plays a huge part in the success of UX professionals. While some companies embrace and prioritize UX, others don't. Before accepting a new role, I now do a ton of research to make sure I'm not making faulty assumptions about the work I'd be doing and the environment I'd be walking into.

For years after transitioning careers I was also afflicted with "Imposter Syndrome," worried that someone would eventually discover I was a "fraud" because the bulk of my background and experience was not in UX. In all honestly, I admit that I still struggle with Imposter Syndrome today. What I've eventually learned is that Imposter Syndrome is an issue for most who have transitioned into UX from other careers, and while it's understandable to feel this way, it's not warranted. Those with diverse career backgrounds are actually often at an advantage as UX professionals, as they tend to bring unique skillsets and knowledge to the table that can make them stand out.

In fact, feeling like an imposter can be somewhat of a constant as a UX professional given how quickly tools and technology change, and I've learned that the best way to deal with it is to just be transparent about what you know.

Putting pressure on myself to know everything when I was initially making the career change—to be the mythical UX unicorn—was yet another early career mistake. This pressure ended up being counterproductive and unhealthy; I'd start taking on several classes and volunteer projects, just to eventually drop them due to burnout. What I know now is that UX is a massive umbrella of information, and while multiple skillsets are a good thing, it's impossible to know it all.

I hope my story will help you avoid some of my early career mistakes and faulty assumptions as I transitioned into a UX career. That said, I guarantee you'll make your own unique mistakes along the way. When you do so, don't sweat it too much, as making career mistakes is a normal part of the learning process. If I can overcome the challenges I shared with you, I have no doubt you can overcome yours too.

Chelsey Glasson is a UX researcher whose skills have impacted a wide variety of enterprise and consumer technologies at diverse companies including Google, Salesforce, Udacity, and T-Mobile. Motivated to help others avoid her early UX career mistakes, she often writes and gives talks on the topic of UX careers. She also taught a Udacity.com design fundamentals course with Don Norman and Kristian Simsarian in order to help UX newbies explore the exciting world of UX. Follow Chelsey on Twitter @chelseyglasson.

Deciding to Stay or Leave

Throughout this chapter, we talked about the process of landing a job. But as you can see, you're going to have to put a lot of time and effort into this transition. If you are currently employed but unhappy, consider whether the problems can be fixed. UX positions remain remarkably hard to fill, and you can use that to your advantage. Remember that if you are doing a good job at your current workplace, it will end up costing your employer a lot of time, money, and effort to replace you, not to mention the time it takes to get a new person up to speed.

Try to imagine a potential solution playing out for what is troubling you. If it's a solution that you can't initiate on your own, figure out who can, and try to talk to them. Either you may be able to find a way to adapt better to your situation or your workplace may be able to adapt to your needs. Even better, for the longevity of your career at your current workplace, perhaps there is some reasonable compromise that could keep both you and your employer happy.

Leaving

Sometimes nothing is specifically wrong, but you are just ready for something new. Sometimes it's just not possible to fix what is wrong.

As a consultant, I had a situation once where the work was wonderful, but then the powers that be—people who were involved in continuing to fund UX work—left. The new people who came in, while saying that a good user experience was important, decided that they didn't need UX experts, as funds were getting tighter.

While your employment situation may not be quite so black and white as my contract situation was in that case, a change of the guard may represent less value placed on the UX skills that you bring to the table. Or maybe the new managers change the definition of what UX means to the company and the skills that they require aren't those you have or want to have.

There are many reasons why it may be time to go; some are just more obvious than others. Ideally, you'll be able to identify the writing on the wall without being laid off first.

Yes, you can have a fair bit of confidence that there are a number of UX jobs out there, but finding the perfect job at the perfect time and in the perfect geographic location is not guaranteed to be immediate. So keep your job if you can, and start your job search.

Resigning Gracefully

Just like a design review of an interface should usually start by saying what is good before going into the issues of concern, when you do resign from your current job, don't burn bridges. Tell your boss and your company what you've enjoyed about your work. While you may have frustrations, there are certainly things that you have liked. Let them know.

Think in advance if you would consider a counter offer. If you would consider it, wait to formally accept the new position offered to you until you know you are definitely leaving your old one. When you have decided for sure that you are leaving and you know that you need to move on regardless, as best you can, come up with a valid and honest reason as to why you're going to move on. Ideally, related to your UX skillset, mention new and incredible challenges that you are excited about pursuing and other things that clearly don't exist at your current company. And whatever you do, don't say that you're leaving because you don't like working with some other staff person.

Do your best to give your company a two-week notice, even if this is not required in your contract. And certainly consider the idea of offering your company some ongoing support, even if after hours, so that your replacement could, perhaps, email you questions that you could respond to when you have time. Do not offer unlimited transitional help for free, but you can certainly offer this with an hourly rate that is at least roughly equal to whatever you are currently making.

To whatever extent possible, do your best to wrap up your current projects. Remember to keep in touch with the colleagues you've enjoyed working with and connect with them on LinkedIn and other social media. Besides the fact that it can be fun to keep in touch, you never know when they might hold the key introduction to something in the future.

In the next chapter, we will discuss more fully yet another resource you can tap to help you find a UX job: recruiters!

Get more online at uxcareershandbook.com/landing-job

Part 3

Recruiters & Employers

CHAPTER 9

Working with a Recruiter;
Being a Recruiter

By Amanda Stockwell, Vice President of UX, 352 Inc.

Job Seekers: The first part of this chapter is directed primarily to you. Learn about working with recruiters, what they can do for you, and how to choose recruiters to work with as you search for a job. While you could choose to skip the latter portions of this chapter that are directed to recruiters and employers, if you have the time, reading these sections may provide you with some additional useful context.

Recruiters: While you may have turned to this chapter first, consider reading the book in its entirety to better understand the careers that you are recruiting for and the jobseekers who you are placing in user experience (UX) positions. Also, although you can jump ahead to the middle portion of this chapter that is directed to you, you may also gain some valuable insights from the start of this chapter that addresses job seekers.

Employers: The last section of this chapter is targeted specifically for you and includes considerations when working with recruiters. You'll definitely want to also read the text that immediately precedes it, however, which tells recruiters how to work with you. Chapter 10 will then elaborate significantly on additional hiring considerations.

For Job Seekers

"Recruiter" can be a dirty word to some. Even with an abundance of UX-specific recruitment agencies popping up, many professionals in the UX world have had negative experiences with recruiters, often for jobs they are not remotely interested in or which have nothing to do with their UX skillset.

How likely do you think it is that this person is going to find a UX designer in such a mismatched role?

Subject: Full time position—<u>UX Designer</u>

To: amanda.stockwell@gmail.com

Hi Amanda,

Hope you are doing good!

Just to update you that I got your profile from our internal Database and I am trying to reach you to discuss about an open & highly burning position matching your skill set and experience.

Location(s): Charlotte, NC

JOB DESCRIPTION

* Ability to develop new approaches to complex design problems.
* Knowledge of new technologies (such as PHP 5, CSS, HTML5).
* Knowledge of JavaScript—rich interactive client interfaces (e.g. Ext.js), JSON, AJAX, DOM manipulation, Node.js.
* MySQL or other database experience.
* Experience using SOAP and RESTFUL web services.
* Solid understanding of scalable design principles.
* Knowledge of written View controller code in any MVC applications.
* Experience in Ajax, JQuery, Java and web services.
* Experience in Web application framework (spring, apache, flex, struts, play).
* Web container level experience (tomcat, jetty).
* OI layer level experience (akka, netty, node.js).
* Solid understanding of Linux or Unix operating systems.
* Experience building web apps in a load balanced environment.
* Experience working with and configuring web servers and databases.
* Understanding of storage systems, firewalls, VPN, networking and/or virtualization technologies.

However, just like UX professionals, recruitment agencies and recruiters are not all the same, and some are certainly more knowledgeable about recruiting for UX positions than others.

There are several types of recruiters and recruiting firms out there: some place only full-time positions, some serve companies looking only for part-time or short-term contracts, and some fill both types of roles. There are times when those recruiting firms that provide short-term or contract roles could be your actual employer and essentially contract you out to their clients, parallel to a long-term consulting arrangement with a consulting agency. In addition, some recruiters and recruiting firms have specialty areas within UX career pathways, while others focus on particular clients or segments that their agency serves.

Payment models for recruitment firms also vary, sometimes even between different contracts within the same company. Some firms are paid a set fee just for finding a candidate. Sometimes a recruiting firm gets paid a fee at certain intervals based on the candidate's salary. Some agencies that contract out their employees make their money by marking up candidates' hourly rates to the client. Sometimes recruiters receive a bonus after a candidate they found has been at a company for a certain amount of time.

The variety of payment structures and employment types can influence how recruiters behave and therefore a jobseeker's experiences in interacting with them. Regardless, most of the time external recruiters or recruiting agencies make money only if an employee gets and stays at a job, at least for a little while; so it's in their best interest to find good fits between their candidates and the roles they have to fill.

Working with Recruiters

Even as someone who works closely with a recruiting agency, I've certainly also been on the receiving end of a "Dear Experienced IT Professional" email asking me to move across country for a 3-month contract at a fraction of my normal pay, and I can understand the frustration UX professionals can have with recruiters. If you receive a sterile cold-call or impersonal template email from a recruiter who clearly does not understand your work or the role they are recruiting for, delete the message and move on.

Successful UX recruiters become knowledgeable in the UX skills and career pathways for which they need to hire and work to build relationships within the UX space. These are the recruiters who can be of most value to you in your job search.

What Recruiters Can Do for You

Working with recruiting agencies can be a huge asset to you when you are actively searching for a UX job, whether you are just starting out or are several years into your career. You can be open with them about your past experiences and what exactly you're looking for so that they can help you find the best fit for you. It's common for candidates to be talking to several recruiters at once, so you can get multiple perspectives and become aware of a larger degree of possibilities this way.

Recruiters are often privy to information that is not publicly available, such as unadvertised open positions or the range of salaries that a company is willing to pay, which can help you find open roles or negotiate terms of an agreement. They might have insight into a company's unpublished hiring plans and could potentially frame your skills appropriately for additional near-term needs at a company; this is usually not an option if you are contacting a company cold. They may also be able to provide insight about a company's culture from speaking to business representatives and possibly other candidates they've placed.

Recruiters and recruitment agencies represent multiple related open positions. They typically serve a breadth of role types and levels, so if you apply to a particular role that you aren't quite a fit for, they may have immediate suggestions for another role within the same company or a similar role at a different company. These recruiters can also introduce you to opportunities that you wouldn't have necessarily thought you were qualified for but that may be a good fit because the company is interested in someone with similar industry experience or someone who is a good match for their company's culture.

Recruiters may be able to supply detailed feedback about your resume, portfolio, and experience that you might not otherwise hear or feel comfortable asking for—both before and after they submit your materials to an employer. They typically are told reasons why a candidate isn't a good match in order to help them refine their search for a perfect candidate. If you find out that an employer has rejected your candidacy for a job, don't hesitate to ask the recruiter why, so that you can gain insights that would help you with future job applications.

You may be eligible for a referral program. Even if you are not the one to fill the job they are looking for, because of difficulty finding UX candidates to fill roles, there are frequently referral programs that pay from several hundred to several thousand dollars if a person you pass to a recruiter is placed in a role. If you know someone who would be a great fit you can both help a colleague and make some extra money.

Recruiters are useful people to stay in touch with. Staying connected with a few trusted recruiters can also be beneficial for those who are happy in their current job role. If you have regular interactions with a recruiter, whether by email, phone, or social media connections, you could be helping to keep yourself at the top of their list of potential candidates when they start recruiting for exciting new opportunities.

> There can be many benefits to working with and establishing solid relationships with recruiters—they may have inside information, be aware of multiple positions over time, and be willing to provide valuable feedback to help you frame your skills and experiences appropriately.

Choosing a Recruiter or Recruitment Agency

It can seem that you just have to work with whatever recruiter shows up in your inbox. It's true that you're likely to get contacted by any number of recruiting agencies, especially if you take that critical initiative to put yourself out there on the web. However, you can take control of your career by actively evaluating recruitment agencies and specific recruiters to see which ones fit best with your goals and needs.

First, find out if an agency prioritizes UX roles. This can be obvious if the firm is a specialty shop and they solely recruit for UX roles, but you can also look for a recruiting agency that publicly states UX roles as one of their specialties and advertises employing UX subject matter experts as part of the screening and hiring process. You can check out an agency's website and other resources that they provide, such as whitepapers, blog posts, or other articles to learn about their UX lens and perspectives. Also, look on the web to see if you can learn if the agency has involvement in UX events beyond just sponsorship—see if their staff are connected with and attending learning events, showing an active interest in getting involved in the UX community to find appropriate talent.

For agencies that actually hire talent directly and then place them at client companies, you can investigate the company's potential compensation and

Work with recruiters who understand UX

contract packages to see what would be a good fit for you. If you're only interested in full-time, more permanent roles, you may want to find a specific firm that fills only those types of positions. If, on the other hand, you're open to contract-to-full-time roles, short-term contract roles, or part-time roles, you can tell the agencies that contact you what you are looking for and see if they are amenable to finding staff for these types of positions.

Recruitment firms that prioritize UX may be more likely to have recruiters who will prove beneficial for you. These may include specialty shops, firms that employ UX subject matter experts, and firms that make a point to be involved in the UX community.

If you find a specific recruiter at an agency with whom you relate well, stay in touch with him or her, and foster an ongoing relationship. On the flipside, if you don't have a great experience with one particular recruiter, you don't have to write off an entire agency.

Last but not least, remember that you can be in contact with as many recruiters or agencies as you please and that your commitment starts only when you accept a particular job.

Working with In-house Recruiters

So far, we've focused on working with recruitment agencies, but many companies employ in-house recruiters to focus solely on finding the best employees for their teams.

An internal recruiter should know their company inside and out, have a close relationship with the hiring manager, and know the other members of the team for which they're recruiting. They're likely to be able to give you the best view into the real day-to-day life at a company and may be able to give you some information about who you'll need to impress to get the role. This can be great insight, but keep in mind that they are actively trying to sell their company to candidates, so they may not want to be as forthcoming about challenges or ongoing issues. On the other hand, an internal recruiter should have a very good gauge to know if you are truly a good fit for a role.

In-house recruiters may be less reliant on commission than third-party recruiters, which means they are less likely to try to push you to a role that isn't a great fit for you. Their key objectives will be to look for the best fit to grow a team, and their loyalty is to the same company you are applying to work for. With that in mind, consider speaking to an internal recruiter as the first of many interviews, and start crafting the story you want to tell the company from the outset.

Finally, if you're particularly interested in a job at a specific company, it can be valuable to build a relationship with an in-house recruiter. They can be your advocate for a role, and if they like you but aren't able to offer you a specific role, they can keep you in mind for future positions before they are publicized, or suggest you for an alternate role.

What Recruiters Can't Do for You

Have you communicated your value? Even the most experienced recruiters (at recruitment agencies or in-house) won't understand nuances of your work unless you clearly communicate your skills and value. It can be tough for recruiters to know for sure when candidates really have legitimate UX skills. Make it easier for them to understand you by following the branding, resume, and portfolio tips in Chapters 4 and 5.

Have you already applied to the company? Recruiters often can't help you if you've already applied to and gotten rejected from or didn't take a job at a particular company within a certain period of time that could last from months to years. There are usually contracts that require that recruiters bring what the companies define as "new" candidates.

Are different recruiters hiring for the same job? It's definitely possible that several recruiting firms are trying to fill the same jobs, especially if a company is having a really hard time filling the role. That's not necessarily all good or bad, but be aware that you could be approached about the same job from multiple sources. If you are already working with a recruiter for a particular role at a company, let a new recruiter know, since they may not be able to submit you if another agency already has submitted you for the same job.

CORY'S RECRUITER FAQ: READY ANSWERS FOR RECRUITERS' QUESTIONS

As I am well branded and out on the web as an experienced UX professional, I find that at least once a day I get an email from a recruiter offering some new job for which the recruiter thinks I'd be a great fit. While I appreciate knowing that I'm findable and in lots of databases of potential candidates, I never find that I can give an unqualified yes to a recruiter to submit my name to the employer. I created a Recruiter FAQ post so that I didn't have to keep making the same points to recruiters. I don't send a link to this blog post to all recruiters who contact me, but I have sent it when it looks like there is at least a chance that things might work out.

I encourage you to come up with your own recruiter FAQ. It doesn't have to be as publically available as mine is. It could simply reside in a word document or a link to a Google doc that you can send out. If you'd like to use my original Recruiter FAQ as a template to adjust to your own job requirements, you can copy and adapt from http://lebsontech.com/recruiter-faq/

For Recruiters

64. That's my record for number of recruiter emails I've received in one week as a UX researcher. Want to know how many I immediately deleted? 63. That's right. All but one. You want to be the recruiter who sends the one email UX professionals don't delete.

UX roles are notoriously difficult to source and fill. You can't do anything about what constantly feels like a larger number of job openings than there are qualified candidates looking to fill them, but you can do your best to understand the people that make up the UX industry, which will help you tailor your recruiting approach and make good matches.

UX professionals have been on the positive side of a mismatched supply and demand ratio for several years. They are often in high demand, are well compensated, and don't find themselves in a position to try very hard to secure a job. As a recruiter, therefore, you need to take a careful and well thought out approach when searching for UX professionals. You need to **sell** the benefits of a job, the challenges a candidate will have the opportunity to address, the great environment, and other reasons why a professional might want to give up a current job or explore your offer over the other offers in hand to accept your role.

Much like other very specialized roles, it's often hard for others outside the profession to understand exactly what UX professionals do. Recognize that there are a variety of differing skillsets that UX professionals have, and just because someone is a UX professional does not mean that she or he will meet the criteria for the UX job opening you are looking to fill. UX professionals are like snowflakes: even though they may all self-brand as UX, they're often quite unique from each other. Take the time to really learn about the different UX pathways in Chapter 11. Realize that often UX professionals have a lot of experience in only a few of these pathways, and they may have more general familiarity in only a few additional areas.

Sending a UX practitioner a job description for a role that doesn't appear to play to their strengths or seems to require skills they don't practice is a way to turn them off quickly. Beware of sending out job descriptions that require skills from just about every UX pathway in Chapter 11, even if you are aware that these skills don't necessarily exist in a single person, at least not with any great level of expertise. If you are seen as a UX unicorn hunter, you will lose credibility.

Yes, it takes more time, but be sure to fully investigate a UX professional's background, and carefully compare it to the job description you have. If they seem to have more research skills, don't send them roles that are heavy on visual design and technical skills. Also, instead of insisting they'd be a great match for a particular role, simply reach out to find out if they're interested, and if not, what kind of role they are looking for. And at the very least, apply at least a base level of personalization to your emails to show that you really know who you are emailing and have, in fact, been reviewing their resume.

Above all, remember that **UX professionals are often inundated with requests and could resort to deleting recruiter emails, voicemails, or LinkedIn requests very quickly.**

Finding Potential Candidates and Staying in Touch

You have likely found yourself under a lot of pressure to find the right candidate for UX positions, and find them fast. While there is no magic rock under which all the talented UX professionals are hiding, there are definitely some ways recruiters can get and stay in better touch with these highly sought after professionals.

- **Get out there and go to UX-oriented events**, conferences, meetups, professional groups, and social networks that are geared to all aspects of UX. These in-person opportunities are a great way to network with a lot of potential candidates at once.
- **Try a viral networking approach.** People in the UX community are well connected to each other. If you have a client who provides a great environment, can offer flexibility, or has a really interesting design problem to solve, articulate this in such a way that even those not looking for a job will want to let their UX network know. A job that sounds incredible could be as useful as cash in helping get others to spread the word.
- **Keep in touch with people you meet**, offering references for other jobs and connecting folks that you meet. UX professionals are much more likely to come to you or send a colleague your way if they know you,

feel confident that you understand UX, and trust that knowing you offers value to their own career.

Screening UX Professionals

Understanding a UX professional's background and qualifications can be tricky, especially with all of the recent buzz around the field and the associated influx of candidates claiming UX proficiency. Here are a few tips to help determine a UX professional's overall expertise set:

- **Ask about their overarching understanding of a UX methodology and framework.** They should be able to articulate the user-centered design principles involved in creating great user experiences, regardless of which aspects of the product cycle they typically work on. Do they understand the value of incorporating feedback from users? Do they understand that an attractive site is not necessarily a usable site?
- **Look beyond job titles, which are often inconsistent.** Instead look for previous methods the potential talent has used and deliverables they've created to better understand how well they match your particular job description.
- **Look beyond resumes and even portfolios to assess their legitimacy as a UX professional**. Consider whether a candidate shows an interest in UX beyond their jobs. When you Google them is their name at all associated with UX Meetups or events? Have they posted UX-related content on a blog or periodically on Twitter?

Really investigate whether a candidate would make a good fit within the team structure and overall culture of a job and has the other soft skills required of their role. If someone has all the right skills but a personality that would clash with the team, suggest that they look for something different. Both the individual and company will appreciate it, and you will earn credibility in the eye of the UX professional.

When screening someone for a particular role, be as clear as possible about timelines, and provide feedback as soon as possible. Top UX candidates are likely to have multiple opportunities and need to make decisions quickly; so checking in, even when there is no update, can make them feel confident that you value their time and perhaps give them a reason to hold off accepting another offer.

Working with Employers

Another challenge that you may face in the UX space is that your clients don't know or can't articulate what they need. Use your understanding of UX to work with your clients and help them to better express their staffing needs.

Focus on the employers' overarching goals. Why are they hiring someone now? How do they expect a new UX team member to add value? What types of UX-oriented deliverables is the candidate expected to produce?

Find out about that particular client's definition of UX and what, exactly, they expect the new hire to do on a day-to-day basis. While they may ask you to find a "UX professional," their actual need may not represent what UX professionals would consider a typical UX job. Or they may be looking for one skillset but trying to frame it within a different UX career pathway.

Find out how the UX work will be broken out among different UX team members. This is especially true for hybrid roles that are supposed to fill multiple UX pathways within a larger team. If a candidate is expected to cover both interaction design and information architecture needs, be aware that it's likely the candidate will want to know what percent of time will be spent doing what. This information will also help you to know which of these two skillsets you should focus on more when looking for a candidate.

Identify what UX skills your client does NOT need. Sometimes, it can be just as helpful to know what not to focus on as you consider possible candidates. So that you don't end up sending clients candidates whose real UX strengths are only in areas that aren't a priority.

Convince employers not to put requests for UX certification in job descriptions. While there is plenty of good UX training available, a training program that offers "certification" is not necessarily better than a training program that does not. In fact, as we talked about in Chapter 2, while it may be easy for employers to want a quick marker of eligibility, among those who are experienced in UX, there is cynicism about, and criticism of, employers who add requests for certification into job descriptions.

Resist the appeal of the UX unicorn. While it's appealing to imagine that you'll find one person who has true expertise across all elements of UX, it's rare that you'll find someone who truly excels in all aspects of UX; and if you do find this needle in a haystack, they are likely going to be incredibly expensive to hire.

For Employers

For those who have been tasked with working with a recruiting company or non-specialized internal recruiters to find UX professionals to join their team, it may be easier said than done to communicate the needs and nuances of your team, but a bit of prep work can make the recruiting process easier for everyone involved.

Getting the Most Out of Your Recruiters

Know your needs before you try to describe them to a recruiter: Why are you hiring a new UX professional? How do you want this person to improve the UX of your products? What projects will this person work on? In what way? Focus first on what you'd expect this person to do within the broad scope of UX and then secondarily on what UX pathways their skillsets will match.

Be explicit about what deliverables the new hire would be producing, and try to provide a general breakdown of the ratio of responsibilities. That is, if you need to hire someone to cover multiple facets of UX, specify how much of each niche will make up the person's daily, weekly or monthly workload.

Prioritize must-haves and nice-to-haves. Be honest about what skills you can and cannot live without, including UX areas of expertise, personality traits, industry experience, and other non-skill-specific characteristics or experiences you require. The more explicit you are with the recruiter, the more successful they will be in bringing you appropriate candidates.

Share portfolios and experience of people on your team (or that fit the profile of someone that you'd like to hire) to give recruiters a concrete example to follow.

When working with an outside recruiting agency, inform recruiters about your team and company culture so the recruiter can effectively screen for a culture fit. Consider inviting the recruiter to your office for a few hours to better understand your team processes and personalities.

Be realistic about price. UX professionals are really tough to find and often have multiple offers. Recruiters can bring you talent, but they can't convince them to be interested in a below-market rate. Also, describe the specific benefits of joining your team beyond money so that the recruiter can better sell your open position when there are competing options.

Keep in mind that recruiting for UX positions can be incredibly challenging, and the more closely you partner with your recruiter in general, the more successful they are likely to be.

For more information about Amanda, see her bio at the end of Chapter 5.

 Get more online at uxcareershandbook.com/recruiters

CHAPTER 10

Employer's Guide (And What Job Seekers Should Look For)

By Pamela Walshe, Vice President, People & Client Experience, AnswerLab

Job Seekers: Each of the chapters through this point has been directed primarily to you. Now, as you'll see, we're about to address your present or future employers. You may be saying to yourself, "Oh—looks like I should move on and skip this chapter." However, consider reading it to gain some insights and find out what employers are planning and thinking about when considering your employment—or at least what they *should* be thinking about.

Employers: While you may have noticed this chapter upon picking up the book, don't consider only reading this one chapter. While this chapter distills some critical points that you should consider when employing user experience (UX) professionals, and frames those points largely for you, the earlier chapters leading up to this point, as well as the chapters that follow, also supply you with critical knowledge that you need to understand UX professionals.

As you likely know, it's a challenging job market where the demand for UX often seems to far exceed the supply of qualified UX professionals. Therefore, it's especially important that you think carefully about your hiring strategy and organizational environment to give yourself the best chance of hiring and keeping the best UX professionals for your organization.

Identifying Needed Skillsets

When growing a UX team, the first step is to clarify precisely what type of practitioner(s) you need. Review the next chapter on UX career pathways to better understand the full range of roles that you could consider. Beyond these core skillsets, however, also consider carefully the:

- soft skills and personality you need
- level of seniority that is required
- need for practitioners or leaders
- job structure you are hiring for.

Soft Skills and Personality

To consider what you want as soft skills and personality, start by thinking about your current top performing employees. What soft skills and personality traits do they have that contribute to their success? For example, these are typical markers of employees who are most successful at AnswerLab, a user research consultancy:

People who . . .	Will thrive because . . .
Have great presentation and storytelling skills	They will influence others by keeping them engaged, creating buy-in, and building empathy for users.
Work collaboratively	They will create better work by integrating the ideas and feedback of others.
Love to learn	They will continually keep up with trends in the industry including innovations in technology and changes in the marketplace.
Are articulate and communicative	They can connect and interact clearly with both team members and clients/stakeholders, avoiding or successfully navigating through conflicts of opinions or ideals.
Have good problem-solving skills	They will overcome obstacles and be adaptable in the face of change.
Project confidence	They are readily perceived as knowledgeable and worthy of respect.

Level of Seniority the Team Needs

It's also important to think through what level of seniority is needed in the role you are looking to fill. Do you have a hands-on manager who can oversee and groom a more junior level employee, or do you need to hire people who are savvy self-starters or who can independently lead complex UX projects? Do you have the resources to invest in training a less experienced practitioner, or would you benefit from someone who could potentially mentor and educate others in your organization?

While the answers to these questions aren't always black and white, they are important considerations that will affect the success of your employees and your UX team in the long run. Instead of simply using your hiring budget as a guideline for who you can "afford," carefully consider what level of seniority the organization needs, and invest wisely. A new hire that seems affordable given your budget may be less valuable than a more expensive candidate over time if you don't have the resources to develop that less experienced new hire or if you need to subcontract work to an external agency because the less experienced staff is unable to do it.

JUNIOR-LEVEL UX PRACTITIONERS

Junior-level staff are usually best suited to environments that have a strong existing foundation of tools, processes, and mentorship that will set them up for success and support their growth over time.

An ideal approach to ramping up more junior UX professionals is to embed them in teams where they can directly contribute but also have the opportunity for close mentorship from other more experienced practitioners while they build their skills and confidence.

At AnswerLab, typically about half of our new hires each year are relatively "junior." Our strategy is to identify promising raw talent and to shape them into UX professionals according to our own philosophy and our quality standards. We support them with a robust training and mentorship program that enables us to develop and grow them into senior consultants over time with the intention to build tenure within our team from the associate level to principals, strategists, managers, directors, and beyond.

Pros of Junior UX Staff
- Relatively inexpensive compared to more seasoned peers
- Opportunity to mold/shape the employee into a UX professional that embraces your organization's philosophies
- Can act as a "second pair of hands" while getting up to speed

Cons of Junior UX Staff

- May be perceived as less useful to the project by more senior staff
- May lack the confidence needed to be perceived as an authority
- Requires investment from management to develop "the basics" if little or no experience
- May be successful at executing tasks but will take some time to build the skills of problem solving and working independently

SENIOR-LEVEL UX PRACTITIONERS

Senior-level UX hires will thrive in an environment where they can apply their skills and expertise with autonomy, see the impact of their work, influence the strategic direction of the business, and (for some but not all) mentor others.

Pros of Senior UX Practitioners

- Deeper and broader experience leads to more strategic work overall
- Although more expensive, can potentially provide greater value by operating more efficiently and successfully managing a larger volume of work
- Better positioned to "hit the ground running" and work independently
- Can wield experience and be seen as authoritative and influential by colleagues/clients

Cons of Senior UX Practitioners

- Can command high rates/salaries due to specialized skillsets
- May be more set in their ways and less adaptable to organizational differences from prior work

Note that while for the purpose of illustrating pros and cons we focus on the two ends of the experience spectrum, you can also consider mid-level practitioners who will often end up as somewhat of an amalgam of junior-level and senior-level staff.

PRACTITIONERS OR LEADERS

When building a UX team, you also need to consider whether your current needs are for practitioners or leaders (or both). When asking yourself this question, consider your immediate needs, but also look to your overall business goals. Consider what you will need one to three years from now, and be sure you take those needs into account.

Beware of assembling an entire team of UX professionals who are only skilled at executing the work. You need to make sure that some of your UX practitioners are also leaders. The most successful UX teams are those with strong leaders who can set a UX vision for an organization, can evangelize the value of their team, and can successfully procure the resources needed to execute on that vision. When seeking a UX leader for an organization, look for established (but perhaps generic) leadership qualities, and also seek out these unique UX-related characteristics.

Leaders need to have a passion for UX. UX is fundamentally about having empathy for the users and ensuring that their needs are considered in every major business decision. The successful UX leader first and foremost must care deeply about the value and necessity of a team that can create a high-quality experience for users. Simultaneously, they must be an effective storyteller who can convey the importance of meeting user needs (while satisfying business goals) to stakeholders.

Leaders need to have a solid UX background. In addition to having specific expertise in one or more of the UX career pathways described in Chapter 11, having a good general understanding of all relevant UX career pathways discussed in that chapter is also important. It establishes credibility with members of the team who want a leader who can understand what they do and can make appropriate decisions, provide direction, and generally understand what it takes to get the work done.

Hiring is about more than just UX skills

JOB STRUCTURE

There are further considerations for job candidates depending on what kind of job structure or situation you are hiring for.

Hiring in-house employees to join the team. In-house UX teams could work throughout the lifecycle of a particular development effort or could span multiple projects or development efforts. If you need to hire for these teams, look for individuals who are successful at developing relationships, collaborating with others, and seeing things through over the long term, and also those who strive to develop deep subject matter expertise.

Building a brand new in-house UX team. When building a new UX team within a company, selecting the right first hires is critical because they will set the culture and reputation of the team going forward. You will need astute practitioners who can wear different hats and be creative in resource-strapped environments. In these early stages of team development, it's important to be sure that you hire individuals who demonstrate a strong aptitude for leadership and can help to evolve the team or UX practice over time.

Hiring for a consulting agency. Consulting agencies' needs can vary greatly based on the engagements and clients they're working with at any given time. Beyond core skills and any specialized skills that are needed, when hiring UX consultants, consider that successful candidates need to be able to thrive in rapidly changing environments: timelines shift, client expectations are highly variable, and consultants may need to jump from team to team as consulting work comes and goes.

LOOK FOR AN OCTOPUS (AND NOT A UNICORN)

By Baruch Sachs, Senior Global Director of User Experience, Pegasystems

For years now, I have been engaged in what can be described as the Great Gold Rush of building a UX team. Instead of prospecting for that glittery mineral that has broken the hearts and busted the wallets of many, I and many others have been searching for something equally destructive: The UX unicorn. I am here to tell you to stop. Much like the creature itself, a UX unicorn is a myth.

I have reviewed countless resumes, portfolios, and predictive indexes. I have spoken to numerous colleagues in the UX profession and outside of it who are searching for this perfect candidate.

This is not to say that there are no UX professionals out there who have the capability to strategize, research, design, and code, single-handedly raising your product's UX to dizzying levels. I should know, as I have hired 17 of them in the past 2 years. However, none of these people had *all* of these skills before I hired them. What this experience has taught me is that we should not really be searching for unicorns. Instead, we need to find flexible and adaptable people who have the *capability* for a wide range of skills.

FIND AN OCTOPUS

If I were to choose an animal that best describes what I look for in the ideal, all-inclusive UX professional, it would be an octopus. Instead of the mythical and vague attributes that we look for in UX unicorns, an octopus's attributes are concrete and readily apparent in value. Let's look at the octopus and its attributes for a moment and align them with the qualities we look for in a UX person on a team.

- Highly intelligent
- Behaviorally flexible
- Able to basically reinvent themselves by regenerating a limb
- Employs multiple defense strategies depending on context
- Able to get in and out of the tightest places with ease

Now these are characteristics that any hiring manager can get behind! These abilities of an octopus are the core of a successful person in any line of business. Instead of looking for more mythic and subjective qualities of a UX unicorn, I have started to look for these octopus-like qualities instead, and I have to say, while my search may not have gotten easier, it is much more focused and successful.

I have started looking not just at the depth of experience, but the breadth. I ask questions around difficult situations and how they would handle them. I also have them meet with folks within my company but from outside my own UX department to see how they interact. Success with these people is very telling as to whether I may have a potential UX octopus.

No one is an immediate perfect fit. Unrealistic expectations have plagued the UX profession for years, and it is showing no real signs of stopping. However, we can get ahead of this. Stop looking for the unicorn. Start looking for a flexible, adaptable octopus with UX know-how who can pick up additional skills as needed.

In his first job out of college as a technical writer, **Baruch Sachs** found himself designing better UIs so that he could write less. For the next 15 years, he would develop a wide range of skills in the areas of interaction design, user interface development, and product management and successfully lead efforts to improve UX across various industries. He founded and continues to lead the global UX team at Pegasystems where he consults with Fortune 100 clients on how to transform their enterprise user interfaces into delightful experiences. He still enjoys designing more, and writing less.

Designing an Effective Interview Process

Job Seekers: While we talked about the job search process in Chapter 8, also read this section carefully to know what you may (and should ideally) expect in an interview from potential new employers.

Teams—especially those that work collaboratively—are dynamic organisms that can be dramatically impacted with the addition of new members. For this reason, consider a collaborative hiring process in which several members of the team can participate in at least some aspects of the interviewing process. The intention is not to attempt to gain complete consensus on hiring decisions (likely impossible anyway), but rather to give visibility into the decision-making process and let the team know that their voices are heard. Whether the team involvement is minimal or great, including team members will enable you to be transparent about how and why decisions are made, and to gain buy-in for the incoming new hire.

Do Your Research Before an Interview

In Chapter 4, we talked about how job seekers should brand themselves for success and should network and be part of the UX community. Then in Chapter 5, we talked how job seekers should be constructing their resumes and portfolios. As an employer, you are on the other side of this equation, so how should you use this information?

Carefully review submitted materials. Even before candidates are invited for an interview, closely assess everything that you can learn about the candidate from their application. You likely already know that you need to look for a resume that illustrates the appropriate experience and portfolio materials that show high-quality work.

Review their online presence. Find the candidate online and see if the brand that they are promoting for themselves in the materials they submitted matches what you find when you look them up on the web or through social media.

Look for passion in UX. Look for indicators of UX passion in both their materials and online presence. Does UX permeate the candidate's online presence? Do they strongly associate with other UX professionals and the greater UX community? Do they participate in UX-related activities outside of their paid work? Do they talk about UX in social media or through a blog? Remember that while what candidates provide to you is a great starting point, often it is the searches you do that expose the most details about who they are.

Gain Insights from Simulations

The insights gained from the materials that candidates provide and from online searches are critical to understanding who those candidates are. However, also try to see those skills in action by simulating the most realistic situation possible.

Using such exercises has enabled AnswerLab to differentiate top-tier talent from the rest, while also helping to get a true read on level of seniority, as years of experience is not always the best indicator. Additionally, since these scenarios are designed using real-world case studies, they give the candidate direct insight into the day-to-day responsibilities of the role.

Consider having candidates participate in one or more of the following types of exercises:

Written exercise involving a real-world case study: Candidates are required to respond to a real-world case study in which a business leader or client has requested UX services. The candidate is required to draft a response outlining their approach to the business challenge and recommending next steps.

Hands-on research or design exercise: Depending on what role you are hiring for, creating a real-world design or research challenge that requires the candidate to apply relevant skills within a limited timeframe can provide insight into how quickly the candidate can think on their feet within the constraints you've set forth. For example, candidates for UX researcher roles at AnswerLab are required to moderate a mock research session so the company can observe the candidate's moderation technique.

Presenting their work: Presentation skills are key for most UX roles, especially at the more senior levels. Requiring candidates to present the work that they did in an exercise like that above or perhaps to present some work in their portfolio as if they were presenting it to stakeholders provides an opportunity for the team to observe candidates' communication and presentation skills firsthand. Audience members can also ask questions, requiring candidates to think on their feet and demonstrate their skill in addressing tough questions.

Evaluate Culture Fit

Work environment and culture is one of the primary drivers for employee engagement and should not be overlooked as part of your hiring process. Each individual that joins a team has the potential to either elevate or distract the other members of the group. At AnswerLab, culture fit is core to our interview process in two key ways:

Social hour: Each later-stage on-site interview with candidates also includes a social hour where employees have the opportunity to get to know the candidate in an informal social setting. Everyone in the company from all functional areas of the business are invited to drop in; these are generally scheduled around lunch and take place at a communal area. The intention here is to step away from the interview setting to see how discussions and interactions naturally develop. When this goes well, the candidate is clearly at ease, engaging with others and readily jumping into the group conversation. When it goes poorly, there is visible tension, awkwardness, and difficulty making conversation. There are rare occasions where the answer is not so clear-cut (candidates may be more tense or nervous than usual), but usually this process is quite insightful and addresses the question "would you want to spend 40+ hours a week working with this person?).

Behavioral questions related to culture and core values: One of the most effective ways to get insight into culture fit is to use questions requiring the candidate to describe first-hand experience exhibiting the behaviors that you value. Give careful consideration to your existing core values, and also think about the dynamic that exists within your team today to craft questions that will elicit whether the necessary qualities are a part of the candidate's natural make-up. For example, here are sample culture questions that AnswerLab uses:

This question . . .	Will help you understand . . .
Thinking about how you conduct yourself in your personal and professional life, can you identify three core values that describe who you are?	Unaided, does the candidate naturally speak to core values that are in alignment with the company core values?
Describe what a "perfect" work day would be like for you. What would you be working on? What about it would be satisfying?	Is what they describe realistic in your work environment?
Describe what a "nightmare" work day would be like for you. What is going on? What makes it so terrible?	What is their tolerance level for "things going wrong?" Are they easily ruffled or flustered? Does their example day sound much easier or more difficult than the challenging days you've witnessed in the organization?
Tell me something funny that happened to you recently.	Can the candidate think on their feet? Are they able to be humble and not take themselves too seriously?

Creating a Productive Work Environment

Don't underestimate the impact that a work environment can have on the productivity, overall engagement, and longevity of employees. We define "work environment" broadly to include not only the physical environment, but also the policies and processes that impact how and when people perform their work and how employees are developed and rewarded.

Consider the Specific Needs of UX Professionals

While there are many pathways within the broader field of UX, all of these roles share some common elements that are important to consider when attempting to create a highly functioning work environment for UX professionals.

Creativity: "Creatives" is common slang used to refer to UX professionals. This field is about creating solutions to human problems—whether it be identifying and creating for a new customer need or experience, or improving an existing product.

> **To entice and keep UX professionals:**
>
> - Give as much flexibility as possible in work hours and workspaces to allow creativity to flourish.
>
> - Provide physical and virtual workspaces for collaboration.
>
> - Support opportunities for employees to evolve their skills and gain exposure to new tools and methods.

Creativity needs room to thrive, which can include everything from dedicated rooms in which people can ideate to flexible work hours to tap into creativity at self-designated times of optimal performance for each individual. Conversely, creativity killers may include overly dense work environments without quiet spaces to escape to, or rigid work hours that do not let people work at times when their own creativity is at its peak.

To whatever extent possible, value and reward work performance, regardless of wherever and whenever the work is done. Employees should certainly still be accountable for meeting stakeholder or client needs and timelines, and they must be present whenever there are core business activities (however your business defines these), but they should have as much autonomy to structure their work lives as possible.

Collaboration: Collaboration is also core to the UX work environment and is essential during ideation to generate the best ideas. This is true, for example, with designers looking to create elegant and usable design solutions or for researchers tailoring their research techniques to meet key research objectives. Creating great user experiences is also inherently a cross-functional effort, and as such, it's important that team members have the opportunity to easily engage with each other throughout a project. Readily available collaborative workspaces—both physical (open meeting areas) and virtual (ready access to shared online meeting tools with opportunities for shared screens and video)—create the environment in which a free flow of ideas can occur, as well as enable project teams to remain aligned throughout a project's evolution.

Rapid growth/change in technology: UX continues to evolve to meet the continual changes in technology. Employees will thrive in environments where they are encouraged to evolve their skills and gain exposure to new tools and methods. Perhaps even consider subsidizing team members' purchases of new software and technology that may not meet immediate business needs but would help employees to stay on top of new trends.

Pamela Walshe has always been fascinated by human behavior—seeking to understand how beliefs, culture, and technology influence what people do. She graduated from UC Berkeley, earning a BA in Anthropology and her master's degree from the iSchool. Pamela has 10+ years of experience in UX, working in both large corporate organizations (Wells Fargo, Charles Schwab) and nimble startups (AnswerLab, Spring Studio). In her role at AnswerLab, she leads the UX Research Practice and is passionate about growing teams and creating a dynamic working environment. Under Pamela's leadership, AnswerLab has won Fortune's Great Places to Work Award for Small Businesses 3 years in a row. Follow Pamela on Twitter @pamelawalshe and find her at linkedin.com/in/pamelawalshe.

Using the Rest of this Book to Help You Help your UX Staff

We've talked about important hiring considerations, how to use the interview to differentiate between UX professionals, and some basics about creating a good work environment to get the most out of your UX team. But as we mentioned at the beginning, there is more to know about employing UX professionals than just what is in this chapter. Use the advice throughout the other chapters to better understand what you should be doing now:

- **Promote professional growth**: In Chapter 3, we talk about why UX professionals should never stop learning, and Dan Brown talks about how good employers promote professional development. Help employees come up with professional development plans, and subsidize their efforts. Make sure to provide opportunities for mentoring of junior staff, but don't forget that senior staff should never stop learning either.

- **Help your staff to get connected**: A theme in this book (covered in most detail in Chapters 3 and 4) is to advocate for UX professionals getting out there, networking, getting connected to the larger UX community, and participating in that community. Help your staff to get out there. Let it be known that you support this. Even consider contributing to the UX community by sponsoring or even organizing public events. Also remember that the more people that your staff know, the larger your corporate network, and the greater the likelihood that your business will be no more than one degree of separation away from knowing the right people to hire next.

- **Illustrate your (corporate) value**: While Chapter 5 teaches UX professionals how to illustrate their value through resumes and portfolios in order to seek a job for themselves, a lot of these same principles apply on an organizational level too. In an agency or consulting environment, certainly helping staff to illustrate and explain their prior work could help your company get future work. But even for your in-house employees, being able to articulate successes can be key to getting stakeholder buy-in.

- **Understand how to work with recruiters**: Chapter 9 discusses the recruitment process, and at the end it talks about how you as an employer may find yourself working with recruiters. In fact, however, all of your recruiters may be in-house, or if your company is small enough, the recruiter may just be you. Take this recruiting advice to heart and consider how you can perform your best as you recruit new talent.

- **Understand that there are different career pathways, and don't require unicorns**—Chapter 11 reviews a variety of different UX career pathways and associated skills. Learn about these pathways and fully understand what skillsets are associated with each one. While it is likely that you will find UX professionals with skillsets that span multiple pathways, do not expect that you're going to find it *all* in one person. You're either going to be setting yourself up for failure with a vacant position, or you'll hire a jack of all trades and a master of none. If you do manage to spot that rare genuine unicorn, you could be paying more than you ever imagined possible to hire and keep them. As Baruch Sacks pointed out, if you need someone with many different skills, find someone with core critical skills, and then provide robust training opportunities for the rest of the skills you need.

Let's now go explore those UX career pathways in detail in the next chapter. Not only will you get a good overview of what kinds of UX professionals are out there, you'll learn more about what you can expect each type of UX professional can really do for your company.

Get more online at uxcareershandbook.com/employers

Part 4

Career Glimpses: What, Specifically, Can You Do?

CHAPTER 11

UX Career Pathways and Primary Skillsets

For most of this book so far we have focused on the convergence of user experience (UX) careers: all of those foundational elements that are generally relevant regardless of your actual UX job type. In this chapter, however, we will delve into details about specific UX career pathways and skillsets.

UX as the Umbrella

UX is a very common global umbrella for many of these skillsets, and one that represents the framework of this book, but there are always going to be differing opinions on which careers really fall under this umbrella. Similarly, as discussed in the introduction, not everyone will agree that UX is *the* umbrella at all, and I've seen many of these career pathways legitimately and coherently grouped under a different (or perhaps just renamed) umbrella, such as interaction design or experience design.

The important point here is that in this chapter we have a collection of different career pathways and organized sets of skills, many of which overlap. When you search for a job, you may find job descriptions that purely represent one career pathway, but more often you'll find descriptions with multiple career pathways represented.

Curse of the Unicorn

As we initially introduced in Chapter 1, you're also going to see job descriptions that loudly broadcast a desire for UX unicorns. Employers figure why bother hiring specialists when they can just get it all in one! They can get someone who does interaction design, user research, development, and visual design, with expert skills in all of these areas—what a wonderful package! If only unicorns were real, or at least common place.

While it is important that you get a sense of the diversity and scope of UX as presented in these career pathways, you do not have to be (and shouldn't try to be) an expert in everything. You may start out as a UX generalist, but as you advance in your career, you will likely find that advancement means having some specialized skillsets. Over time and many years, expect to increase your skillset with more skills, possibly in more career pathways. Over the years, with many types of deep experiences, some highly diversified UX professionals may begin to approach unicorn status; but don't expect that to be a short road, or one that everyone needs to achieve. And don't try to represent yourself as a unicorn early on in your UX career.

> The idea that you need to be a UX unicorn—highly skilled in most, if not all, areas of UX—is unrealistic and unnecessary for a majority of UX professionals. Instead, aim to become expert in one or a few related UX career pathways. You can continue to add more skills over time.

He wanted a big scoop of everything

Picking your Superpowers

In Chapter 4, we talked about external coherence—for career success, you need to fit reasonably well into a mold that will make sense to employers, and that structure will most likely be one or more of the career pathways that we examine in this chapter. Then it is time to pick your superpowers. What are your strengths? Which career pathways look most intriguing and play to your strengths?

As you go through this chapter, you'll see that there are so many different career pathways that it may be hard to choose just one or even a few. Ultimately, however, you're going to want to find your niche. You'll want to find a job that inspires you and that you want to put your energy into. You may need to have some flexibility since your absolute perfect job may not exist—but hopefully you can find something really close.

What you want to end up doing in UX lies at the junction of who you are and what you know. Both people and technology will need to be somewhere in the mix, but in different ways and to different degrees. While reading this chapter, and even as your career develops and evolves over time, look to identify your own intersection of skills and nature.

DISCOVERING WHO YOU ARE IN UX

By Tracey Lovejoy, Team and Leadership Consultant/Founder, Lovejoy Consulting

After working as a UX researcher at Microsoft and running UX teams, I transitioned into Leadership Development and Coaching where I work with UX professionals around the globe. I spend a lot of time with UX students, and the most common questions I hear are, "How do I figure out what I would be particularly good at in UX?" and "How do I determine what I'm most going to enjoy?" The answer to these questions lies at the intersection of your strengths and your UX interests.

STRENGTHS

Finding your strengths, your areas of innate talent, will allow you to more easily identify work that will be engaging. There are several ways to go about pinpointing those strengths.

You can start by asking friends, family, teachers, colleagues, or managers to share three to five things that you were always excellent at, along with examples. Look for patterns from this feedback. Alternatively, you can take a guided assessment. A favorite of mine is Gallup's Strengths Finder 2.0 (http://strengths.gallup.com/).

Once you have a list, it is important to internalize how your strengths support you in the work you do (or would like to do), then get comfortable referencing your strengths in conversation. To accomplish this, write down two stories from your work (paid or volunteer) or school history that illustrate each strength. Then share those stories aloud with at least two people. This exercise, similar to how you would construct your elevator pitch as discussed in Chapter 4, is excellent preparation for interviews, which often have questions asking you to reflect on a situation. This allows you to have many work examples that you can readily use for the specific question. This preparation will help you to come across as confident, rather than as anxiously searching for an answer.

UX INTERESTS

The other key element in discovering your UX career pathway(s) is to clarify what UX activities most interest you. I often hear "I know I love UX, but job listings are specific and I'm not sure in which direction I want to go." The possibilities can seem overwhelming.

To identify your favorite UX activities among those that you've done in school or on the job, pay attention to how you feel during each part of a project. Questions to ask yourself:

- When do I feel the most energized in my work?
- When do I feel the most drained or uninterested?
- Which tasks do I lose myself in?
- Which tasks would I not miss and/or prefer to hand off to others?

In addition, you can align activities to career pathways for insight. Here are some examples:

- Do you feel most energized when you are talking with customers and gathering user needs and feedback? (Consider user research or perhaps human factors.)
- Are you most engaged when the making starts to happen? (Consider interaction design, information architecture, or content strategy.)

- Do you love to control the look and feel? (Consider interaction design or visual design.)
- Do you prefer the big picture and get energy from being part of the entire process of a product? (Consider some aspects of UX leadership as discussed in Chapter 12.)

Answers to these kinds of questions help you get clearer on what you might most enjoy.

INTERSECTION OF STRENGTHS AND UX INTERESTS

With knowledge of your strengths and UX interests you can compare them to various UX career pathways. Here are some examples from representative students, Helena and Rodrigo, who were both struggling with which direction to go.

Helena asked her fellow students about her strengths and came up with perseverance, excellence in meeting deadlines, and attention to detail. Helena realized she didn't mind missing customer visits, but she gladly worked long hours translating insights into ideas, turning ideas into something real and then iterating on the flow of the user interaction. She ended up applying for UX designer positions, focusing on interaction.

Rodrigo talked to former colleagues who said he was empathetic, reliable, and had a skill of making sense of lots of information. In projects he was most energized during the early investigation when he was talking to customers and brainstorming ideas right after, but he struggled to make himself sit down and try to translate insights into designs. Rodrigo decided to focus on a career that integrated user research and information architecture pathways.

Take the time to examine your own strengths and UX interests to discover who you are. Not only will doing so propel you towards career satisfaction, it will also give you confidence when choosing and interviewing for jobs that your unique qualities really are a great match for the job!

Tracey Lovejoy spent 12 years at Microsoft where she cultivated exceptional teams as a UX manager and investigated questions as an ethnographer and user researcher. After leaving Microsoft, Tracey founded UX Careers Unlimited with Gayna Williams and started coaching UX students and professionals around the globe. Tracey also founded Lovejoy Consulting, which specializes in team building, empowering teams to move in unison so they can tackle any challenge as a group. Tracey received her MA in Social Science from the University of Chicago. In her free time she spends time with her two small children, husband, and five rambunctious pets.

ATTRIBUTES OF UX PROFESSIONALS
By Susan Farrell and Jakob Nielsen[1]

Qualities that you may share with UX professionals:

- They know a lot of different things, and they keep **learning**.
- They like solving problems and **puzzles**.
- They care about people and want to **make a difference** in the world.
- They like to **simplify** things.
- They like to **tinker and invent** things.
- They think **thinking** is interesting.
- They love to **learn new things** (and are okay with their own ignorance).
- They **understand people** and can closely observe them.

UX candidates must have:

- **Empathy**—feel users' frustration and understand their points of view.
- **Soft skills**—for example, can talk with anyone easily.
- **Technical vocabulary**—speak engineers' language (data and precision).
- Understanding of **how systems work** (basics).
- Understanding of **how people work with systems** (specifics).
- The **ability to convince** people to fix things.
- **Tenacity**—don't give up easily.
- The **ability to explain** things to anyone.
- **Writing** and **communication** skills.
- **Patience** ("shut up and listen").
- **Perceptiveness**—observational skills.
- **Concern for people** with different abilities and education.
- Love of **good design** and its **analysis.**
- **Curiosity**, the drive to learn new things.
- A tendency to **want to improve things**, to streamline them.

Traits that can sink you in UX include:

- Perfectionism—be excellent, but ship [the product]
- Procrastination—must manage time
- Lack of interest in technical topics
- Disinterest in ongoing self-education
- Lack of self-awareness and self-control
- Attachment to plans rather than ability to adapt

Single tracking

You can find success with only one career pathway. Single-pathway professionals have become experts in their area and clearly know the ins and outs of their career pathway. If you end up as one of these people, you'll know exactly what jobs to look for. You'll enjoy your super-expertise and reputation for really knowing your stuff. As a caution, however, by only being able to take on one kind of work, you also limit the job openings that are available to you, or if you're a consultant, you'll have a finite set of project work to choose from.

Career Pathways Vs. Skillsets

UX professionals who have a primary career pathway plus multiple secondary pathways are more common than single-tracked experts. It's fine to be a multi-faceted UX professional so long as you're able to maintain a level of external coherence as someone who can fit well into common UX-type jobs. In fact, it may be easier to think of these career pathways as common skillsets that can be mixed and matched as an amalgam of who you are and the kind of work that is available.

Career Pathways Described by Those Who are Deeply Embedded

While I wrote the career pathway descriptions for two of the areas in which I am personally expert—user research and evaluation, and accessibility—the remaining sections are written by those who are most expert and embedded in each of these other career pathways.

Each section details day-to-day activities that you may experience in that career track, typical challenges that you may face, common job titles, other career pathways and skillsets that are frequently combined, and some thoughts about ideal training.

Keep in mind that these career pathways are glimpses into a variety of activities that UX professionals may involve themselves. While all the contributors and a number of reviewers have strived to make sure that all of these pathways are as generalizable as possible, each pathway can—and often is—a book in itself. Therefore, **for a more comprehensive review of**

each particular career track, refer to the companion website
through the specific links at the end of each section or by following the
link below to see a listing of all the additional pathway resources. You will
find additional links and information, including references to any relevant
compensation data that are publically obtainable.

Get more online at uxcareershandbook.com/pathways

CHALLENGE: IDENTIFY THE CAREER PATHWAYS IN THIS JOB DESCRIPTION

As you review the career pathways that we discuss, see how many of them you find in this job description. How likely do you think they are to find someone who has this set of skills, much less 10 years of experience with them?

Role: Interaction Designer/UX/Information Architecture Specialist

Experience level: 10+ years

Duration: 6 months

Job description:

- At least 10 years of experience as an Information Architect, User Experience Designer/Architect, User Interface Designer, or Interaction Designer
- A portfolio that demonstrates the ability to strategically create compelling user experiences that factor in business goals, development capabilities, design standards, and user needs
- Strong understanding of interaction design principles and current global UI/design pattern standards
- Demonstrated ability to work with and influence stakeholders to determine business strategy in the digital arena, develop and execute big ideas while maintaining collaborative working relationships
- Ability to make strategic decisions and mitigate risk in order to produce timely, high-quality deliverables under suboptimal conditions
- Significant experience designing with business, technical, and design guideline constraints
- Experience in working on multiple projects simultaneously
- Ability to adapt existing processes and deliverables when necessary to meet project needs and improve efficiency and quality
- Demonstrated ability to design complex transactional user interfaces and interactions for web, mobile, and cross channel experiences
- Experience creating conceptual models, site maps, interaction flows, design patterns, UI specifications, taxonomies, and metadata frameworks
- Demonstrated experience in defining research criteria, leading or participating in user research, and translating user research into design decisions
- Ability to track and predict industry trends
- Experience creating interactive prototypes (e.g., Dreamweaver, Axure, Flash)

ROLE DESIRABLES

- Bachelor's degree in Human-Computer Interaction or a similar field; an advanced degree in human computer interaction, user interface design, human factors, or design planning is preferred. Significant relevant work experience may substitute for an advanced degree.
- At least 2 years of experience integrating mobile/responsive design into Information and/or Experience Architecture.
- Self-starter who can make significant progress with minimal guidance.
- Experience creating accessible designs.
- Ability to be flexible in a very fluid and dynamic environment.
- Must be extremely well organized and capable of handling multiple (and sometimes conflicting) priorities effectively.
- Blend of corporate and agency experience is a plus.
- Proficient with: InDesign, Visio, Axure, and Microsoft Office.

INTERACTION DESIGN

By Kim Bieler, UX Product Manager, Fonteva

As an interaction designer, you're responsible for how an interface behaves. Most of the time that interface belongs to a digital product such as a mobile app, ecommerce shopping cart, payroll system, or touchscreen kiosk—but it could also be for a medical device, a smart watch, or a game controller. Here I focus on interaction design for digital products. If you are more interested in the interaction design of physical devices, see the pathway for Human Factors and the section about user experience (UX) for industrial designers.

Designing behavior can range from high-level product strategy (what should this product do?) to low-level decisions about interface components (how fast should the swipe interaction happen?). As an interaction designer, you might work alone and be responsible for the end-to-end design and production of a mobile game, for example, or you might be part of a large enterprise software team, working with product managers, business analysts, developers, quality assurance, and technical support.

A general principle of interaction design is that the best design is invisible—that is, it doesn't assert itself or get in the way of the user's objectives. As an interaction designer, your job is to understand what the users' goals are and help them get there with as little effort as possible, while balancing that with business requirements and technical constraints. Frequently, user needs and business goals are in conflict—*the user wants to interact with her friends on social media, the social media provider wants the user to click on ads.* In that case, the designer must find or negotiate a compromise that preserves the usability and desirability of the product.

What Does an Interaction Designer Do?

CREATE WIREFRAMES

Turning concepts and requirements into screens, workflows, and experiences is a critical skill of the interaction designer. There are dozens of ways to envision the product experience—storyboards, videos, comic strips, role play, Legos—any medium is fair game if it gets your ideas across effectively. Most of the time, however, the organization or client will expect you to **deliver traditional wireframes and prototypes** using tools such as Visio, Omnigraffle, Balsamiq, or Axure.

A wireframe is an outline of the interface showing the screen elements (banners, text, buttons, widgets, images, tables, links, footers, menus) and their relative positions and sizes. Wireframes can be rough and sketchy or tight and polished. The main purpose of the wireframe is to help team members, stakeholders, and clients understand what the final product will look like. As a design tool, wireframing forces the designer to understand all the elements that need to be on the screen, how they should be prioritized and organized, what actions can be taken, and what happens after an action is initiated.

A wireframe can encompass a whole screen, or it can focus on a single widget or interaction within a screen. Complex widgets may require dozens of wireframes to illustrate all the possible states and outcomes. For example, consider an interface where users can create, delete, and edit their own comments, reply to other comments, and attach links or images. Each of those interactions must be thought through and designed.

Because they are flat, two-dimensional representations of the interface, wireframes are not good at conveying dynamic interactions such as drag and drop, hover states, or animation. Sometimes it's easier to show how a complex widget will work, rather than wireframe every single state. In that case, you may create an interactive or "clickable" prototype.

DESIGN PROTOTYPES

Just as with wireframes, prototypes can be rough or polished. A common lightweight technique is paper prototyping, where screens are drawn on paper and the designer swaps out drawings to simulate screen transitions. **Paper prototypes** are an effective way to quickly validate your ideas and make changes on the fly.

A plethora of applications and online tools exist to help you make **clickable prototypes** that allow users to interact with your wireframes—Axure, Justinmind, Balsamiq, and InVision are just a few. Clickable prototypes allow you to simulate a working application without having to involve developers. Clickable prototypes are also useful for reviewing workflows and conducting initial rounds of usability testing.

As the interaction designer on a project, you will need to decide how lightweight or detailed your wireframes and prototypes need to be. You may be required to use a particular tool, or you may have free reign to choose the best tool for the job. Whichever situation you find yourself in, you'll need to exercise judgment and restraint to ensure that you're not *overdesigning* your deliverables and wasting time perfecting the details.

UNDERSTAND AND ADVOCATE FOR THE USER

You must understand your users—who they are, what they care about, and why they would want to use your product. The better you understand your users, the better able you are to address their fundamental needs through your design.

When **advocating for the user**, if you're asking the team to go out of their comfort zone or do extra work, you will be most persuasive if you have solid research findings to back up your design. You must observe what users do, as well as understand *why* users do what they do with your design. No interaction designer should feel confident about the success of his or her design without **validating it through usability testing**. Usability testing can also keep you humble—when you realize that your awesome, cutting-edge design simply doesn't work for users. Expect to either work with a dedicated user researcher or conduct your own user research using the skills described in the user research and evaluation pathway.

TURN REQUIREMENTS INTO INTERFACES

New products or features within existing products have requirements: detailed descriptions of what the product or feature needs to do. In some organizations a business analyst or product manager is responsible for coming up with the requirements and handing them off to the interaction designer. In that case, it's your responsibility as the interface designer to **understand the requirements and translate them into a user interface**. Even if you're handed detailed requirements, there's still plenty of room for creativity—business requirements rarely specify the screen layout, images, design elements, interactions, and animations.

In other organizations, the product manager may provide only a brief, high-level description of the feature. And if you work in an agency, you may not even have a product manager. Instead, the project is described by a statement of work or contract, based on discussions with the client. In those situations, it's up to you as the interaction designer to flesh out exactly how the product or feature will work.

An effective way to generate requirements during the design phase is the lean UX method. Rather than do all the research, design, and documentation up front, and then hand the whole thing over to developers to build, the lean UX approach is collaborative, iterative, and agile. It emphasizes **sketching and white-boarding** rather than detailed documentation. Design happens not in the privacy of your computer, but iteratively in collaboration with developers and customers. Features are developed, rolled out, and tested quickly on the assumption that you won't get it exactly right the first time.

COMMUNICATE THE DESIGN

As an interaction designer, you will work with many different disciplines across the team, such as visual designers, programmers, managers, writers, subject matter experts, business analysts, technical support staff, and sales staff. These disciplines have different processes and goals, and you will need to effectively communicate with each of them. **Software products are a team effort—you will not be successful working in isolation.**

Understanding these various stakeholders and team members is not that different from understanding the product's users. You must understand what their goals are, what they care about, and what they need from you to be successful. That means listening, demonstrating empathy, and accepting feedback professionally. If your team is not all in the same location, you will need to proactively communicate what you're working on and what you're planning to do next so they feel included and informed.

You must work to keep the team focused on solving the design problem for the user. That means having an extraordinarily clear and well-articulated understanding of the problem yourself. Everyone has ideas and opinions about design, and it's your job to give those ideas a fair hearing, weighing them against the design goals.

UNDERSTAND THE TECHNOLOGY

All products have technology constraints, and as the designer of the product's behavior, you must understand and work within those constraints in order to best leverage the strengths of the chosen technology and avoid recognized weaknesses. Spending the time to understand the technology also builds bridges between the designer and developer. You'll find that you're better able to communicate your design needs and, more importantly, you'll be better equipped to negotiate when you get pushback.

Interaction design positions for web products also often require at least **some level of understanding about how to design for desktop, mobile, and tablet devices**. Having some knowledge of or experience with HTML, CSS, and JavaScript is an asset.

RUN MEETINGS AND WORKSHOPS

Workshops are a critical tool in the interaction designer's arsenal. They are useful at all stages of the design process—at project kickoff, for research distillation, during the ideation phase, and for sprint planning, design critique, analyzing test results, and project retrospective. Running a workshop or meeting requires a sophisticated skillset and is best learned by frequent practice.

The first step in running a workshop is to plan the goals: what will the output of the workshop be? What do you want to achieve? The next step is figuring out whom to invite: who needs to be there to make the workshop successful? The third step is deciding on the workshop activities: what activities will result in the desired outputs? All this information feeds the meeting agenda and invitation. As the workshop leader, your job is to make sure the meeting stays on track and that everyone is focused on the goals.

Challenges

RECOGNIZING WHEN YOU'RE BEING HANDED A SOLUTION, NOT A PROBLEM

Often the design problems you will be asked to solve are not, in fact, problems. They are solutions. "We need a mobile app." "We need to make the button bigger." "Customers are telling us they need a Help screen."

A mobile app is not a design problem. A properly articulated design problem sounds more like this: "Patients avoid our emergency room because they think they'll be waiting for hours. If we could somehow give them up-to-the-minute wait times, they'd see that it's usually less than half an hour." This states the problem and doesn't say anything about how the service will be delivered. Perhaps a mobile app is a good solution. But a better solution might be a highway billboard. Or a television commercial. Or a text message service.

As the project designer, you need to recognize when you're being handed a solution. Then you need to ask a lot of questions until you're confident you've gotten to the *real* design problem that underlies the request. Once you understand that fundamental problem, a whole world of solutions will suggest themselves.

RUSHING TO A SOLUTION

Interaction designers want to solve problems and want to solve them now. The most common mistake is to rush to design before understanding the problem or having had a chance to explore many possible solutions. This is particularly hard to avoid in agency settings where clients are paying for results, and they expect the good ideas to start flowing in the first kickoff meeting. Instead of giving them your off-the-cuff (and perhaps dead wrong) ideas, ask questions and get them to talk. Instead of rushing to the computer and launching Photoshop, pick up a whiteboard marker or pencil. Instead of running with the first idea you have, spend another hour brainstorming five more ideas.

Your first solution is usually obvious and safe. The best solutions happen when you force yourself to design past the obvious into new and uncomfortable territory.

IDEAL TRAINING

It's possible to get an interaction design job with a **bachelor's or master's degree** in any number of fields along with a strong portfolio, rather than a formal design-oriented degree. Traditionally, interaction designers have degrees in human-computer interaction or industrial design. These days, however, you can also find targeted bachelor's and master's degree programs, certificate programs, and training courses related specifically to interaction design and UX. These are available at academic institutions, at professional in-person training programs, and through a variety of online learning options.

POTENTIAL JOB TITLES

- Interaction Designer
- User Experience/UX Designer
- UX Architect
- Product Designer

CAREER PATHWAYS THAT MAY BE COMBINED WITH INTERACTION DESIGN IN JOB DESCRIPTIONS

- Development
- Visual design
- Industrial design
- Service design
- User research and evaluation

You can also learn a certain amount from reading, but the rest you need to learn by *doing*. You can learn interaction design on the job, as long as that job puts you into close daily contact with the production of digital interfaces. If you plan to teach yourself, find problems to solve. While solving problems at work may be ideal for your portfolio too, if no such opportunities exist at your workplace, consider a volunteer interaction design effort or else do a speculative redesign of an existing product. A smart, thoughtful speculative project is sometimes enough to get a hiring manager's attention.

 Get more online at uxcareershandbook.com/interaction-design

 **Kim Bieler** is a product manager for UX at Fonteva. Before that she led a team at FireEye, and designed the 1.0 version of FireEye's innovative endpoint product. Previously, she ran her own creative design firm for 13 years. Kim served as local leader for the DC chapter of the Interaction Design Association from 2010 to 2012 and has presented on design and business topics at IA Summit, UserFocus, EDUI, UXCampDC, and RefreshDC. Her focus is on applying design tools and thinking to professional effectiveness—whether that's designing a resume, managing a team, or using enterprise software. She blogs at uxresume.com.

UX FOR DEVELOPERS

**With Chris Castiglione, Co-founder &
Head of Content, One Month**

As a developer, your job may involve writing some code, pushing that code to GitHub, and then testing out the features in production. Or maybe you are developing within a WordPress environment, or perhaps customizing another out of the box content management system to meet specific corporate needs.

If you haven't been involved in user experience (UX) discussions, you may think of your job as something that is exclusively about coding: you code properly and meet the needs of your employer and specific business requirements. But coding will really only get you so far. As you may know if you have been involved in those UX discussions, good development is actually not just about writing and dealing with code. Good development is also about a good UX.

Great products aren't just about output, they're about outcomes. What's the difference? Output is the features you're building. Outcomes are the reasons why you are building those features. To develop something great, therefore, you need to understand not only *how* to build the product, but also *why* you are building it. *How* is the output; *why* is the outcome.

Being successful as part of a project team requires a developer who has knowledge of relevant programming languages (your tools) combined with problem-solving skills (how you use your tools to meet project needs) as well as an understanding of UX to frame the development effort.

By understanding principles of good UX, and being able to articulate them to your current employer, a new employer, or potential clients, you'll give your professional credentials a boost. You may be more likely to be tapped to help make decisions about the interface. And if you want to eventually move into managing a development team, those UX skills will likely be a necessary qualification.

How Might You Use UX skills in Your Job?

COMBINE YOUR CODING KNOWLEDGE WITH INTERACTION DESIGN

While interaction designers should have at least some basic coding knowledge to do their jobs, your deep knowledge of the selected development platform means that you can likely visualize and explain exactly what interface choices are going to work or not. And you may be able to propose other approaches that will help meet the larger project goals, based on an expanded knowledge of what else may be technically feasible.

VALIDATE YOUR EFFORTS BY THINKING ABOUT USER REACTIONS

While your UX knowledge will help you to think through how something should be developed initially, as you test out your code after development, you'll be able to think through how someone—who is not a coder and not you—may react to the interface. Does something that seemed to make sense to you and the team before development not play out quite so smoothly for users? Perhaps you'll be able to improvise a bit by reviewing the code and figuring out how to improve things before you open it up to a wider team review.

DO USER RESEARCH

While a larger project team may have one or more UX professionals who have the responsibility for user research and evaluation efforts, if you're at a small company or startup, perhaps they don't have anyone designated to do user research. It may be hard to watch people as they evaluate, and perhaps have difficulties with, aspects of what you developed (and as discussed in the user research section, you'll have to watch out for biases that you could inadvertently introduce by wanting people to like what you created). But by having user research skills, you could provide a valuable service to your employer who otherwise wouldn't be doing any user testing. User research also presents a valuable feedback loop for you. As you actually get to interact with users, you'll be able to better predict how products should be developed to be most valuable to target audiences.

CONSIDER METRICS

Beyond more formal user research, in order to determine whether users are working well with what you have developed, you can help come up with a set of metrics to measure user interest and engagement. Perhaps you'd use off-the-shelf web analytics tools, like Google analytics. Perhaps you could develop a custom survey within the interface itself to periodically poll users about their experiences. Maybe you can reach out to the marketing team and see what kind of metrics they have already, and what kind of metrics they still need. Your development knowledge again will help you understand ways that data can be collected, and simultaneously, being a recipient of the data will help you better understand and anticipate the users for whom you are developing.

BE A PART OF AGILE DEVELOPMENT TEAMS

Agile development is a software development method that ensures you release your code in small increments, and that you collaborate with the other people on your team while you do it. The philosophy of agile development is widespread in the development community, and for developers it may be surprising to learn that many of the principles of agile come from UX.

Agile is iterative: you develop, you are part of the team that evaluates, and then you develop again. Agile development almost guarantees (or at least should guarantee) that you'll be a part of a cross-functional team. And being able to understand and speak the language of UX means that you'll be able to better integrate into and add value to that team.

CREATE ACCESSIBLE PRODUCTS

In this chapter, we also review the role of an accessibility specialist who likely knows something about development, but not as much as you do as a developer. If you learn and understand the principles of accessibility, you will be able to develop products that are accessible from the outset. Even if you develop them to be fully accessible, however, someone will still need to manually confirm that the end-products are accessible—and that person can even be you. With your ability to code for accessibility from the outset, you likely won't have many surprises after this manual check, but even if you do, you could expect to have an easier time accounting for those surprises.

Challenges

DEVELOPER STIGMAS

You may find that when others on the team meet you, they will think that by the very nature of your profession you will be focusing only on the code and not the user. They may think that they'll have to stick up for the users, and that you're going to push back. You'll need to explain to them that developers can care about UX as well, just as much as anyone else, and not only do you care very much but you want to and expect to be a part of the team that thinks through good UX for the product.

SPEAKING THE LANGUAGE OF UX

The language of development is, perhaps, both specific and technical. It is a language of precise, accurate, and clean code. If you're embedded in a development world, you'll be able to use specific technical terms naturally and with ease. But be aware that not only will your core product audience not understand these terms that you've absorbed over the years, but neither will at least some of the team members that you work with.

The language of UX is often a bit more "squishy" and perhaps even touchy-feely when compared with technical jargon. Just like someone who strives to be multi-lingual, you'll have to carefully watch the terminology and labels that you put into the interface to make sure that they represent the language of the users. In addition, when you are speaking to the product team, you may need to avoid, or at least define, some of the technical terms and jargon that would otherwise be the most efficient way to articulate certain aspects of the interface.

Begin your UX Journey

If you are interested in UX, but are not yet very steeped in UX knowledge, you need to first learn more about the principles of good

UX (see Chapters 2 and 3), and consider how you can code to meet UX goals. You will also need to work on framing your development skills in terms of a solid UX.

If you already have a solid knowledge of UX, make sure to articulate to teams, employers, potential employers, and clients what that knowledge is. Let them know that "UX" is more than some letters that are sitting on your profile. Explain to them how you are well positioned to help, not only by writing the code, but by simultaneously understanding the users for whom you are developing.

Strong development skills combined with well-rounded UX knowledge and skills is a winning combination, and you'll likely be able to leverage these skills towards incredible career advancement.

Get more online at uxcareershandbook.com/development

Chris Castiglione is an engineer, an artist, and the co-founder of the Y Combinator backed One Month—the "For Dummies" of online education. In 2013, he taught at Columbia University, and he is currently an adjunct professor at The School of Visual Arts in NYC. Follow Chris on Twitter @castig and read his writings and musings on his blog (castig.org).

USER RESEARCH AND EVALUATION

By Cory Lebson

As a user researcher, your mission is to understand and represent a product's actual users through every phase of the development lifecycle. Simultaneously, you need to understand the technologies being employed and what business constraints exist. You need to speak the language of business, the developers' language, and the language of a product's primary user groups, and you need to translate among them.

As a researcher, you constantly encounter new situations and must always be ready to improvise. Your improvisation may be figuring out how to update your research plans at the last minute to accommodate scope changes. It may be adjusting methods while already in the field, thinking fast when things don't go as expected. You'll also find that research conditions are often not ideal. You'll be making tradeoffs to balance budget considerations, project deadlines, and internal politics.

What Does a User Researcher Do?

DETERMINE WHO THE USERS OF THE PRODUCT ARE

If a product is already established, you will likely have some kind of market research data. If you don't, you may be tasked with trying to collect this information and/or start to pull together data sources that have never been combined, be it historical research, web analytics, call center data, competitive analysis data, or anything else that has been or is being collected.

PROVIDE INPUT AND EVALUATIONS BASED ON KNOWLEDGE

When research is called for, the team will turn to you to figure out the best research method. You may also be asked to apply your knowledge by participating in strategy meetings, design workshops, and discussions. You could be asked for formal or informal **expert/heuristic reviews** of existing products where you apply your knowledge and background as an independent usability expert, ideally separate from the core designers of the product. People will look to you with respect because you are a researcher, which implies a level of critical thought and evaluation. (And you'll demonstrate these skills on the job too!) You may also have extra insights from being a researcher on several projects simultaneously or on similar projects over time.

CONDUCT RESEARCH TO LEARN MORE ABOUT WHAT USERS WANT

Exploratory research: Whether you are given information on the product's users or you need to find that out for yourself, you will likely be involved with exploratory research to aid in understanding how users work (with previous versions of the product or on tasks like the ones the product is meant to support) and to find out what users want.

Exploratory research may be **ethnographic research**, where you watch users during their normal day-to-day activities perhaps with previous versions of the product or perhaps using competing products.

You might use a slightly more structured technique, such as **contextual inquiry** or a **cognitive walkthrough**, where you ask participants to show how they do typical activities with the product or how they accomplish goals that the product might eventually support.

While these activities can be done remotely, using standard remote meeting and screen sharing tools, that loses context; so when possible, you will probably prefer to do this kind of exploratory research in person.

Card sorts: While you may not be an information architect, you might still do some formative information architecture research, such as to figure out how a new set of concepts or topics should be organized. You'd give potential users a stack of cards (paper or virtual) that represent topics on a web or mobile site and ask them to sort those cards into groups in ways that make sense to them.

You may also do a **first click analysis** where you see the first place they'd click on a page when presented with a task.

USABILITY TEST EXISTING PRODUCTS AND PROTOTYPES

To make sure a product or a prototype is usable, you'll know that it's a good idea to propose a **usability test.** The refrain "early and often" is frequently heard from user researchers, which means that you may need to make the case that usability testing doesn't just happen once work is completed and a product is about to launch, but should be conducted at specific intervals from a low-fidelity mockup stage to a finished product, thus allowing for iterative improvements.

While you may sometimes find yourself in an environment where you do large-scale studies, in many cases, a study can have perhaps only 10 or 15 people testing over two or three days. Another alternative is to do a leaner kind of research, and you may only test with five people but do this at some specific regular interval.

You may find yourself in a research environment that provides **eye tracking** during usability studies, which does require more users to be able to properly quantify the data.

There may also be times when you let people interact with a system on their own, and then you have them enter their reactions electronically, for example, in what's called a **diary study**. You could do this as part of your early exploratory research (where you learn about how they use the product or do the tasks today) or with a prototype or early version of the new product or new release.

DO QUANTITATIVE RESEARCH

Many techniques in a user researcher's toolbox are **qualitative**—in-depth sessions with limited numbers of people. You may also find opportunities for quantitative research, for example **surveys of users** or perhaps usability studies that have enough participants to be valid as quantifiable data. It is definitely important to have some basic quantitative analysis skills regardless of what kind of research you are doing, and a statistics class in college will most certainly provide you with valuable context. However, if there is really heavy-duty statistical analysis, you will generally not be expected to do this without the support of someone with advanced statistical knowledge.

ANALYZE DATA AND REPORT ON IT WITH RECOMMENDATIONS

Once you have done the research, you **analyze the data** and tell others what it showed, usually in some sort of **research report** and/or **presentation**. You aren't just rattling off what you saw during testing or a summary of the data collected. You also include interpretation in light of your knowledge of usability standards. Most likely, your report will also include **recommended solutions** based on the findings, so you are essentially applying design-oriented knowledge.

A user research report could be a big dense Word document, but beware of eyes that glaze over. Your report could be a slide presentation, a set of bullet points, or a discussion at a meeting.

USE RESEARCH TO PROVIDE INSIGHTS FOR DESIGN

You may be expected to use your research data to:

- **Build personas**—fictional representative users built from findings to help design teams more concretely understand who they are designing for
- **Suggest scenarios**—user stories from your findings of how people might use the product to accomplish their goals
- **Explain context**—help designers understand the physical, cultural, and social situations in which people will use the product

TEACH OTHERS

As a user researcher, you'll probably end up being a teacher, too. While you may not formally instruct in principles of user experience (UX), you may find that through your discussions, evaluations, research, and reports, you are helping others, including developers, product managers, and senior management, understand UX principles with what are very specific and useful examples, that is, those of the product being designed.

Challenges

BIAS

Research does not exist in a vacuum and by its nature, all research—whether qualitative or quantitative—has some embedded bias, no matter how insignificant. You always need to be on the lookout for this and do what you can to avoid making mistakes that impact your research findings. During a usability study, you could reflexively say the word "good" or "that's great" when a participant uses a site as you expected, or you may not be aware of your body language, for example, if you nod your head when a participant does something right.

If you are put in the role of being both the designer and the researcher evaluating your own product, it will be particularly hard to evaluate the product objectively. I overheard a designer who was moderating a study say something to a participant to the effect of "I really tried to make this design change so that the product would be helpful to someone like you. Would you find it useful?" If you are also the designer, try to participate in the research without interacting directly with the participants.

NEED FOR PUSHBACK

You may find yourself part of a design or development team that does not see research as a critical need. You'll have to advocate for the value of the research activities. Other times, stakeholders may be confident in their knowledge about user research, but their knowledge may not actually be correct. For example, your employer or client may ask you to use a focus group to assess product usability, and you will need to explain that focus groups are great for understanding people's desires and beliefs, but people sitting around using a product as a group (usually) does not represent real-world usage. While advocating for user research or particular methods is important, don't be branded as a research purist! Certainly be ready to advocate for what you think is best, but if you don't succeed, letting it go and being flexible will be better for your job and career.

Ideal Training

A **bachelor's degree** is the minimum level of education you should have. A **master's degree** is not absolutely necessary but is often a plus when you are looking for jobs as a user researcher. A **Ph.D.** can be a hiring plus where employers value your academic experience but could also be a risk in other environments when hiring managers are afraid that this may mean that you are too academic or too much of a research purist. If you do have a Ph.D., be ready to squash inappropriate stereotypes.

Valuable areas of study include social, cognitive, behavioral, or

---

POTENTIAL JOB TITLES

- User Researcher
- User Experience (UX) Researcher/Specialist
- Usability Engineer/Specialist/Expert
- Design Researcher
- Human Factors Engineer/Specialist (which may not actually indicate someone doing the human factors work that is discussed in the pathway on Human Factors)

CAREER PATHWAYS THAT MAY BE COMBINED WITH USER RESEARCH IN JOB DESCRIPTIONS

- Information architecture
- Interaction design
- Content writing/information design
- Content strategy
- UX strategy
- Human factors
- Accessibility
- Market research

experimental psychology; human-computer interaction (HCI); human factors; computer science; industrial design; and human-centered design.

Alternatively, particularly for those who have academic degrees that aren't directly related and/or have had alternative careers, several universities have UX-related certificate programs that can help prepare those new to research careers. Furthermore, you can find opportunities for professional training workshops and seminars in user research outside of academia.

Get more online at uxcareershandbook.com/research

UX FOR MARKET RESEARCHERS

By Brianna Sylver, President, Sylver Consulting

If you're a market researcher who has experience in qualitative research and have made your career in understanding customers, the distinction between market research and user research might seem irrelevant to you. You may think, "I can do what those user researchers are doing. Or, I already do that!"

From a technical perspective, you may be doing something similar. You may do research to fuel the product development process and be proficient with qualitative data collection techniques like ethnography, contextual inquiry, and customer diaries. But that said, market research and user research don't quite have the same goals in mind.

Users Vs. Usage

Market researchers focus on collecting and understanding data about the current or anticipated users of a product. User researchers start with a base understanding about who those users are and focus their research on how user attributes and behaviors will impact their use of that product. They then work with design teams to figure out how to apply solutions within the framework of user experience (UX) best practices. In other words, instead of being focused on collecting user data and explaining about users as their final output, user researchers are focused on solving design problems through research.

Shifts are occurring in UX that will help market researchers become further integrated into UX work. More and more, UX teams are looking to UX research to help set strategy, not just provide input to the design team. This prioritization of strategy dovetails well with the goals of more traditional market research. Additionally, if you are working in a large corporation, you may find that the company is now embracing UX even more than before, allowing you new opportunities to build bridges based on your in-house market research reputation.

How Can Market Researchers Add UX Value?

SUPPORT THE UX TEAM

Even if you've only been doing traditional market research up to this point, you may find that UX professionals already appreciate the data that you and your team provide, particularly **broad-scale, often quantitative-based, market knowledge/context** for the organization and its products. Also, market researchers may take on responsibilities that provide additional valuable inputs to a UX team, such as **trend monitoring** and **competitive intelligence**.

BRING METHOD BREADTH AND RIGOR TO STUDY DESIGN

If you've come to market research by a traditional pathway, you've been exposed to a variety of qualitative and quantitative methodologies. You may be an expert in some and not in others, but you likely have **wide knowledge about the types of methods/techniques** out there and understanding of when one method is likely better than another to answer a particular research question. And like user researchers, you know what is needed to reduce study biases that your non-research-oriented colleagues may not be fully aware of.

As a market researcher, you may have stronger quantitative research skills than UX team members, and you can apply these quantitative skills by **creating and analyzing survey data** and using other methods that focus on product usability and usage. Your background may also add particular value if you can provide insights on how to structure **hybrid qualitative/quantitative studies** to provide understanding along a product development journey.

Challenges

MARKET RESEARCHER STIGMAS

The phrase "market research" sometimes provokes negative stereotypes in the UX community. If you're a quantitative person, you may be thought to only produce numbers without meaning behind them. Numbers don't provide inspiration like stories do, and UX professionals very much value stories to provide insights. You may also be thought to be inflexible with methodology, and UX teams may assume that you're uncomfortable with creative thinking and process. Be prepared to explain to them that you are comfortable with a focus on qualitative UX research methods and adapting, if necessary, to a more user-centered design approach.

NEEDED MENTAL REFRAME OF WORK, ROLE, AND SCOPE

To fit into UX as a market researcher, you must seek to understand not only the methods of UX research, but also the tenets of the UX discipline. If you're a qualitative market researcher, you likely already know and feel comfortable with some of the pillar methods of UX, including focus groups, ethnographic research, contextual inquiry, and customer diaries.

However, because UX is more concerned with behavior than with attitudes and desires, focus groups are less often used in UX than usability testing. So you may have to learn more about usability testing. While you likely have one-on-one interview experience, you may need to adapt your technique somewhat for one-on-one usability testing.

It's the tenets of the UX discipline—UX standards and trends—that you'll really need to immerse yourself in. You need to fully understand what it means to create a good UX, and then you need to use that understanding to frame design advice that you give.

You also need to see yourself as a change agent—a facilitator—within the organization, helping your team to explore customer touch points and articulating ways to bring additional value and relevance to the experience that customers have with its products. In the UX world, actionable insights are an expectation of your work product.

In addition, you'll need to be a user/customer advocate as a user researcher, much more so than as a market researcher. Instead of simply expressing the attributes or attitudes of users, you will need to use and interpret what you learn to speak *for* the users—and the experiences that they expect of their products—based on your research findings.

Be Part of the UX Team

You can begin your journey to UX now. If you already have solid and diverse market research skills, start tweaking those skills to tailor them for a UX mindset. Immerse yourself in UX knowledge as discussed in Chapters 2 and 3. Challenge any biases that you may encounter. Hone your pitch on how and why your skills can be valuable for UX and the specific team you'd like to work with. Demonstrate how your skills add understanding to their user journey.

Always remember that as a market researcher, you do bring a valuable and diverse methodological toolkit to UX—and you can use that toolkit to make a difference.

Get more online at uxcareershandbook.com/market-research

Brianna Sylver is the founder and President of Sylver Consulting, an international innovation research and strategy firm operating at the intersection of market research, UX, and design strategy. Brianna and the team at Sylver support Fortune 500 organizations in defining clarity and purpose around their innovation and growth agendas. Brianna has gained recognition for her contributions to the fields of innovation, UX, and consumer insights by the Product Development & Management Association (PDMA), HSM Management (Brazil), and the Qualitative Research Consultants Association (QRCA). She writes on topics of innovation, communication, UX, and entrepreneurship. Follow her on Twitter @BriannaSylver.

INFORMATION ARCHITECTURE

By Abby Covert, Independent Consultant, Abby the IA

An information architect (IA) helps people decide how the pieces of something should be arranged to best communicate the intended message to intended users. If that definition sounds general, it is meant to. Because while IAs specialize deeply in terms of tools and methods, they generalize in terms of the media and materials they work in. For example, as an IA, you might be hired to set the structure of how products are presented to users on a large ecommerce website. You might later be hired as an IA to help a restaurant chain optimize their printed menu system. The materials that IAs work in are context, language, and meaning. An IA's job is to ask questions, dig into complexity, and propose structural approaches to improve the project or product, regardless of the medium or material that the work is eventually executed in.

IAs help people to decide how to organize and structure things to make sense to other people. IAs are indeed user-centered, but they are primarily supporting the efforts of designers, technologists, and business stakeholders. They help those people to craft a better user experience (UX) by facilitating agreement and understanding of the best ways to structure information to reach and communicate with the end users. They help by explaining both the language that works best for end users, and the implications for how end users will perceive the meaning of the language that the product uses.

What Does an Information Architect Do?

UNDERSTAND BACKGROUND AND CONTEXT

As with user research, information architecture relies heavily on understanding users and involves the kinds of formative research that you read about in the User Research section.

Evaluating the product or project against best practices: As an IA, it is important that you get familiar with best practices and research in the type of product or project you are working on. You can then evaluate the current state of the product against those best practices. Evaluation criteria will differ based on industry, medium, and context. For example, you may need to inform a client that the right alignment of prices on a restaurant menu has been demonstrated to drive down the average order value. A large part of an IA's upfront research into a new context is to find and become familiar with these very specific best practices.

Stakeholder research: Understanding the people who are behind the decisions being made is an important part of fully understanding a system. As an IA, you often spend a healthy amount of time getting to know the decision makers for the product being developed.

User research: Often an IA cannot fully understand a system without seeing it in use by real users and having the chance to ask them questions. As with any other step in an IA's process, this research is often done in collaboration with other team members specializing in research. **Card sorting** is a specifically helpful user research task for the information architecture. During this activity, a user is asked to group and label items as it makes sense to them. The results allow an IA to understand what is called the "mental model" that users have around a specific set of tasks. **Conversational research**, **ethnographic diary studies**, and **contextual inquiry** are other popular research methodologies that IAs use.

FACILITATE AGREEMENT ON DIRECTION

Identifying goals: Once you have identified the organizational problems of the system, your job becomes turning those problems into opportunities for improvement in light of your understanding of organizational goals. For example, there may be different ways to arrange content to best influence someone to sign up on a website instead of calling a phone number.

Controlled vocabulary development: Once you and your team or client have solidified the goals, you can make decisions around language. A controlled vocabulary is the documentation of the language that should be used to support the goals. A good controlled vocabulary will include both guidance on language that is helpful and language that may be harmful to the goals. For example, consistently calling people "survivors" instead of "victims" in the aftermath of a natural disaster can set a much more positive tone to response and recovery efforts. You know that it is little tweaks like these that can have big impacts on how people perceive information systems.

DEVELOP SYSTEMS AND RULES FOR HOW THINGS ARE ARRANGED

Developing taxonomies: A taxonomy is the way in which you classify and group things within a system. The things you are grouping might be pieces of content, products being sold, or posts users have generated. Regardless of what it is you are arranging, many taxonomic decisions generally represent the whole of the system that a user interacts with. For example, on a website like Amazon.com, there are several taxonomies working together. Three of the most prominent are:

1. The navigation taxonomy allowing us to browse by category > sub category > genre
2. The faceted filter navigation allowing us to further limit a list of items by things like brand name, price or review rating
3. The algorithmically driven features like "people who bought this also bought . . ." and "because you bought _____, you might need _____"

Each of these taxonomies had to be thought about architecturally before they could be designed and developed.

Developing rules, roles, and permissions: No matter how simple a system seems on the interface level, there is almost always an iceberg of complexity underneath the surface of what users experience. Often it is the development of these rules, roles, and permissions that allows the user to have a simple and elegant experience on the surface. Your job is to fully survey what lies below the surface to make sure that complexities are being dealt with and not ignored. Often the best way to communicate what you uncover is by creating diagrams and maps. Diagrams and maps allow you to point to something that is otherwise very hard for people to see and therefore discuss fully.

TEACH AND ADJUST THE AGREED-TO MODEL

Play testing: Once a system has been architected, it needs to be tested internally. You will have designers, technologists, and business people use and critique the proposed structures with the intent of improving them. Generally this is best done in a **workshop setting** where work and questioning of the work can be done in tandem.

Ideally, usability testing and/or co creating an information architecture is done with users in the same time frame as play testing with stakeholders, to assure that the goals of both groups remain in alignment.

Governance: A system needs to be flexible but hold its own when it comes to fighting off decay that can occur over time. You must make sure that a taxonomy includes directions on how and when it should and should not be changed over time.

Critique: You will often be called in to critique the work of others in design and technology to assure that the architectural recommendations are adhered to or the process of making changes is managed according to defined rules of governance.

Challenges

BEING THE ONE TO SAY SOMETHING DOESN'T MAKE SENSE

It is an IA's job to find structural faults that are not serving the goals of the project.

Once found, it is incredibly hard to be the one who calls out the mess in front of a team. Especially if those people also made the mess you are looking at cleaning up. You need to develop the right framing and tone for delivering news like this.

While it is hard, it is also necessary. Most teams need this moment of realization; otherwise they will perpetuate the same problems over and over. Someone has to be the brave one.

DEALING WITH ANXIETY

Change is hard. Complexity is hard. Language is annoying and mushy. Semantic arguments are not everyone's idea of a good time. Information architecture is fraught with dealing with problems people might not want to deal with. It is not only an IA's job to point out the problems that exist. It is also your responsibility as an IA to make the path to a solution clear for those who may be anxious about the journey. It is often the job of an IA to draw pictures that allow people to get beyond their own perspectives.

EMBRACING AMBIGUITY

There are many ways to arrange anything, but stakeholders often want black and white answers—either the organization of something is right or it is wrong. Yet there is no such thing as THE right way. It is whether or not you have achieved your intent that matters. It is the responsibility of an IA to let people know this fundamental principle so that they don't get caught searching for perfection, while missing the opportunity for progress instead.

Ideal Training

Ideally, before dabbling in IA as a specialty, IAs are able to educate themselves on a variety of media to better understand how each medium affects messages. Not all IAs have formal education in IA as a practice; but when they do, it is generally at the **master's degree** or **PhD** level in information and/or library science. That said, some undergraduate graphic design and interaction design programs are starting to include IA in their curricula. Alternative educational pathways such as conferences, workshops, and community centers are also starting to become interested in teaching information architecture.

POTENTIAL JOB TITLES

- Information Architect
- User Experience Architect
- Experience Architect
- Librarian
- Taxonomist
- Ontologist

CAREER PATHWAYS THAT MAY BE COMBINED WITH INFORMATION ARCHITECTURE IN JOB DESCRIPTIONS

- Interaction design
- Content strategy
- Content writing/information design
- Service design
- UX strategy
- Technical communication
- User research and evaluation

Get more online at uxcareershandbook.com/information-architecture

Abby Covert is an independent IA living in New York City. She speaks and writes under the pseudonym Abby the IA, sharing information architecture content with the design and technology communities. She is the author of *How to Make Sense of Any Mess*, a book about information architecture for everybody. She teaches information architecture at The School of Visual Arts and serves as president of the Information Architecture Institute, a global non-profit membership organization focused on empowering IA leadership, currently serving members in 73 countries. Follow Abby on Twitter @abby_the_ia.

UX FOR SEO PROFESSIONALS

**By Erin Everhart, Lead Digital Marketing Manager—SEO,
The Home Depot**

Historically, Search Engine Optimization (SEO) and user experience (UX) careers haven't played nicely. SEO professionals (SEOs) were not focused on what happened once users got to a website, and UX professionals were not focused on how users got to the website initially. UX professionals employed tactics that were good for users, and SEOs implemented tactics that were good for search engines.

But SEO has gone through a major transformation over the past 10 years, largely driven by updates to Google's search algorithm. While SEO professionals love to hate algorithm updates, Google and other search engines have to keep improving because users are constantly getting savvier as they more rapidly bounce from websites that don't meet their needs. Whatever the updates are, there is one underlying factor in all of these improvements: search engines now want to rank what's best for the user, not just what's best for the bot that indexes a site.

Good SEO Means Good UX

There's a lot in the backend code structure of websites that's fundamental to good SEO—things like URL structure, proper canonical tags, and optimizing CSS and HTML, but when it comes to what your users see, good SEO looks a lot like good UX.

Good, Quality Content

Your website will not rank highly in search engines unless it has good, quality content. Likewise, best practices for UX demand that content be easily digestible and help users to achieve their goals. Websites with this type of content are exactly what search engines want to rank high.

Sharing and Linking

Strong UX increases customer retention and improves your conversion rate, but it also increases the likelihood that people are going to share and link to your website. Users aren't going to convert on bad websites, and they're certainly not going to share them with their friends. Quality links from relevant sources, and even social shares to a lesser extent, will likely remain a heavy ranking factor. Since search engines want to rank what users want to see, quality links and social shares are one of the ways that search engines determine if others will value what you have to offer.

User Engagement

Google knows a lot about your users. It knows when a user clicks on a website listing on its search engine results page and immediately bounces from that website back to the search listings. It also knows how much time users spend on your site. While at the time of this writing, Google has not announced overall time on a website as a ranking factor, given that Google has already stated that good mobile UX is a ranking factor, it is likely that time spent on a website is already being used for ranking in some way.

Integrate UX into Your SEO Work

Since good SEO is impacted by good UX, you need to make sure that you and your team create a successful UX in order to rank highly in search engines. As an SEO, you should gain and maintain the UX knowledge necessary to help facilitate that successful UX. Learn about what makes for good UX and how to gauge the UX with qualitative and quantitative user research. Then start integrating these into your SEO workflow.

Do User Research

Understanding your users is fundamental to creating a user-friendly, well-ranked website. **Review web analytics** to better understand user search behavior. Conduct **focus groups** and **deploy web-based surveys** to figure out what users expect and to provide better context around their search behavior. And for more depth, consider **interviews** with users as well as **usability testing**. If you can fully understand what users want and how they are reacting to your site, you can better use appropriate language to attract the target audience to your website, and once there, provide a web resource that keeps their attention.

Create Personas

Once you have the necessary information about your users, you can build **personas** that represent the main types of people who use your website. While personas often include demographic information and motivation for using your site, take these personas one step further by mapping your keyword research to each persona. And remember that these keywords are not just words; they reflect the need and intent of each of your target audiences, as well as variations in search behavior that will allow you to optimize your pages appropriately.

Convince Your Team that UX Matters for SEO

Hopefully you're already convinced that SEO and UX need to go hand in hand for search rank success. Your biggest challenge, however, may be to make the case to the web team. While you might have been hired specifically for your SEO skills, you may need to update the team and key stakeholders explaining why UX matters more and more for SEO success. You will need to be able to explain to them that successful SEO doesn't just mean the SEO practices of years past, but now also means creating exactly what users want.

Get more online at uxcareershandbook.com/seo

Erin Everhart is the Lead Digital Marketing Manager—SEO at The Home Depot where she leads a team that focuses on content marketing, SEO, and digital strategy. Previously, she was the Director of Digital Marketing at 352 Inc. where she built a 9-person digital marketing department, growing it to 20% of the company's revenue in less than four years. Erin's expertise in website strategy, digital marketing, and conversion rate optimization (CRO) has helped small businesses and Fortune 500 companies alike improve their digital brand by increasing traffic, demand, and customer satisfaction. She is a University of Florida journalism graduate and speaks at conferences nationwide.

CONTENT STRATEGY

By Ahava Leibtag, President, Aha Media Group LLC

As a content strategist, you help brands define what their content says, how the content appears on different devices, and the workflow around producing and managing the content. In this role, you may be involved in managing:

- **People**: the talent needed to create and sustain content for a brand (for example, sales and marketing, customer support, etc.)
- **Process**: a clear and thoughtful workflow to create a consistent product and/or consistent product branding
- **Technology**: the platforms used to prepare, publish, and distribute content

What Does a Content Strategist Do?

As a content strategist within an organization, you may do several different types of work.

DEFINE EDITORIAL AND BRAND MESSAGING

You may work with editorial and brand messaging to create style guides, personas, content governance (as opposed to web governance), and voice and tone guidelines. Editorial and brand-oriented content strategists care about consistency and **make sure the team is keeping content and messaging consistent and focused** by answering five questions:

1. To whom are we speaking?
2. Who are we as a brand?
3. What are we trying to say?
4. How do we say it?
5. When and where do we say it?

Editorial and brand-oriented content strategists are also responsible for trying to make sure that content clearly articulates the problem that the brand is solving for its target audiences with a consistent and cohesive message.

ENSURE APPROPRIATE AND THOUGHTFUL WORKFLOWS

You may also be responsible for **creating, establishing, and maintaining efficient content-creation workflows**. When you go to Starbucks, the barista doesn't consult a recipe book to make your decaf grandé skinny vanilla latte. That's because the brand promise of Starbucks is that you can get a personalized cup of coffee anywhere in the world within four minutes. If she has to take time to look up how to make every cup of coffee, Starbucks loses customers.

Similarly, many experts in content describe content strategy as a repeatable lifecycle for content, meaning you get the same consistent product every time. Just like Starbucks wants that skinny vanilla latte to taste the same every place in the world, content strategy seeks to align content as a product such that it delivers the same message in a consistent way every time.

Content strategists who specialize in workflow are process specialists. They understand that the right people need to be in the right roles to create a consistent, coherent product.

ENSURE CORRECT DELIVERY AND DISPLAY

How does an airline make sure that ticket prices are up to date on all the different travel search engines available to shoppers? How does a car engine parts manufacturer keep suppliers informed? How does a publisher make sure content appears appropriately on every single kind of device, scaled to fit onto that screen?

If you're a more technical content strategist, you may sometimes be called a content engineer or a content technologist. You **make sure that content is semantically structured to ensure appropriate delivery and display**. These types of content strategists use technical terms like DITA, XML, structured content, adaptive content, metadata, and intelligent content. They are able to visualize complex content models that allow for the reuse and repurposing of content without a person having to tell the content where to go each time.

Challenges

CREATING AND MAINTAINING CONSISTENCY

You may find that it is a major challenge to get people to agree to follow the same rules and procedures day in and day out. For example, in a large brand there may be many divisions, and different divisions may refer to the same things in different ways. To overcome this key challenge, you will need to create tools, like style guides or editorial guidelines, to help your employer or clients. Other tools that content strategists typically use include **content inventories, content analyses, content migration plans, and content audits**. You may also provide training to people within the company to make sure that they follow the rules and maintain content cohesion.

GETTING EVERYONE TO AGREE ON A STRATEGY

In large organizations and often even in small ones too, you may have trouble getting leadership to agree on a single content strategy to follow. Particularly when different departments disagree about which audience groups are most important, or what they are supposed to say, it can be hard to keep everyone in line.

Below are some examples of what you may hear and need to deal with:

- "We want to say something different than that other department."
- "We can say it about the brand even if it's not true."
- "Trust me, everyone knows what this acronym means."
- "It's just a blog post—why do I have to put metadata in the CMS?"
- "Why does it have to be edited? I was an English major."
- "Our SEO strategy says we have to use critical keywords several times on the page so I used the keyword for every fifth word."
- "Can't we just build a microsite?"

These differing needs and ideas are what bring complexity to content strategy. As a content strategist, you must stay firm and keep reminding people of the two major tenets of content strategy: aligning content with business objectives and supporting users in accomplishing their tasks.

Ideal Training

Content strategists typically have a **bachelor's degree**, and sometimes a **master's degree**. They do not often start out with a "content strategist" position. Even if you're doing content strategy work now, as described above, you may find that your current job title is something else. In fact, as you read this you may be saying: "Oh that's what my job is really called!"

Content strategists who work in editorial and brand publishing typically are current or former copywriters, journalists, editors, creative writing majors, or information scientists.

Content strategists who work in workflow may be editors, writers, project managers, process engineers, or information scientists.

Content strategists who work with technology typically start as developers, information scientists, information architects, database engineers, or CMS authors.

POTENTIAL JOB TITLES

- Content Strategist
- Content Engineer
- Content Technologist
- Brand Manager
- Web Author
- Communications Strategist

CAREER PATHWAYS THAT MAY BE COMBINED WITH CONTENT STRATEGY IN JOB DESCRIPTIONS

- Content writing/ Information design
- Information architecture
- Technical communication

 Get more online at uxcareershandbook.com/content-strategy

 **Ahava Leibtag** is passionate about content and prides herself on tackling the toughest content projects—from healthcare to higher education to hip-hop (seriously). She has more than 15 years of experience in writing, messaging, and marketing, and is a well-recognized content expert. Ahava is the President and owner of Aha Media Group, LLC, a content strategy and content marketing consultancy founded in 2005. Her first book, *The Digital Crown: Winning at Content on the Web*, was published by Morgan Kaufmann in November 2013. She encourages you to become a content strategist if problem solving is your passion.

CONTENT WRITING/INFORMATION DESIGN

By Ginny Redish, President, Redish & Associates, Inc.

As a content writer/information designer, you make sure that the information in the product is useful and usable. Content is useful and usable when the people who need that content can find what they need, understand what they find, and act appropriately on the information in the time and effort that they think it is worth.

Within this career path, you may be a generalist or you may have one or more specialties:

- **Content area** (for example, environment, health, insurance, science, etc.)
- **Medium** (for example, print, social media, web)
- **Type of content** (for example, marketing, news, technical information, etc.)
- **Type of organization** (for example, commercial, government, non-profit)

The broader your interests and skills, of course, the more career options you'll have.

We've called this career path both "content writing" and "information design" because creating great content for any medium is not only about what to say and how to say it, it's also about how to present it well in whatever media you use.

What Does a Content Writer/ Information Designer Do?

PLAN, SELECT, ORGANIZE, WRITE, EDIT, REVISE, AND FORMAT INFORMATION

The type of content and the topics you work on will vary based on the business that employs you or the clients you have as a freelancer or consultant. For e-commerce, your content may be primarily persuasive marketing copy. For a government agency, your content may be more neutral factual reporting. For a non-profit, you may be explaining projects or advocating a position or persuading people to change their behavior.

Whatever the topic or the medium, as a content writer/information designer with a UX perspective, you plan each piece of content by focusing on both the goals of your client and the needs of your audience:

- **Purposes:** What do you want to achieve? What—very specifically—do you want people to do after they read what you write? In answering these questions about purposes, you focus on the goals for your content.
- **Personas:** Who is your audience and what should you keep in mind about them? How busy are they? Do they know the technical words your subject matter experts want to use? Will they really read everything—or will they skim and scan?
- **Conversations:** What do these people want and need to know? What is your key message? What questions would they ask if they had you on the phone? In answering these questions about conversations, you focus on the content you must have to achieve your purposes.

As the users' advocate for useful and usable content, you should understand the concepts and principles of plain language so you can prepare content that works for both the organization and the user.

Whether your content is meant to inform or persuade, you will almost certainly have to work with other team members. This may include subject matter experts whose information you are using; other reviewers, for example, if your content has legal implications; content strategists to be sure your content is "on message" with the overall goals of the organization or client; editors who can help save you from embarrassing typos; designers and developers who are responsible for the overall interactive or visual interface; and user research specialists who can inform you about your audience with personas, conversations, and usability test results.

WORK WITH SUBJECT MATTER EXPERTS (SMES)

In many cases, as a content writer, you will be working with someone else's information.

Sometimes, you will be **responsible for all the writing**. You will interview the SME to gather information for what you write.

Sometimes, the SME will write the first draft, and you will **serve primarily as editor**—helping the SME get to a useful, usable piece.

Whether you act as writer or editor, you may have to negotiate with the SME (and possibly others) to be sure the information is technically accurate (also sometimes legally accurate) and also useful and understandable to the readers. Part of your job is to **advocate for the user**, and you can do so by getting SMEs and others to understand how people read (and don't read), when people are likely to skim and scan, how the presentation (design) will help or hinder people from getting the information, and so on.

WORK WITH CONTENT STRATEGISTS AND OTHER TEAM MEMBERS

Your content must serve the organization's business goals. Everything you write or edit must support the organization's content strategy. Therefore, you and the content strategists will work closely together. You may even serve both roles.

WORK WITH OTHER WRITERS, EDITORS, ILLUSTRATORS, DESIGNERS, AND DEVELOPERS

You are always your own best first editor. You are never you own best last editor. An important aspect of being a successful UX content writer/information designer is the ability to put your ego away and to accept constructive suggestions from your peers.

As a content writer/information designer, you should be familiar with basic theory and practice of information design, such as the gestalt principles–how to group information, use space well, align information, and so on. You should know something about typography although you may find yourself working closely with a visual or graphic designer when choosing type fonts and sizes.

As visuals become ever more important in content, you may want to **match (or sometimes even replace) text with relevant pictures**, technical illustrations, infographics, and other visuals for making complex information clear. You should know when to use lists and tables, when to put information into a chart or graph. Sometimes, you may be in charge of selecting pictures. However, you don't have to be a skilled illustrator, infographic designer, or videographer. You only have to be able to work well with people who have those skills.

WORK WITH THE ORGANIZATION'S STYLE GUIDE

Although you may be a lone writer—the only one producing content for the organization or client, that is likely to be a rare situation. You are much more likely to be one of several (or many) content creators. As a UX practitioner, you will realize how important it is for the people who get your content to have consistency in the messages, tone, style, formatting—even sometimes the wording—of what they have to deal with.

That consistency usually requires that you and your colleagues have and follow a style guide. You may be responsible for **creating or maintaining the style guide**. You will certainly be responsible for knowing about and using the style guide.

Challenges

BRINGING UX TO THE CONTENT; ADVOCATING FOR PLAIN LANGUAGE

You may find yourself dealing with a lot of legacy information that is not organized or written as clearly as it needs to be to successfully let people find, understand, and use the content. You may need to **convince SMEs and others (managers, legal staff) that plain language can be not only clear but also technically and legally accurate** and sufficient.

CONVINCING DESIGNERS AND DEVELOPERS THAT CONTENT IS CRITICAL

Although many designers and developers today understand that people come to websites and apps for the content, you may still find some who think they can wait until the end of a design or redesign project before thinking about the content. Content can't wait. You may have to advocate and **push to be involved from the very beginning so design and content are planned together.** You may have to show visual or interaction designers that information design is also critical—and that you can help make sure that choices in color, typography, spacing, heading size, etc. will help, not hinder, the users.

BRINGING ORGANIZATIONS INTO TECHNOLOGY SPACES—SOCIAL MEDIA, RESPONSIVE/ADAPTIVE DESIGN, ACCESSIBLE DESIGN AND WRITING

As a content writer/information designer with a UX perspective, you alone (or jointly with a content strategist) may be the person who helps the organization **shape content so it works well in new media and new technologies**.

If your company does not have an accessibility specialist on staff, you may also even **be the person who pushes the organization to support everyone by making all the content accessible**.

OVERCOMING A FOCUS ON TOOLS

Unfortunately, many job descriptions for content writers/information designers focus on the tools the organization uses to prepare and publish content. They ask for someone who knows how to write or format in a specific software package. You may have to convince interviewers that your writing ability and your understanding of the user-centered process of creating great content is the strength they want—and that you can learn to use the tools (if you don't already know them).

IDEAL TRAINING

Content writers/information designers often have a **bachelor's or master's degree** in one of these fields: Business communication, Communication, English, Journalism, Technical communication. Others have a college degree in the specific field they write about. Discovering that they have a flair for and passion for clear writing about that field, they move into a career as a content writer/information designer.

Others (even without a college degree) may come into content writing/information design through personal professional development, attending workshops and conferences, or taking a certificate program. Several universities offer courses leading to certificates in UX with a focus on clear writing and information design. To find them, you might search with some combination of these words: UX, content, information design, certificate program. Some professional societies, such as the Society for

---

POTENTIAL JOB TITLES

- Communications Specialist
- Content Specialist
- Copy Writer
- Editor
- Information Designer
- Marketing Communications Specialist
- Social Media Writer/Editor
- Web Writer/Editor
- Writer

CAREER PATHWAYS THAT MAY BE COMBINED WITH CONTENT WRITING/INFORMATION DESIGN IN JOB DESCRIPTIONS

- Accessibility
- Content strategy
- Technical communication

Technical Communication, offer webinars and online courses for professional development.

Get more online: uxcareershandbook.com/information-design

Janice (Ginny) Redish has been a passionate evangelist for clear communication and usability for many years. Through her consulting company, Redish & Associates, Inc., Ginny helps clients and colleagues with all aspects of creating great user experiences. Ginny has been called the "mother of usability" for her early work in user-centered design and writing and for co-authoring the first book on usability testing. Reviewers rave about her most recent book, *Letting Go of the Words—Writing Web Content that Works* (2nd edition, 2012). Ginny is a graduate of Bryn Mawr College and holds a Ph.D. in Linguistics from Harvard University. Follow Ginny on Twitter: @GinnyRedish. Connect with Ginny on LinkedIn at linkedin.com/in/ginnyredish.

TECHNICAL COMMUNICATION

By Tom Johnson, Senior Technical Writer, Experian

As a technical writer, you help people understand complex technical information. In the United States, many technical writers work in a variety of industries creating documentation, especially for software applications. For example, when people click the help button in an application, your documentation appears and helps guide them through tasks.

If you work in manufacturing engineering industries, you might create documentation for machinery, medical devices, consumer goods, or other physical products. In this case, your user guides often ship with the product.

In a company that employs engineers, you will probably also find technical writers, because technical writers provide the documentation that accompanies products that engineers build. You might create reference and user guides for software APIs, work on massive projects such as providing maintenance guides for aircraft, or write troubleshooting articles about mobile devices for help center agents. The number of contexts for technical writing is as diverse as the technology landscape.

Regardless of the context, the end result is usually the same: through the documentation you create, users learn to use applications or products efficiently to accomplish real-world tasks.

What Does a Technical Writer Do?

CREATE DOCUMENTATION

Your principal deliverable is usually **documentation for a product, published as an online help site or printable user guide**. The documentation primarily focuses on tasks that users perform with the product. You also typically include conceptual information related to your users' goals with the product. Your guide will most likely have a table of contents, a search feature, cross-references, screenshots, and navigation, among other features.

CONTRIBUTE TEXT FOR THE USER INTERFACE

Beyond creating documentation, you might also **shape the text in a software interface**, including error messages, tooltips, button names, getting started text, and wizards. Unlike with content in a user guide, you may have to make a persuasive case for some button names and labels. This is because there are more competing stakeholders with the user interface than with the user guide text.

As a master of language, you can play a vital role in shaping the language used in the user interface. In many cases, users never leave the interface, even when they get frustrated and need help, so this is a key area where you should focus your efforts.

MAKE INFORMATION VISUAL

Nothing turns users off more than long walls of text. To help users understand complex information, you supplement your text with screenshots, conceptual illustrations, video tutorials, diagrams, workflows, and multimedia graphics.

Even with areas of text, you still **make it visual** by adding bulleted or numbered lists, subheadings, callouts and notes, paragraph breaks, sidebars, and other visual elements. Making documentation visual helps make it appealing and readable.

CREATE STRATEGIES FOR CONTENT RE-USE

In addition to creating content, you also **employ strategies for reusing the content** across different deliverables. For example, you may need to provide five different variations of mostly the same content for different product versions and audiences.

Rather than primitively copying and pasting content from one output to another, you reuse content using special tags, and add product and audience attributes to the content to filter the page when you specify your output. Reusing content reduces inconsistency and minimizes word count for translation.

SET UP AUTHORING AND PUBLISHING TOOLS

In addition to creating content, you also **set up the tooling to support authoring and publishing of the help content**. Whether you're using a help authoring tool, wiki, custom website, or other platform, you often need to set this up. You might configure access rights, set up search, construct documentation portals (home pages for lots of different guides), design the style sheets, and more. Deciding which publishing tool to use based on your requirements is a decision you may also make.

Challenges

UNDERSTANDING HOW A PRODUCT WORKS

Before you can write documentation, you have to **figure out how your product works**. You might wade through poorly written specifications or other engineering documents to gather information. You might explore the product through trial and error, or look over the shoulder of engineers as they explain how something works. Just figuring out how a product works can take weeks of meetings, explorations, and interactions with team members.

GETTING INFORMATION FROM ENGINEERS

You need to **interact heavily with engineers**, who may or may not want to take the time to explain things to you. Engineers can also be unreliable in estimating what users need to know, so you'll have to assess what they say about the level of information your users will need. Therefore, you need good interviewing skills and must be comfortable asking questions until you understand the product well enough to explain it to others.

In addition to talking with engineers, you also have to **interact with users** to understand their business goals, level of knowledge, and other needs. You might interact with users directly, such as in training sessions or on-site visits, or indirectly through forums, email, and support logs.

WORKING IN ISOLATION

As a technical writer, **you work long periods of time in isolation**, often in front of a computer. You may be the only technical writer in your organization, immersed in a department of engineers who constantly speak in programming jargon that you may not initially understand. Even if there are other technical writers, you may not get to work with them, as you could be assigned to different projects. Expect to find yourself in situations where you work alone for long periods of time.

WORKING IN TEAMS

Although you may spend a lot of time working by yourself, **you may also be part of a larger team**. You may be writing only one part of a large set of documentation. You and your colleagues may have to produce documentation that has a single voice and style. Agreeing on that voice and style and helping each other maintain it may be part of your job. Therefore, skills in peer review—both giving and taking constructive criticism—may be important.

FOLLOWING DESIGN TEMPLATES AND STYLE STANDARDS

Many companies have set up templates for documentation, and you **must tag your content to match the templates.** For example, you might need to code each note, tip, or caution with a specific style so it shows up on screen or in print with the right font, size, and color.

Many companies also have a corporate style guide, which may cover everything from how to punctuate a bulleted list to whether "web site" is one word or two.

Templates and style standards can make your job easier because you don't have to decide anew each time you write. On the other hand, if the templates don't work for you, you'll have to negotiate with the owners of the templates and style standards to make changes. If you work for a startup, most likely you will be defining the templates, style, and publishing formats yourself.

WORKING WITH REVIEWERS

In addition to getting information from engineers, **you need good negotiating skills** to work well with editors and with technical, managerial, and sometimes legal reviewers. After preparing a draft of your documentation, you submit it to engineers to review it for accuracy. Then you submit it to product managers to look to review the messaging. You may then submit it to a team editor who checks your content against a company style guide. Finally, legal groups will sometimes look for intellectual property rights surrounding images or code libraries you're using.

MEETING REGULATORY STANDARDS

One challenge in some industries and locations is **complying with regulatory standards for your content.** In manufacturing engineering jobs in Germany, for example, your documentation might need to comply with specific regulations required by governing standards boards. These standards ensure that the documentation leads to safe operation of the equipment or includes proper documentation of risks. The financial and medical sectors also require compliance with regulatory standards.

LEARNING NEW TOOLS

Many job descriptions for technical writers focus more on tools and technical knowledge than on skills such as thinking clearly, organizing information well, and writing in a user-centered style.

As you read descriptions of jobs you are interested in, you may find that you need to **learn and practice particular tools** to make yourself a good candidate for those jobs. Currently, the number of authoring tools in the tech comm space is diverse and fragmented, with no tool being predominant among technical writers. By learning a few tools, however, you can demonstrate enough technical competence to convince employers that you can learn other tools.

Ideal Training

A **bachelor's degree** is all that is required. A **master's degree** can be helpful in expanding your capacity to organize and manage complex information, but it is not required.

Many colleges and universities offer programs in technical communication. The Society for Technical Communication (STC—the technical writers' professional organization) lists more than 170 programs leading to a Bachelor of Arts or a Bachelor of Science degree. If you are first considering college, you might want to look into the Academic Database at www.stc.org.

However, you don't have to earn a degree specifically in technical communication. In fact, many technical writers fall into technical writing from a variety of other backgrounds.

Engineering backgrounds (especially computer science) provide strong foundations for technical writing. If you have solid writing skills in addition to technical depth, this provides a knockout combination in the job market.

If you have a humanities background and want to put your writing skills to work in a technical context, you can also have a lot of success. You can often learn the technical information on your own, depending on what you're documenting.

If you're starting out in college, an ideal focus could be to double major in computer science and English. Most of the jobs for technical writing in the United States are in software, and the API documentation space is especially hot. (An API, or "application programming interface," allows different systems to interact with each other, sharing data and performing other functions.)

Other helpful degrees (besides English and engineering) would be a focus on graphics and design, digital media, or library science. If you want to go into medical or life sciences writing, get a degree in a related biology or chemistry field.

Many colleges also offer a certificate program for people who are transitioning into a career as a technical writer. These programs are usually geared to working professionals, offering classes online or in the evenings and focusing on practical skills.

Regardless of your formal training, you can learn along the way as discussed in Chapter 3 to overcome hurdles in technical knowledge.

POTENTIAL JOB TITLES

Most jobs in technical communication will use the title "Technical Writer."

However, technical writers often prefer titles that give more emphasis and credit to the many non-writing tasks they do, such as:

- Information Developer
- Knowledge Engineer
- Technical Communicator
- User Assistance Professional

CAREER PATHWAYS THAT MAY BE COMBINED WITH TECHNICAL COMMUNICATION IN JOB DESCRIPTIONS

- Content writing/Information design
- Content strategy

Get more online at uxcareershandbook.com/technical-communication

Tom Johnson is a senior technical writer based in Silicon Valley, California. His blog, I'd Rather Be Writing (idratherbewriting.com), is a hub for innovation and exploration in the tech comm field. He writes about web publishing, visual communication, information architecture, API documentation, and more. Tom also has a podcast in which he interviews tech writing luminaries around the world. He is a frequent presenter at conferences, chapter meetings, and other tech comm groups. Tom is an influencer and thought leader in the field, and he has appeared numerous times in MindTouch's Top 10 influencer lists. You can contact him at tomjohnson1492@gmail.com.

HUMAN FACTORS

By Angie Hernandez, UX Lead, Design Interactive, Inc.

Human Factors Engineering, as a discipline, is rooted in the military, aviation, and transportation industries but has grown and flourished in a wide variety of other industries such as government, healthcare, consumer products, software, and manufacturing. A Human Factors Engineer's (HFE's) primary responsibility is to **ensure human needs and capabilities (both physical and mental) are incorporated into interactive system design**. An HFE's skills can be applied to a wide variety of systems like mobile apps, medical devices, home appliances, or large industrial power plants. Each industry and company has their own complexities. Once you figure out the engineering environment and the kind of procedures and processes you will be working with, you can determine how HFE will best contribute to the development of the system on which you are working.

As an HFE, you will be required to **work with a wide variety of teams in the development effort**. You may work with other engineers like hardware designers, computer programmers, analysts, and most importantly, project managers. Managers typically provide guidance and direction for the project you are on and will oversee your work. You may also work with teams devoted to certain other specialties such as occupational health and safety, maintainability, training, marketing, or operations.

Lastly, you may work directly with Visual Designers, Information Architects, or other user experience (UX) career pathways mentioned in this book. An HFE may be asked to perform tasks typically assigned to these teams or may be asked to oversee certain aspects of their work. Ultimately, an HFE must maintain the big picture of the whole system and be cognizant of how UX contributes to the usability of the whole design.

What Does a Human Factors Engineer Do?

REQUIREMENTS AND STANDARDS COMPLIANCE

HFEs have to ensure that human capabilities are accounted for in a new system design through requirements. Requirements are the rules and instructions that a system is built to. They describe everything from how a system should operate to what it should look like. As an HFE you will first need to **figure out what the usability/user requirements are**. Requirements can be derived from many sources, but often the first step is to **identify the industry standards and regulatory guidance** that you must comply with. The standards and guides may provide direction on how to "do" human factors (such as the Human Factors Guidance from the U.S. Food and Drug Administration) or may contain specific detailed statements on how the system should be designed. Military standards, for example, contain directions on how big openings should be so that tools fit inside them, or where labels and warnings should be placed so that users of varying heights can read them.

As you collect the requirements, you need to figure out how they apply to the system and how you are going to make sure the system meets those requirements. You will need to **formulate a plan**, which will be your governing "how to" document. Typically these plans are referred to as **Human Engineering Program Plans (HEPP)** or **Human Systems Integration Plans (HSIP)**. However, many of the HF activities will be written out in project proposals, contracts, or statements of work. The techniques and methods identified in these documents will largely depend on the industry you are working in.

ANALYSIS AND SYSTEM DESIGN

Once the project has kicked off, you will be continuously working towards fulfilling your project plan and checking that the emerging product matches the requirements that you've defined (**requirements verification**). Working with the engineering teams, you will be iteratively **participating in design working groups, requirements meetings, and status updates**. You may be **reviewing drawings or schematics** and re-reviewing when the design changes or moves into a more production-ready model.

Usability Issue Tracking: Along with requirements verification, you may do iterative **heuristic evaluations** to identify any emerging usability issues that come up. You may need to talk with experts to understand any potential problems that might constrain the design. For example, you may reach out to a few surgeons to understand how they might use a new surgery tool or how they might store it in an operating room. As the design matures and changes, it is most important to do usability testing of prototypes or partial designs with your end users to make sure the product is on the right track.

Anthropometrics and Ergonomics Evaluation: If the system has a hardware component, you may need to **conduct an ergonomics evaluation**. In this evaluation, you test whether a typical end user can physically interact and access the system's user interfaces. Interfaces may require physical interaction, such as with buttons, levers, or access panels; interfaces may require perceptual access such as viewing a display or labels. Using anthropometric databases, you can **develop test cases of potential user size dimensions**. A good rule of thumb is to ensure your system can be used by the best and worst cases. For example, levers or switches should not be placed so high that the shortest potential user cannot reach them. On the flip side, you should not place levers and switches so low that they hamper the tallest person from reaching and using them. Ergonomic evaluations are often used to point out issues that may potentially cause harm or health concerns such as repetitive stress injuries. An HFE may also need to turn to someone with accessibility skills who can consult on systems that need to address the ergonomic needs of users with a particular disability.

VERIFY AND VALIDATE SYSTEM DESIGN

Verification is often described as determining whether you've "built the system right," and validation is determining whether you've "built the right system." **Verification testing** essentially is the final check that the system was built correctly, or that all HF requirements have been met and that any remaining usability issues are mitigated and documented. The verification process happens iteratively as the design matures.

Validation will be the formal check with a production-ready system and actual end users. To validate a system, you will typically do these tasks:

- **Risk Analysis**: You determine the riskiest or most critical tasks to be done on the system. These tasks are often the most susceptible to human error or safety concerns or are most critical to a user's success.
- **Scenario Development**: You develop scenarios for end users to perform during testing. Scenarios are situations in which users would work with the system. Scenarios are used by other teams as well to conduct system validation testing. Quality Assurance, for example, may use these to understand the user tasks and pathways they need to inspect to ensure the system is operating as intended.
- **Usability Testing**: While you may have done interim, iterative usability testing during development, you will now conduct a formal usability test. This allows you to validate that the final system design allows users to do the expected tasks, especially the riskiest and most critical tasks,

successfully and easily enough to make them satisfied with and willing to use the system. In a usability test, typical end users go through the scenarios and attempt to accomplish tasks to meet their goals. A formal validation usability test is similar to, but also somewhat different from, typical iterative usability testing during development. For example, if you are timing how long it takes people to do these tasks, you will probably not include think-aloud during the test.

Challenges

FIGURING OUT THE ENGINEERING ENVIRONMENT

As a new HFE on a project, the initial challenge you will encounter is learning and adjusting to the engineering process you need to work in. Each company may adapt engineering processes and practices differently or may even have their own spin on conventional processes. How to best integrate within these processes will take collaboration between many different teams and require excellent lines of communication.

WORKING WITH OTHER TEAMS WHO MAY NOT UNDERSTAND HUMAN FACTORS

How much an industry embraces HF will often determine how well HFEs are integrated into the engineering process. In a perfect world, HF will be key to stakeholders in engineering design decisions, and HFEs will be consulted on any changes to the system. In many cases, however, the HFEs are brought in to consult on a system that is already built or has already been launched. Major changes could incur high costs, which managers may not be interested in pursuing. Engineering teams may not value HF as a priority. You may have to educate people on the value of HF and always be illustrating value through demonstrating improvements in the system.

Ideal Training

The level of education needed to be a HFE will largely depend on the environment you want to work in. At the minimum, you will need a **bachelor's degree**. HF programs typically live in industrial engineering or psychology departments, but other degrees (for example, design, computer engineering, and safety) may also have a concentration in HF. Typically, a bachelor's degree may limit you to entry-level opportunities. However, some industries accept a bachelor's degree level with some experience.

A **master's degree** is a typical education level requested across industries. As a master's degree holder, you will be expected to know about a variety of HF techniques.

A **Ph.D.** is sometimes desired for very specific roles and settings within a program. Ph.D. holders typically are found in universities and research labs or roles that have policy or program management duties.

Some certificate programs exist that can augment your education. You may also choose to become a **Certified Professional Ergonomist (CPE)** or a **Certified Human Factors Professional (CHFP).** Certification requires vast knowledge of HF principles and standards.

POTENTIAL JOB TITLES

- Human Factors Engineer/Specialist/Analyst
- Human Systems Integration Specialist/Scientist
- Human Computer Interface (HCI) Designer/Engineer
- Industrial Engineer
- Usability Engineer
- Engineering Psychologist
- Crew Systems Designer/Engineer
- Systems Engineer—Human Factors Focus

CAREER PATHWAYS THAT MAY BE COMBINED WITH HUMAN FACTORS IN JOB DESCRIPTIONS

- Interaction design
- User research and evaluation
- Industrial design

Get more online at uxcareershandbook.com/human-factors

Angie Hernandez is a UX Lead for Design Interactive, Inc. (DI) in the Washington, DC area. She has been in HF for the last 9 years within a variety of teams and projects. Prior to DI, she worked in a healthcare system conducting usability testing to help improve the user experience and safety of medical products. She has also had the privilege of working in Navy and Marine Corps acquisition projects to improve the hardware and software interfaces for service members. Angie received a BS and MS in Human Factors and Systems from Embry-Riddle Aeronautical University. Find Angie at linkedin.com/in/angienator.

UX FOR INDUSTRIAL DESIGNERS

By John Payne, Principal, Moment

With a history going back to the Industrial Revolution, industrial design has always been a pragmatic discipline focused on creating usable products. It emerged as a modernization of the craftsman approach that had produced the tools and furnishings people used in the pre-Industrial Age. When mass manufacturing caught on, it gave rise to a new type of design discipline—focused initially on the problems of manufacturability and safety. This evolved into the industrial design discipline we have today, addressing every aspect of the design of manufactured products.

Industrial designers have a long history of working on the same issues that user experience (UX) professionals wrestle with today. Many of the methods employed in the design of physical products informed and inspired methods in the field of UX and its focus on the digital world.

If you are an industrial designer interested in expanding your purview into UX, be assured that many of the skills and approaches you use are directly applicable to the field. You have one foot in the domain already. But recognize that how you apply those skills, the product that you apply those skills to, and the form that your output will take all need to change. You can do it, but you will have to pick up some new skills to be effective in this emerging discipline.

Overlaps Between UX and Industrial Design

There are a number of distinct overlaps between your practice as an industrial designer and that of a UX practitioner. In the interest of time and your attention, let's focus on three. This is not a comprehensive list, but simply an overview of ways the practices of the two fields complement each other.

Problem Solving

Design thinking: the application of design's problem-solving methodologies to new arenas of business was popularized by the iconic industrial design firm, IDEO.[2] As a successful industrial designer, you have likely employed design as a problem-solving methodology. The objects being designed may be different, but the process through which the team proceeds is really quite similar to UX design.

A Focus on Usage

As with UX professionals, industrial designers are trained to design for use, and both groups share the same approach to uncovering user needs: primary research. **Generative research methods like ethnography, participatory methods like co-design, and even evaluative methods like usability testing** are examples of ways that both industrial designers and UX practitioners ply their trade.

A Product Orientation

Finally, industrial designers bring a product-oriented mindset to a problem. They seek to **design something that will have lasting commercial value** for both the consumer and the business that provides it. That exchange of value justifies putting a product into the market and the expense to keep it there. Successful UX designers also maintain the belief that only through a clear exchange of value can you create sustainable engagement with a customer.

Challenges

There are also a variety of key differences between these two fields, which may reflect challenges for industrial designers who want to do UX work.

PHYSICAL VS. DIGITAL

The most obvious difference between the two disciplines is that industrial design addresses physical products and UX primarily focuses on digital products and associated customer interactions around those products. As an industrial designer, whether you work on furniture and housewares, or electronics and other complex "machines," you likely need a talent for creating three-dimensional forms, from renderings to computer models to physical prototypes. To do equivalent work in UX design, you will need to apply your skills in two dimensions, focusing on sketching, wireframing, and developing clickable prototypes.

MANY VS. ONE

Another key difference between industrial design and UX is that industrial designers typically work on products that will be produced en masse. As an industrial designer, you also likely need to think through the entire product development process, from raw material to manufacture and use, all the way to end of (product) life. UX designers, on the other hand, usually have a different product lifecycle to adapt to, that of a product roadmap. With sometimes only one instance of a product, a website for example, the concern shifts to how a singular product experience will evolve over time, when new features will be introduced, and how those features will be integrated to create a cohesive whole.

SPECIALIZED SKILLS

As an industrial designer, you may take on challenges requiring additional skillsets. For example, you may focus on esthetics and styling only; or alternatively, you may engage in engineering design and design for manufacture; or perhaps, you may concern yourself with issues of usage and ergonomics, like a human factors specialist. Each of these specialties requires additional sets of skills.

Similarly, UX professionals often have additional specialty skills. Some focus on strategic issues of a product experience. Others spend time on screen flows, user interface design, and prototyping. As an industrial designer in UX, you may need to obtain some of these additional highly specific UX skills, depending on where your focus lies.

UX and Industrial Design Synergies

There have long been physical products with digital components. Unfortunately, it is common practice to design each aspect in isolation, only bringing the digital and physical together at a few points during the process. When a company as successful as Apple puts both design processes under the same umbrella, as they recently did,[3] it signals the commercial importance of the partnership of the two design disciplines, industrial design, and UX. The overlap of these disciplines will only increase. As more and more products emerge that are balanced combinations of the physical and digital domains, designers who can work across these two disciplines will emerge as leaders in their field.

Get more online at uxcareershandbook.com/industrial-design

John Payne is a principal at Moment and leads the Experience Design and Strategy practice. His background in Industrial Design gives him a unique perspective on UX design methodologies and innovation techniques. In addition to his work at Moment, John has taught graduate and undergraduate courses in design at Parsons and NYU, serves on the organizing committee of EPIC (Ethnographic Praxis in Industry Conference), and sits on the board of Public Policy Lab. John received his bachelor's degree in Industrial Design from Auburn University and his Master of Design degree from the Institute of Design at IIT.

VISUAL DESIGN

By Krissy Scoufis, Associate User Experience Director, 352 Inc.

Visual design communicates a message, idea, or concept by using established design principles and elements. Deliberate use of typography, color, imagery, line, texture, and space enriches a user's understanding and experience with a product. Although art must be interpreted, successful design should be understood by all without the need for explanation.

As a visual designer, you draw upon your creative instinct and artistic ability to design appealing tangible artifacts based on information that you get about the users of a product and how they'll interact with the interface. You have an understanding of how people perceive and react to visual elements. Your focus is not on whether an element is simply attractive but how it should be visualized to best resonate with the intended audience. You envision innovative design solutions and explore their viability within the realm of what is possible.

The visual design role is highly collaborative, and you will actively seek feedback from your team during the development process. You need to be comfortable making design decisions and supporting your choices with both knowledge and data. You will need to articulate your creative visions to the other content writers and the other designers as well as the development team and product owners.

What Does a Visual Designer Do?

DISTILL PROJECT RELEVANT IDEAS INTO DESIGN SOLUTIONS

As the team gathers relevant information and functionally illustrates ideas for a project, the visual designer will begin to translate that information into easily digestible visual elements using knowledge of design principles and usability heuristics. Patterns may have emerged from stakeholder interviews and user research that lead you to specific types of graphical solutions. Your team will look to you to get some of these ideas mocked up so that they may be explored further.

Depending on the scope of the project, the deliverables in this stage may vary; however, they are typically in the form of **sketches, mockups, wireframes, interaction models,** and **user task flows**. You and the rest of the team will use these low fidelity models to **explore alternative solutions**. Your team may put your designs in front of representative users with a usability test. As areas of improvement are identified, you **iterate based on feedback**, and will potentially have them tested again.

CRAFT DESIGN CONCEPTS

Leveraging feedback and the results of prototype testing to drive design decisions, as the visual designer, you will **translate low-fidelity models into initial design concepts**. You may use a prototyping or design tool like Photoshop, Sketch, Illustrator, or InVision. Having skills in tools like these is essential.

You may be asked to **present your design concepts in an informal review to your team** or a more **formal presentation to the product owner**. You will need to effectively communicate your vision and be prepared to defend your design decisions and proposed solutions.

POLISH FINAL DESIGNS

Often referred to as "pushing pixels," the visual designer will carefully **pull together requirements for the final design**. It is at this stage you sweat the small stuff and focus on every detail. You may be asked to **craft custom icons**, **controls, and brand messaging**. You will **design out every unique page or element** in the project. During this process, you will apply your knowledge of design principles, usability heuristics, persuasion, and the human psyche to create esthetic interfaces that are pleasing to use and forge an emotional connection with the user.

BE A TEAM PLAYER

In many situations you will **work with a team of content writers, developers, and user researchers**. The best solutions evolve from many diverse ideas. Team collaboration is a great way to generate those ideas, so it is important to be open and receptive to collaboration. Page layout will be partly dependent on the content that needs to be included in the project. You will usually work very closely with a copywriter, content strategist, marketing specialist, or others to craft the messaging and content hierarchy. You will also consult with other user experience (UX) team members to ensure navigation elements and page layout correctly represent the information architecture and user task flows.

WORK WITH ESTABLISHED STYLE GUIDES

You may need to **work within an existing style guide or set of brand or design guidelines**, which you must thoroughly review to understand how new elements can be seamlessly incorporated while maintaining the integrity of the current styles. One of your goals is to provide a consistent experience for the user, and that may mean matching an existing look and feel.

CREATE STYLE GUIDES AND PATTERN LIBRARIES

The visual designer may **provide input into a long-term design strategy** and direction to ensure consistency across channels. This can be documented through **pattern libraries**, **style guides**, **style tiles,** or **design spec documents**. As your project grows, this is critical to facilitate a seamless experience for your users. These artifacts can be used to save development time, reduce code bloat, and build a common language for the development team.

Challenges

BALANCING FIDELITY

In every stage of development, balancing fidelity, or the amount of detail you apply to your design solutions, can be tricky. Incorporating the right amount of information is important because too little or too much detail may present communication challenges. Details will bring clarity to your design intention, but adding too much information too soon can cloud expectations and prevent the delivery of useful feedback. Product owners or usability study participants may get too hung up on "missing" details that have just not been fully fleshed out. Conversely, if a design has too much detail and a product owner does not like one element on the page, they may discard the entire design instead of critically analyzing the individual elements. Perfecting design ideas early on in the project discovery phase can take a lot of time that may be wasted if those concepts are discarded.

HANDOFFS TO A DEVELOPMENT TEAM

If you are working with a team, your pixel perfect designs will eventually be handed off to developers to bring them to life. The way elements you designed are intended to respond to user input may have been carefully thought out but may get lost in the design to development translation. Specific and desired design states should be carefully documented to add clarity to the design and make it easier for developers to design what you intended.

POTENTIAL JOB TITLES

- Digital Product Designer
- Visual Designer
- UX Designer
- Experience Designer
- Visual Interface Designer

CAREER PATHWAY THAT MAY BE COMBINED WITH VISUAL DESIGN IN JOB DESCRIPTIONS

- Interaction design

Ideal Training

Visual designers have usually earned a **bachelor's degree**, often with a focus in art or design. A Master's degree is not required. Hands-on experience and a representative portfolio to demonstrate design competency are usually required to get a job.

Get more online: uxcareershandbook.com/visual-design

Krissy Scoufis is a visual designer, researcher, and UX advocate who brings nearly two decades of experience to her role as the Associate Director of UX at 352 Inc. In that role, she works directly with clients to help them best understand their users and craft digital experiences and products to fit users' needs. Krissy's passion for lifelong learning and mentorship led her to organize an internal UX ambassador program to teach others about the value and processes of UX and found the Tampa Bay UX Meetup group, the first of its kind in her area. When not crafting design vision or speaking up for users, Krissy can be found near the ocean with her family. Follow Krissy on Twitter @UXTampa.

ACCESSIBILITY

By Cory Lebson

As an accessibility specialist you function as both disability advocate and technical practitioner, making sure that electronic products and resources are usable by everyone. You are concerned with issues that could impact a range of users, including those with visual, auditory, motor or cognitive disabilities. While accessibility specialists may be involved in all kinds of electronic and information technology products, if you are doing accessibility work within the larger framework of user experience (UX), you will most commonly deal with the accessibility of web and mobile resources.

You can also tout that accessibility, often called "universal usability," really helps everyone whether or not they have a disability. For example, you are helping users with slow web or mobile internet connections, and also providing search engines with more opportunities to correctly index web content.

As an accessibility specialist, you know accessibility guidelines backwards and forwards, and they become part of your everyday lexicon. In many cases, you will be familiar with the W3C Web Content Accessibility Guidelines (WCAG) 2.0. You will often use these, or similar regulations, to do your work. If you are in the United States and dealing with Federal (or sometimes state) government agencies, you will be very familiar with Section 508 of the Rehabilitation Act as well. Other countries have their own specific permutations on accessibility standards.

You use your knowledge of accessibility guidelines to review products, hopefully while they are being developed and before they are made public. You advise and educate the project teams on accessibility, and you advocate for proper coding techniques from the outset. It's easier to bake accessibility in at the beginning than to retrofit.

Finally, you will probably learn and master a variety of assistive technology products, such as screen readers (to read text that is seen on the screen out loud), screen magnifiers, and speech recognition software.

What Does an Accessibility Specialist Do?

TRAIN DEVELOPMENT TEAMS

When you come aboard in a company or on a project as the accessibility expert, the team probably expects you to be there. Yet in many cases, they don't understand what exactly you do or what accessibility really means. That's when the role of **educator and advocate** comes in. Almost invariably, you will find yourself in the role of providing guidance. You likely have enough technical knowledge to be able to talk with the development team in a language they understand, and to explain and demonstrate what it means to have an accessible site that can be used by all users, including those with and without disabilities.

REVIEW RESOURCES

The bulk of your work is to make sure that what is being produced by the project team is going to be accessible for users with disabilities. Your job is much more than checking off boxes against a checklist, however. In fact, you'll find many gray areas, and you'll have to make judgment calls as to whether things truly are or are not accessible.

When you are doing **code reviews**, you may start by simply going through the resource as an actual user would, without any supplemental software. You also likely need to examine the code—both by actually looking at source code and by using (often free) tools that easily make certain aspects of code readily visible.

Sometimes, you'll be tasked with using a baked-in screen reader, or you may use other accessibility software that is built into desktop and mobile operating systems. Other times, you'll be asked to use commercial software to go through and confirm that what appears to be accessible in a code review really comes out as accessible.

Less commonly, like a user researcher, you may do **usability testing**, where you recruit actual or representative users of a product who have certain disabilities. You'd let these users run through common tasks to see whether there are hurdles in actual usage that you may not have identified previously.

Your primary deliverable is often some kind of **synthesis of all of your findings in a comprehensive report**. This could take the form of a formal written report or a spreadsheet that inventories the issues and potential fixes. Alternatively, you might enter your findings directly into bug tracking software that is used to keep track of all problems, accessibility or otherwise.

You may also coordinate a final review with testers who may not be representative users but who do have particular disabilities and make a living out of running through webpages and electronic documents with whatever tools they use normally to make sure that they don't encounter anything problematic.

REMEDIATE PROBLEMS

While you may not be technical enough to remediate actual software code, you could work hand in hand with the development teams to **make sure that code gets remediated properly**. If you are actually doing the remediation work, most likely, it means that you **fix documents**. You go through documents that are going to be made publically available and fix problems that you find; Microsoft Word and PowerPoint, and Adobe Acrobat and InDesign files are typical formats that you may be asked to remediate.

Challenges

ADVOCATING AGAINST ONLY USING AUTOMATED TOOLS

Inevitably, at some point you'll be asked to simply use some sort of automated checking software to test the accessibility of a website and may be told that your role is simply to explain the results from this tool to the development team. You will find yourself in the position of explaining to the team that while there are some things that an automated tool can correctly identify, or at least flag for subsequent review, automated tools should never be used without a manual validation. Accessibility checking algorithms can certainly be very robust, but they cannot replace you actually confirming that the meaning of the content that should be conveyed to users, is, in fact, being conveyed properly.

THINKING OUT OF THE BOX

Sometimes it will be easy to explain to a development team how to make some quick and easy fixes. Other times, however, you may be put in the position of telling teams that conceptually, the dynamic product that they are developing doesn't have a simple fix to make it accessible. Instead of just telling teams that they must pull the offending features, you need to think creatively. How can all the product features be maintained and be of as much value while still being made to be accessible as well? Not only do these creative aspects add value to your job, but they make you an even more valuable part of the team.

Ideal Training

A **bachelor's degree** is ideally the minimum level of education you should have, although not an absolute requirement, particularly once you have experience. Accessibility practitioners could have any undergraduate degree, particularly those found in the other pathways. A graduate degree is not necessary.

> **POTENTIAL JOB TITLES**
>
> - Accessibility Specialist
> - Accessibility Engineer
> - Accessibility Analyst
> - Accessibility Auditor
> - Accessibility Compliance Specialist
> - Accessibility and Remediation Specialist
> - Document Remediation Specialist
> - Section 508 Specialist (US only)
>
> **CAREER PATHWAYS THAT MAY BE COMBINED WITH ACCESSIBILITY IN JOB DESCRIPTIONS**
>
> - User research and evaluation
> - Development
>
> These two are, perhaps, the most common, but accessibility skills can also be found combined with just about any other career pathway.

If you are working with some US Federal government clients, particularly with the Department of Homeland Security (DHS) components, having DHS Trusted Tester certification could be useful. This certification is only available to you once you are already a government employee or (in some cases) a contractor.

Get more online at uxcareershandbook.com/accessibility

CUSTOMER EXPERIENCE

By Kerry Bodine, Keynote Speaker and Customer Experience Coach, Kerry Bodine & Company

Your job as a customer experience (CX) professional is to improve the quality of customer interactions. Not just digital interactions on a website or smartphone app—but *all* customer interactions. That includes email communications, text notifications, printed bills, paper forms, in-store purchases, in-home service visits, online chats, and customer support calls, just to name a few.

You probably work for a service-based business, such as a bank, health care provider, insurer, credit card provider, utility, airline, or hotel. Product companies certainly need to think about customer experience, too—but they've been slower to create customer experience teams and to look at the interactions that happen pre- and post-product usage.

While newer organizations and startups employ CX professionals to some degree, you're more likely to work at a legacy organization—one that's been around for several decades or more. Over the years, your company has amassed tens (if not hundreds) of thousands of employees, Byzantine reporting structures, complex internal processes, strict policies, and an aging technical infrastructure that prevent it from competing on the basis of customer experience. And you've come in to help fix that situation!

What Does a Customer Experience Professional Do?

CONDUCT CUSTOMER RESEARCH

Typical Voice of the Customer (VoC) programs center on the now ubiquitous **customer feedback survey** to understand what's good and bad about the customer experience. You'll also do **sentiment analysis on your customers' social media posts**, **mine customer call logs** for top issues, **review site analytics**, and **look for trends in your company's purchasing data**. Unfortunately, customer experience research today rarely includes user research techniques such as one-on-one interviews and in-context ethnography—though this trend is slowly changing as more user experience (UX) people join the CX ranks.

Your ultimate research goal is to understand the complete end-to-end journey that your customers go through as they do business with your company, and you'll **produce journey maps**—diagrams that visualize the actions, thoughts, and feelings of a person or group over time—to share these insights with others in your organization.

IDENTIFY AND PRIORITIZE CUSTOMER PAIN POINTS

Armed with all of that research, you'll need to figure out what pain points are having the biggest impact on customers' perceptions of your company—a fantastic opportunity to put your statistical background to work. Of course, you'll need to **marry the top customer pain points with your company's growth objectives and business constraints** in order to prioritize the issues to be fixed. Customer experience isn't just about making customers happy; it's about making customers happy in order to drive business results.

IMPROVE THE EXPERIENCE

Define new interactions: Your UX design skills may help you design a new online mortgage application form (although you may want to get special training in online forms design). But what about call center and retail store interactions? You can't script these conversations with pixel-by-pixel precision. Quite to the contrary, you want to encourage flexibility and authenticity in frontline employees, while also ensuring that the experience will be relatively consistent and on-brand across touch points. **Future-state journey maps**, **scenario-based theatrical rehearsal**, and hands-on **co-creation workshops** with both employees and customers will be your go-to tools.

Change the way your company does business: Here's where things get tricky—in order to change the customer experience, you often need to recommend fundamental changes to the way the company operates. Let's take the call center for example. If you want to improve the quality of customer service calls, you can't just tell the phone agents to be nicer to customers. (In fact, that will probably produce the opposite of your desired result.) Maybe calls are going south because the agents have to navigate among 26 different screens to complete a relatively simple transaction. Maybe the agents haven't had proper training. Maybe the agents are unmotivated because they are measured by the wrong metrics or because they aren't paid enough. Or maybe your company's hiring practices aren't getting the right people in the door to begin with.

It's *your* job as a CX professional to identify the root causes of your customers' pain points, and they're often hidden far behind the scenes. Then you need to work with the appropriate people in your organization—like operations, legal, finance, or human resources—to change the way things work.

MEASURE YOUR RESULTS

Your executive team will want to make sure that the investments they're making to improve the customer experience are paying off. So you'll need to **measure the impact of your efforts on several key business metrics**.

Loyalty: Customer loyalty is the Holy Grail for most customer experience teams, and it comes in a couple of flavors. "Retention loyalty" means that customers who have purchased in the past will purchase again—they're *retained* as customers. "Advocacy loyalty" means that customers will refer your company to others prospective customers—they're *advocates* of your brand. The connection between CX and loyalty is easy to understand—it makes perfect sense that customers who have had a great experience will come back again and tell their friends. Net Promoter Score (NPS®) has become the de facto measurement of customer loyalty, and it's calculated by asking one very simple question: how likely is it that you would recommend [XYZ company] to a friend or colleague?

Revenue: Customer loyalty is important to companies because it has a direct impact on revenue. When customers come back again, they spend more money. And when customers recommend a company to their friends, those friends spend money. It doesn't get more simple that that!

Cost reduction: Customer experience improvements can also have a dramatic impact on the cost of doing business. Consider a hypothetical call center that gets a large number of calls about a company's confusing billing statement. If you improve the design of the bill, you'll naturally reduce the number of incoming calls—*and* the number of customer service representatives needed to support those inquiries.

Sometimes it's possible to draw a direct link between cause and effect—like billing statement design improvements leading to a reduction in customer calls. But it's often impossible to draw direct connections between CX initiatives and CX metrics, especially when those initiatives are focused on fundamental business practices or corporate culture. The changes that these initiatives produce are broad and can take months, if not years, to fully surface. That's why you'll spend a significant chunk of your measurement efforts looking for long-term trends in the metrics you're tracking.

Challenges

NOT HAVING ANY REAL POWER

You'll probably report to the Chief Marketing Officer or to an operations group. You might work with a handful of peers or even a CX team of one. Regardless of organizational size and structure, one thing is certain: you will not have any direct power to make the changes required to improve your company's customer experience. Rather, you will need to **lead through influence**—helping others realize the customer experience vision for themselves and creating cross-department buy-in about the steps to get there.

GETTING OUT OF REACTIVE MODE

Let's face it: no company has an empty customer experience improvement to-do list. And because so many companies invest large amounts of time, effort, and money into their Voice of the Customer programs, it's easy to get sucked into a never-ending find-it-and-fix-it loop. That will certainly lead to incremental CX improvements and will keep your company on parity with its competitors. But many executives are looking for CX to be a strategic differentiator—and for those companies, parity won't cut it. They need to *innovate* the customer experience. So it's important to leverage your design skills to proactively reinvent the parts of the customer experience that will allow your company to leapfrog the competition.

Ideal Training

Some universities have added customer experience classes to their curriculum, but there are still no formal CX degree programs as of this writing. Most customer experience professionals have a marketing or business background and a related **bachelor's degree** and/or **MBA**. Valuable areas of study include psychology, human-computer interaction (HCI), human-centered design, marketing, market research, and business.

The Customer Experience Professionals Association offers a paid certification program. This is a test-based certification intended for practitioners with 3–5 years of experience, and as such, it does not include any accompanying training.

Most customer experience professionals acquire the required skills and knowledge through a combination of on-the-job training, conferences, and workshops.

POTENTIAL JOB TITLES

- Customer Experience Specialist/Analyst
- Customer Experience Consultant
- Customer Experience Manager/Director
- Voice of the Customer Manager/Director
- Chief Customer Officer
- Chief Customer Experience Officer

CAREER PATHWAY THAT MAY BE COMBINED WITH CUSTOMER EXPERIENCE IN JOB DESCRIPTIONS

- Service design

Get more online at uxcareershandbook.com/customer-experience

Kerry Bodine believes that happy customers lead to happy shareholders. Her book, *Outside In: The Power of Putting Customers at the Center of Your Business*, helps business leaders understand the financial benefits of great customer experiences—and how their organizations must change in order to deliver them. Kerry is a customer experience consultant whose ideas, analysis, and opinions have appeared on sites like *The Wall Street Journal*, *Harvard Business Review*, *Fast Company*, *Forbes*, and *USA Today*. She holds a master's degree in human-computer interaction from Carnegie Mellon University and has designed interfaces for websites, mobile apps, wearable devices, and robots. Find out more about Kerry at kerrybodine.com and follow her on Twitter @kerrybodine.

SERVICE DESIGN

By Lauren Currie, Co-founder, Snook; Programme Leader, Hyper Island

As a service designer, you put people at the heart of your design approach to create services that people want to use. You design every single interaction a person has with a service from start to finish. Unlike many other user experience (UX) career pathways in this book, your scope of effort extends far beyond a user's interaction with the technology itself.

While the salience of service design is rapidly growing on a global scale, there are some parts of the world (like the UK) where service design is more widely recognized and acknowledged than other parts of the world (like the United States). In everyday conversation, even among UX professionals, the phrase "service design" typically needs explaining and is best illustrated with an example: you call your mobile phone provider to discuss your bill, or receive a text message to remind you you've used all your data, or pop into the shop on the high street to query your phone insurance policy; all of these interactions are components of the service your mobile phone provider offers you.

There are a vast range of services across sectors that we use in our daily lives, from booking an appointment with a doctor, to going to the cinema, to posting a letter. In most businesses, these interactions with customers are handled by a number of different people and departments over time, and often this journey of interactions has not been consciously designed with human beings and our complicated lives and emotions in mind. Badly designed services have negative consequences: they cause people stress and worry, cost our economy, and are often to blame for lost customers.

As a service designer, you gather insights into people through human-centred approaches and methods and connect what may start as disconnected interactions into a coherent positive experience. You will often use an iterative design processes of idea generation, modeling and prototyping. The outcome of a service design process can have various forms: new organizational structures, a blueprint for an updated service offering, service experiences, and even physical objects.

What Does a Service Designer Do?

PROTOTYPE: MAKE THE INTANGIBLE TANGIBLE

Services are invisible. Therefore, a big part of your role is making the intangible tangible. Like an interaction designer, you **visualise and bring ideas to life**.

At a basic level this might be a **sketch, cartoon, wireframe, or storyboard**. The next level is visualising in a more three-dimensional way. The best way to understand a service is to try to build the physical part of it (the "touch points"). It's essential to get a feel for how something might work and **create something three-dimensional you can test with real people**. This could be in the form of a cardboard model of a mobile app, a Lego model of a scenario, or a mock advertising flyer.

A service designer prototypes elements of a service or an experience. The prototypes can vary greatly in terms of tone and complexity, but the common element is the capacity to test the service solutions being proposed in a "real-world" environment.

CO-DESIGN: DESIGN *WITH* PEOPLE AS OPPOSED TO *FOR* PEOPLE

Co-design is a core aspect of the service design philosophy. It involves anyone from service providers, staff from the wider organization, designers, executives, or customers working collaboratively to explore and innovate any given service. Co-design (closely linked to participatory design and co-creation) is an approach that enables clients and customers (or other people who use services) to **design services together** as one multidisciplinary design team. This approach is different than some other service improvement techniques because it is grounded in the belief that all people are creative and that people who use services, as experts of their own experiences, bring invaluable, different points of view that will inform a better solution. This approach can be used at any stage in the design process, but it adds the most value early on in the process during the research phase.

EMPATHY-LED RESEARCH

Service designers spend time conducting user research in order to understand the people they are designing for. During the discovery phase of the design process, service designers use a range of tools to understand the reality of a specific problem. From **in-depth interviews and observations** to **co-design workshops**, these tools help you and your team understand why people behave the way they do—and gather insights that will fuel the design of a product or service people really need.

Bringing deep customer insight into the organisation yields a potent fuel for teams to break through silos and align their efforts. The ultimate result is the shared understanding required to deliver experiences that engage, connect, and enable valuable customer relationships across channels.

Challenges

BEING IN A NEWER AND CONTINUALLY EVOLVING DISCIPLINE

Service design is relatively new among the various UX careers discussed in this book, and there are still debates going on about what skills are and are not parts of this career. Opinions vary across agencies and sectors.

As an evolving discipline, service design lacks a standard academic underpinning and a clear model of what constitutes good practice. Therefore, it manifests itself in a wide range of forms from simple customer journey mapping, to co-design workshops, to more complex service blueprints, and this is opportunistic but challenging for both clients and designers.

GETTING HIRED

In the public sector in the UK, there is no standard process for hiring service designers (also known as commissioning). Therefore, it's often difficult, costly, and inefficient for everyone involved. Similarly, in many countries, service design is still often perceived as an add-on that happens at the end of a process instead of an incremental process that fundamentally shapes the direction of any new product or service.

POTENTIAL JOB TITLES

- Service Designer
- Service Innovation Consultant
- Service design positions are also sometimes found with other design-oriented titles, such as Co-designer, Experience Designer, Interaction Designer, or UX Designer.

CAREER PATHWAYS THAT MAY BE COMBINED WITH SERVICE DESIGN IN JOB DESCRIPTIONS

- Interaction design
- User research and evaluation
- Customer experience

Ideal Training

A **bachelor's degree** is the minimum level of education you should have. A **master's degree** is not necessary but is often a plus when you are looking for jobs. Companies looking for service designers are typically going to be much more focused on experiences and backgrounds that show aspects of service design than a degree that is associated with a particular field of study. The core of service design is empathy, imagination, and pragmatism, and these skills can be gained from voluntary experiences and other alternative routes. Several institutions around the globe offer master's level training in service design, and several global design initiatives exist that anyone can take part in to expose themselves to the service design community and the relevant tools and methodologies.

Get more online at uxcareershandbook.com/service-design

Lauren Currie is co-founder of Snook, Scotland's leading service design and social innovation agency that uses design to make public services better. Management Today recently named her as one of the UK's top 35 business women under 35. Lauren is now leading the world's first MA in Digital Experience Design at Hyper Island, one of the world's leading creative business schools. Follow Lauren on Twitter @redjotter.

UX STRATEGY

By Jessica Peterson, Director of Digital Strategy and UX, GoHealth

As a user experience (UX) strategist, you are committed to the idea that an excellent UX drives value. You are deeply in tune with the business goals you know you can influence by engineering a delightful, usable, and enjoyable digital experience.

Although "strategist" job titles are sometimes found in entry-level positions for business graduates, the UX strategist role is most often a leadership position. You must be adept in the business skills of planning, prioritizing, and budgeting, but also understand the principles of a great UX. A UX strategist, like all other UX professionals, must convince others that putting users' needs first makes for better products and happier users, and potentially leads to a stronger market position. Your finely tuned investigative skills, honed as a UX practitioner, will be critical as you seek opportunities to tie your work directly to the bottom line of the business. Once you identify the most promising opportunities for UX improvements, you will begin building corporate support for the effort.

Whether working in-house at a company or consulting in an agency, as a UX strategist, you must pitch UX work to executives with compelling arguments based on hard financial data. For example, a UX strategist might build a business case for a large investment in a user-centered web redesign by convincing the business the engagement will produce significantly greater revenue in the first year after release and increase their customers' satisfaction.

Because the business looks to you as a strategic leader as well as an expert in UX, you must be able to envision the future of the experience for the products you work on. To close the gap between the current and future state of the UX, you'll identify the critical activities that are needed to move your business toward its ultimate goals. The activities you identify will likely draw on your skills and knowledge of research, design, content, and information architecture.

A solid UX strategy must address these questions:

- Who are the target users and how will they be using the products?
- What is the competition doing?
- What are our core business competencies?

What Does a UX Strategist Do?

IDENTIFY UX INITIATIVES THAT SUPPORT YOUR BUSINESS'S STRATEGY

As a UX strategist, you will use your strong interpersonal skills to interview important stakeholders about their goals and **identify key supporters of UX** within your business or your client's business. This will serve as the first phase of a **discovery,** or detailed research process that will underpin your UX strategy. You'll need to deeply understand the business strategy that your UX work will support, while uncovering the most important needs of the customers you serve. As a UX practitioner, you may not have deep knowledge of accounting, finance, or operations, but familiarizing yourself with these functions can add great strength to your proposals for the direction of experience design in your organization. In order to create a **UX strategy roadmap** that your business will readily support, you will need to have a good understanding of the project management resources required, the budget and staff you will have to work with, and any critical deadlines your roadmap will have to accommodate.

DEFINE A UX STRATEGY AND COMMUNICATE IT TO YOUR BUSINESS

When you have completed your initial discovery, including stakeholder interviews and fact-finding, and you have agreed on a basic budget and timeline, your next responsibility is to **define the UX strategy** that will help achieve the business's goals.

To create a viable UX strategy, you must understand the needs of the target audience very deeply. UX strategists often have user research knowledge and experience, and may work with user researchers or lead early-stage research efforts themselves.

To capture the information gathered during discovery activities and communicate a plan to the business, UX strategists and their teams may produce a number of **strategic deliverables**. A customer journey map, or **experience map**, is an artifact that visually represents the ecosystem of a user's interactions with a business. This map may take the form of a description of users' interactions and touch points with the current experience (sometimes called a service map) or it may illustrate the future state of the users' needs and wants for ideal interactions, with targeted recommendations for how the UX strategy will help users reach this ideal relationship. Mapping out user interactions visually and connecting them to the emotions and mindsets that influence users' behavior can be a powerful communication tool as part of your UX strategy. For instance, if the customer journey map shows frustration or low satisfaction when users interact with a certain part of the digital experience, it will strengthen your case for funding to improve this interaction.

A detailed **competitive analysis** that focuses on the user experiences offered by your chief competitors can help convince your stakeholders that you are an expert in the market they're trying to master. UX strategists often conduct a competitive analysis as part of their discovery in order to narrow in on any gaps in unique features or pain points in the digital experience that once improved can help your business differentiate and gain a UX-driven competitive advantage. And before any design work begins, UX strategists may help **create a design brief** that cites key elements of the strategy, helping ensure consistency in the audience the team will design for and the goals this new design should achieve.

Challenges

THINKING LIKE A CORPORATE LEADER

UX professionals who have worked as entrepreneurs, at a startup, or in a small business will already have a good sense of the priorities and challenges that corporate leaders face. However, many UX practitioners who come to UX strategy from a creative, design, or technology field have had lots of exposure to the inner workings of product development, but perhaps less exposure to the financial, operations, sales, and marketing aspects of running a business.

One challenge that some UX practitioners may face when choosing to move into a strategist role is how to develop the foundational business acumen they need to make an impact on strategy. Massive Open Online Courses (MOOCs) from the world's elite business schools are available for free online, and can help you shore up your knowledge of business fundamentals without a commitment to graduate school. For a more targeted, practical approach, some UX practitioners may find that shadowing the sales team is a good way to learn about what drives their business. If you can find out what targets the sales team is trying to meet, you can glean some insights into how a better UX might help them sell more, or deepen client relationships—and how this can expand revenue.

GETTING ACCESS TO FINANCIAL DATA AND BUSINESS METRICS

As a member of the UX team, you may not be invited to attend your company's weekly finance meetings. But as a UX strategist, you should work to build relationships with the finance team. Understanding your business's financial performance and how the money moves within your organization can be very helpful to understanding where UX work can make the biggest impact. Work with your manager or your executive sponsor to gain access to data that can be framed as useful, actionable metrics for your UX initiatives.

MAKING INROADS INTO OTHERS' TERRITORY

Strategy means taking a leadership role in deciding how UX initiatives will help a business meet its most important goals. This can be the principal challenge for many UX practitioners looking to move into a UX strategist role. In many businesses, senior leaders in marketing, technology, or operations often drive decisions about strategy. Therefore, as a UX strategist, you may find yourself encroaching on territory occupied by others. If you find yourself in this position, view it as an opportunity rather than a roadblock, and as a chance to use your people skills to improve business relationships. Success as a UX strategist can depend on your skill at being a change agent within your organization.

EXPLAINING THAT STRATEGIST DOES NOT MEAN GENERALIST

You may find yourself looking for UX strategy positions only to find that hiring managers are looking for junior UX generalists and decided that strategists was a better term for the job title. Or you may tell someone in your company that you are a UX strategist, only to learn that their initial assumption is that you are a UX generalist, doing a little bit of this and a little bit of that. Be ready to challenge these assumptions and explain your value as a strategist. It is always possible to think strategically about UX, even if your job title does not include "strategist"—keep persevering.

Ideal Training

A **bachelor's degree** is the minimum level of education you should have. An **MBA** can be a big asset in securing a position that is seen as a peer to the business strategists. Though not essential, it may help you create a strong cross-functional relationship between the business and the company's UX experts.

Valuable areas of study include any or all of the disciplines in the interaction design or user research career pathways. Useful coursework or training can include topics related to competitive analysis, product innovation, or marketing strategy. As a baseline requirement, you should have done some work (and/or professional or educational training) in one or more UX career pathways, such as user research, information architecture, or interaction design.

POTENTIAL JOB TITLES

- UX Strategist
- Strategic Planner
- Customer Experience (CX) Strategist
- Product Manager

CAREER PATHWAYS THAT MAY BE COMBINED WITH UX STRATEGY IN JOB DESCRIPTIONS

- User research and evaluation
- Information architecture
- Interaction design

Get more online at uxcareershandbook.com/ux-strategy

Jessica Peterson, Ph.D., is a UX strategist based in Chicago, IL. At GoHealth, she creates digital experiences that make complex decision-making easier for America's uninsured. She co-organizes ChiDUXX, a professional networking organization for Chicago women in UX. She also teaches and mentors students at @starterleague, a school to teach budding entrepreneurs core digital product design skills. She was named to Crain's Chicago Business Tech 50 in 2014, and has recently been featured by the Illinois Technology Association and Chicago Product Design. Follow Jessica on Twitter @jessability.

NOTES

1. Farrell, Susan and Jakob Nielsen. *User Experience Careers*. p.31 Nielsen Norman Group. http://www.nngroup.com/reports/user-experience-careers

2. David Kelley, a Stanford Professor and founder of IDEO, was instrumental popularizing the term "design thinking" and applying it outside an academic setting. http://en.wikipedia.org/wiki/Design_thinking#cite_note-8

3. Human Interface Design, including software design, recently came under the organizational leadership of Apple's long time industrial design head, Jony Ive. http://9to5mac.com/2014/04/09/jony-ive-shakes-up-apples-software-design-group-iphone-interface-creator-greg-christie-departing/

CHAPTER 12

Pathways to UX Leadership

If you want to get more out of your own user experience (UX) career than just a paycheck, and want to make a difference in the careers of others, consider a path towards UX leadership. As I've advanced in my career, and found myself in different types of leadership roles, I've become more and more aware of how many paths there are to UX leadership. Further, good UX leadership is such a critical need for our profession—both at work and outside of work.

My Own Leadership Pathway

LEADING SMALL TEAMS

For the first ten years of my career, I enjoyed my role as a UX practitioner without considering any real leadership responsibilities. At the end of that period, I started in a new role in a small UX consultancy, and with my years of experience in the field, I became responsible for leading junior staff members who would help me with project work. In addition, I became part of the company leadership team of four, which met periodically to discuss matters of corporate concern.

After I left that job, I took a one-year hiatus from anything that could be called leadership with another more typical UX practitioner role. The next year, in my only stint of in-house corporate work, I was given the title of Director and once again had a small team and a handful of contractors to manage, as well as occasional responsibility for hiring.

LEADING MY OWN COMPANY

I remember thinking to myself that to advance in my UX career, I was supposed to be managing larger and larger teams. But I decided my next step was to go out on my own full-time because it seemed like an exciting practitioner path forward to manage my own small business. This step gave me the vague feeling that I had taken a step backwards in being a leader, as my business was initially just me, even though I was joined later by two staff members and occasional sub-contractors. But I gradually came to realize that managing a company was simply a different kind of leadership, where I had to lead projects, develop and manage client relationships and sometimes client staff, manage schedules, and be responsible for my own employment destiny in a way that I had never experienced before.

LEADING OUTSIDE OF WORK

To this point in my career, I had only considered career leadership as something that one would get paid for. Right around the time I started my own company in 2008, however, I also got my first taste of a different kind of leadership. I was asked to help fill a vacant position and run for secretary of the UPA-DC chapter. I subsequently became extremely involved in volunteer professional organizational leadership, ending up as the president of UPA (switching mid-tenure to "UXPA") DC, and as a board member and then president of UXPA International.

Simultaneously, I began to realize that mentoring and helping others in their careers—through UXPA and in an ad hoc fashion—was also a form of leadership, as were giving talks and writing about UX.

This chapter is not just about getting you to think about leadership in the most stereotypical of corporate ways. Rather, I want you to realize that leadership can take many forms. Of course, if corporate leadership is right for you, go for it. But also consider the other types of UX leadership that might be right for you.

Let's now consider the many ways you can be a UX leader.

Leading in the Workplace

You can be a leader who makes things happen at work. You can do this either as an employee of a corporation or agency or by running your own business.

WORKPLACE LEADERSHIP   UX ORGANIZATIONAL LEADERSHIP   MENTORSHIP   THOUGHT LEADERSHIP

There are many ways to be a UX leader

LEADING AS PART OF A CORPORATION OR AGENCY

As an employee, you could be a project or product lead. Or you could lead a research or design team that works on many projects or products. Or you could be a leader who oversees staff with multiple skillsets that span multiple UX career pathways.

Just as we talked about abilities and interests at the beginning of Chapter 11, workplace leadership is also a combination of ability and interest. You could be really good at being a leader at your workplace, although your work-related leadership responsibilities may take you away from being a practitioner. Some UX practitioners really enjoy transitioning into a corporate leadership role as much as or even more than their previous UX practitioner role.

Whether you come to UX workplace leadership as a UX practitioner moving up or as someone with management experience outside of UX, you need to understand deeply what UX is all about, and you need to understand how UX practitioners' skillsets intersect with the overall project and product needs (whether that is one specific project or product, or many). Does that mean that you need to be a UX unicorn? No. While having a broad understanding of UX is important for everyone, especially for those who oversee projects that require multiple UX skillsets, you don't need to be an expert in practicing every type of UX.

This broad understanding of the field is also important if you are responsible for hiring others. Understanding how each of the Chapter 11 pathways fits into the broader cycle of development will help you better understand who you need to hire, and how to get them (as we discussed in Chapters 9 and 10).

RUNNING A UX BUSINESS

Beyond the projects and products, you could be involved with the day-to-day operations of running a UX-oriented business. Perhaps you could be a solo practitioner where you may work with sub-contractors or co-bid on a project with others. Or you may run a multi-person UX consultancy or agency that does work for others.

While some of the pure business operations matters may require very important non-UX skills, many of your business operations activities could be UX-oriented. For example, you could be involved in business development, which most certainly requires that you understand what your UX-oriented staff are capable of, how they do what they do, and how they can be valuable for future clients. When you bid UX work, you have to understand your clients' UX needs, their level of understanding of UX, how your work will fit with whatever in-house resources they have, and so on.

Leading within a Professional Organization

Having spent nearly a decade in volunteer leadership, both locally in the Washington DC area where I live, and also internationally—touching UX professionals all over the world, I certainly encourage you to get involved in volunteer organizational leadership at any level.

HELP OTHERS

There is a wonderful satisfaction that comes with creating events and establishing resources by leveraging the power of an organization or Meetup. Building on what we talked about in Chapter 4, you can become a leader of a professional organization or Meetup that already exists or, particularly

at a local level, create a new UX-oriented effort to fill a gap. Through your organizational efforts, you can see very directly how you are helping other UX professionals and the UX field as a whole as you promote learning, be it through speakers or perhaps a UX book club. Like a matchmaker, by creating networking opportunities, you can see directly how you have helped other UX professionals form connections with each other—connections that lead to well-matched jobs and new opportunities.

ENHANCE YOUR BRAND

While involvement in UX volunteer work is largely an effort to help others, it can also benefit you and your brand. Think back to Chapter 4 and personal branding. As a local UX leader, you are establishing yourself and your UX brand as a helper and a leader in the field, and as someone who values UX learning and the greater UX community.

You will be respected for your efforts. Your work in the UX community can make you stand out when applying for jobs. In Chapter 4, we established the value of networking for your UX career, and UX leadership is what I think of as the networking express train. You become very visible to many, many UX professionals, essentially broadcasting your brand and your existence as a UX professional much more than could happen through your paid work alone.

HOW CAN YOU GET STARTED WITH LOCAL ORGANIZATIONAL LEADERSHIP?

- **Look around for a local Meetup** or a chapter of a larger UX-oriented organization, and attend events to make sure that you find the organization and types of attendees a good fit.
- **Offer your services as a volunteer** to an existing organization. If you enjoy volunteering for the group, you can work your way up to bigger leadership roles in the organization.
- **If no UX group exists, create one**. You can contact one of the national/international groups that has local chapters and ask to start a local chapter. You may have to demonstrate sufficient interest initially, but in return, you may also have the help of useful infrastructure. Alternatively, create a local Meetup that is entirely independent of any larger organization. Meetup.com gives you lots of information to get started.

Mentoring

As we discussed in Chapter 1, UX is a hot field and it's hard to find qualified UX professionals to fill the number of open roles. Given the difficulty in filling roles, as we discussed in Chapter 10, keeping staff and helping them grow professionally and find workplace satisfaction is a critical business need. As the title of a good mentoring advocacy book says, in no uncertain terms, *"Help Them Grow or Watch them Go."*[1] Being a mentor directly, or fostering mentoring relationships, will ultimately not just help individuals, it will help the organization as well.

ENHANCE THE CAREERS OF OTHERS

In Chapter 3, we talked about the value of finding a mentor. If you are in a position or choose to put yourself in the position to *be* a mentor, you can be a UX leader. As a mentor, you are very personally helping and guiding less experienced UX professionals in their careers. You are not only paying it forward (or paying it back), you are also guiding the future of UX.

MENTOR ON OR OFF THE CLOCK

Mentoring can happen in the workplace or beyond. Whether or not you are a paid workplace mentor, consider finding opportunities to mentor others in the broader UX community. By establishing yourself in the local UX community and going to UX events, you'll get to know others who are newer to the field than you or who are looking for knowledge that you have. Consider something as simple as accepting offers to meet for coffee or a drink to listen to career stories and to give suggestions based on your own background and experiences. As your time permits, also consider establishing deeper mentoring ties—providing instruction and guidance to help others grow in the work efforts, or perhaps with a side project that you both might be interested in.

Being a Thought Leader

In Chapter 4, we talked about getting out there into the larger UX world for your brand and your career. By speaking or writing about UX topics, you are also engaging in thought leadership. You are helping to advance the profession, and your words could touch other UX professionals and help them with the learning that we talked about in Chapter 3.

You can also combine thought leadership and mentoring by helping others become thought leaders. You can help others advance their careers, brands, and professional credibility, for example by reviewing articles, blog posts or talks from others before they are published or presented. You may also co-write or co-speak with those that have less experience as thought leaders than you do.

Two UX leaders Talk About Leadership

While I've talked about my own leadership experiences and used those experiences as a frame for the many ways that you can be a UX leader, I have also had many opportunities to talk with other UX leaders who have had different types of leadership experiences. Michael Rawlins and Kevin Lee have both been corporate in-house UX leaders of large teams, and they now share their own stories and lessons learned. Although their stories are both framed by their corporate experiences, their reflections include a lot of good advice that applies to anyone managing people, projects, or perhaps a team of volunteers in a UX organization.

UX LEADERSHIP: INHERITING AN EXISTING TEAM OR BUILDING ONE FROM SCRATCH

By Michael Rawlins, Principal User Experience Design Architect, ESPN

In your first UX leadership role, you will likely find that you've either inherited an existing UX team or you're being asked to build one from scratch. I've done both. I've been fortunate in my career to manage UX resources in technology startups and Fortune 100 companies, as well as expertly branded institutions like ESPN. Based on my own experiences through the years, here are some tips on what has worked (and why).

INHERITING AN EXISTING TEAM

At a Fortune 100 financial services company, I inherited several UX practitioners to drive a companywide consumer site branding and sub-site consolidation strategy. The previous

UX leader had a solid vision. However, my approach was new and different. It was challenging to ensure buy-in from my business partners while firefighting the fallout from a significant change in direction for the incumbent UX team members.

From that experience, I took away some keys to leadership success when coming into an existing practice:

- **Deal with objections head-on**. Communicate, and be empathetic but decisive.
- **Replace people who cannot adapt to new approaches.** (They can kill a team.)
- **Concentrate on your business customer's needs.** (All will fall into place once you secure buy-in.)
- **Provide a concrete vision.**

Getting recruited into leadership from outside of a company—or getting promoted from within—can be rewarding and exciting. Expect a very short honeymoon phase and ramp-up period. Both your staff and management will be waiting for signs of your vision and direction.

It's important to determine:

- How mature and established is the existing practice?
- How engaged and "bought in" are the stakeholders (senior management, clients, development partners)?
- What are the team's strengths, weaknesses, threats, and opportunities?
- How does the company make decisions (adoption cycle and risk tolerance)?

These factors will affect your ability to quell fears and generate excitement, loyalty, and curiosity. Gain insights into how your stakeholders make decisions so that your ideas and practice methods don't stall. Be transparent with your processes and agendas, and make friends with your peers who are running other teams. And most importantly, know that you will make mistakes (get over it) and lean into your vision.

BUILDING A NEW UX TEAM

A new leadership role may be particularly daunting if you're asked to build a new practice, particularly if this challenge comes with key stakeholders wondering what "UX" actually means for their company. I have been fortunate to build a few practices where I've ensured adoption and sustained growth by doing the following:

- **Secure a high-level executive advocate early on.** Find someone who has the ability and fiduciary level authority to make corporate change. Your ability to secure this executive sponsorship enables you to surface your arguments early and often. It also provides early insight into the financial forces that drive organizational decisions.

- Think like a leader, and ethically **influence your stakeholders with your UX persuasive skills.**
- **Brand yourself and your team as collaborative and innovative.** You'll have other leaders taking you to lunch asking for your secret success formula.
- **Avoid using UX jargon** to make your points. Speak the language of the business.
- **Seek practice partnership from other disciplines** that have been recently adopted (and try to take a page from their playbook).
- **Try to hire employees who are more skilled than you are**, and seek diversity in the employees that you hire.

Finally, whether you are coming into an existing practice or starting one from scratch, be sure to lead strategically, with purpose—and align your objectives and the practice to projects that mean something to the corporation.

Michael Rawlins is the Principal User Experience Design Architect for ESPN (The Walt Disney Company) in Bristol, Connecticut. He also serves as the Vice President of the User Experience Professionals Association International. He is a leader in analyzing the global marketplace for growth and technical innovation opportunities. He has led teams at companies such as Cigna, Open Solutions/FiServ, MassMutual, Hartford Life, and Aetna. Michael also is an instructor at Manchester Community College (MCC) in Manchester, Connecticut. He serves on several technology and industry boards, including the MCC Technology and Communications Advisory Board.

ITERATIVELY IMPROVING YOUR WORKPLACE LEADERSHIP

By Kevin Lee, Vice President, Head of Design, VISA

While transitioning from being a rookie UX designer to a leader was a big professional leap, it was also a roller coaster experience for me. I started out with a "my way" attitude that ended up shutting out others' good ideas. It took some time before I realized that being a leader is about **listening to and embracing the creative ideas that come from your team.**

I eventually learned that I needed to apply the same user-centered design principles that guide product development to my leadership approach. I now continue to **iterate, refine, and improve my leadership skills**. I am constantly looking at my team's reactions to my leadership, and when I realize that something doesn't work, I tweak my method.

Initially, for example, I tried to use a "one-size-fits-all" communication style with all of my designers at eBay. But when this brought about unintended negative reactions from my staff, I realized I needed to modify my communication style.

Be aware, however, that willingness to iterate your leadership style will only be as effective as your ability to **maintain an open and honest feedback loop with your team.**

Finally, if you want to be an effective leader of UX teams, you need to **lead your team by example.**

- **Use your UX skills and knowledge** in creative problem solving.
- Respectfully **identify and articulate stakeholders' needs.**
- **Be proactive in reviewing your team's products early in the process** so that you can quickly identify problems and offer solutions.
- **Be on time** with your own deliverables to your team.

Being a true leader of people in the workplace is more than just a position title. It's something you need to work at and to improve day by day.

Kevin Lee is Vice President and Head of Design at Visa, Inc, responsible for the overall design and UX of all digital products, in addition to driving key strategic initiatives. Previously, Kevin led the design studio at Samsung responsible for overall product strategy and open innovation strategy as well as for launching wearable products. Kevin also led the global design team at eBay and PayPal, and he launched several key products such as checkout, shopping cart, and shopping showcase. He has also been responsible for managing the UX design studio at Whirlpool Corporation and leading a cross-functional design team at GE Healthcare.

Be a Leader and Make a Difference!

As you progress in your career, you can decide whether managing projects, product development efforts, or people might be a good pathway for you. If it fits with your abilities and inclination, then by all means, consider moving into this kind of workplace leadership. But do not feel that this is the only way to be a UX leader and advance your career. Many well-respected UX professionals have made a solid career out of being UX practitioners.

Whether you are a mentor at your workplace or outside of it, or are involved in UX leadership outside of your workplace entirely, know that you are a leader making a difference. You are helping UX professionals advance their careers and knowledge, and this results in a stronger UX field and community that will be better able to meet the UX challenges of the future.

Get more online at uxcareershandbook.com/leadership

NOTE

1. Kaye, Beverly and Julie Winkle Giulioni. *Help Them Grow or Watch Them Go: Career conversations employees want.* Berrett-Koehler Publishers, Inc. San Francisco, 2012.

Conclusion

CHAPTER 13

UX in the Future; Your Career Today

I was participating in a user experience (UX) careers panel discussion and someone in the audience asked: "So, what is the next big thing, and how will that impact UX careers in the future?" This is a great multi-faceted question, so while I gave a brief answer at the panel discussion, to answer this question more fully I turn to Jonathan Follett, author of *Designing for Emerging Technologies: UX for Genomics, Robotics and the Internet of Things*.

The Next Big Thing(s)

By Jonathan Follett, Principal, Involution Studios

The uptake of emerging technologies into both consumer and business applications is happening at an almost frighteningly fast rate. While there will remain a strong ongoing need for screen-based software design and UX, there are increasingly other areas of technology emerging that will require UX as well.

UX is moving beyond the screen, facilitating human interaction with new technologies, and helping to incorporate those new products into our lives. Such new technologies include:

The Internet of Things (IoT): The sensor-laden, connected network of objects and environments, collectively referred to as the IoT, promises to facilitate better understanding of and optimization for everything from the manufacturing process, to rush hour traffic flow, to home entertainment, to heating, cooling, and lighting for building systems.

Wearables and Smart Clothing: These wearable products incorporate sensors into everyday objects on our bodies, like wristbands, watches, sweaters, jackets and glasses, in order to monitor personal health and other metrics, communicate with others, and otherwise interact with information.

Robotics: Robots can take up some of the difficult, dangerous, and repetitive tasks for people, but they will need strong interaction design to work in concert with humans, especially in key areas like manufacturing and healthcare.

Genomics: With its promise of highly personalized medicine, tailored to the specific person and disease, and its seemingly endless potential for improving our understanding of human traits, genomics has the potential to significantly affect the entire healthcare industry. However, the *personal* side of personalized medicine will require long-term, intricate interactions that UX is well positioned to guide. For example, the services that surround genomic sequencing and personalized medicine require ongoing organizational relationships that can last for a patient's entire lifetime. Those interactions, between patients, systems, and the technology of genomics—from initial testing to the creation of personalized pharmaceuticals—must navigate uncharted territory and will require much design work.

Synthetic Biology: The capability to design nature itself makes synthetic biology a most powerful emerging technology. From bio-fuels to bio-inspired materials to 3D printed organs, the products and services that lie within the realm of synthetic biology will require strong design thinking alongside scientific and engineering considerations.

Your Professional Future

There's no doubt that the UX field will continue to evolve to meet the needs of new technologies, so be prepared to evolve in your career as well. Certain skills and experiences will enable you to navigate a changing world more easily:

Learn constantly: We may take for granted the need to learn new things on a day-to-day basis in our jobs, but a systematic approach to ongoing education and training is a must for continuing success, whether it be learning new technologies, new techniques, or even whole new approaches. Being curious, building a personal library, and treating learning as a discipline, not as a byproduct, is key. Previous generations may have been able to learn one set of skills and then refine them over a lifetime of work at just one company, but this is no longer the norm.

Work at a variety of scales: For a UX practitioner, when it comes to product design, being able to both see the big picture and drill down into the details is critical. In software, for instance, this manifests itself in a need to understand both the raw data, which dictates what information can be displayed by a system, as well as the overall context for the use of the software itself, which explains why a person might need to see that information in the first place. The same is true for emerging technologies from genomics to robotics. As a UX professional you'll need to fully understand everything from the materials to the human and business aspects that contribute to a product.

Work across disciplines: The ability to work in cross-pollinated teams—made up of diverse disciplines from biology to engineering, business to architecture—will increasingly become important as UX and software become embedded into many more aspects of our day-to-day lives. If you're involved in UX for medical devices, wearables, robotics, or automobiles, you're probably lucky enough to work in a multi-disciplinary team already.

Be flexible: Being able to manage change and transfer your UX skill sets to another area—perhaps from software to synthetic biology—may be one of the greatest assets you can acquire as you move forward in your career. Consider having a long-term high-level concept of where you might go that can help to frame career change and avoid potentially boxing yourself in.

The hybrid jobs of the future have only just begun to surface. Designing for UX will be needed at the intersections of synthetic biology and computer science, the IoT and architecture, and even robotics and medicine, to name just a few of the possibilities for emerging technologies. Whether you pursue any of these new areas as you evolve in your career, it's clear that UX holds much promise as a key field for integrating new technology into human life.

Jonathan Follett is a principal at Involution Studios where he is a designer, business lead, and internationally published author on the topics of UX and information design. His most recent book, *Designing for Emerging Technologies: UX for Genomics, Robotics, and the Internet of Things*, was published by O'Reilly Media in December 2014. Over his 15-year design career, he has contributed to beautiful, usable software for enterprise, healthcare, and emerging technology clients, from the Fortune 500 to the market leaders of the future. Jonathan is a classically trained pianist who dreams of one day having a family rock band with his two sons. Follow Jonathan on Twitter @jonfollett.

The Here and Now

While the future is exciting to think about, let's focus back to the present day and think about what we've covered and what you now know. You know that you are in an amazing and exciting field. UX is hot across the globe, and your job prospects are bright. So what should you do now to carry yourself into the future of UX, both near and far?

You have to learn. Learning is so important that it earned two chapters devoted to this topic. And as Jonathan pointed out, no matter what the next big thing is, if you keep learning, you will be better positioned to handle it. Get a college degree, consider if graduate school makes sense, attend professional development classes, and learn from your peers with lectures, conferences, mentoring activities, and conversations.

Brand yourself as a UX professional. No matter where you are in a job-hunting process, you need to start this branding right now. If someone looks you up online, they need to see a UX professional. Take advantage of the tremendous power of social media platforms like Twitter and LinkedIn, and build your UX network, ideally with in-person participation in meetups and UX activities.

To get a job today or years from now, you have to illustrate your value through a resume that shows and frames your UX skills and experiences, as well as a portfolio that tells the story of who you are through deliverables you have produced. To be ready, sharpen your resume and make it available, and keep your portfolio updated, even if you are not looking for a job at the present time.

Know yourself and consider your long-term goals when deciding to go for an in-house job, a consulting agency, or even going out on your own. Dissect those career postings carefully, and make things easy on yourself by creating your own UX job board. Consider if recruiters may be able to help you as well.

There are so many pathways by which you can be a UX professional, and your skillset represents something unique and special even while fitting into one or more of those career pathways. Don't aspire to be a UX unicorn, particularly early in your UX career; instead, choose your superpowers.

Strive to be a UX leader; there are many routes to leadership, on the job or outside of it. Be a mentor and help other individuals in their careers too, or be a UX community leader, and by volunteering your time, you can help create something that will help UX professionals across your geographic region or country, or maybe the world.

You can be something amazing. The power to further your career lays within you. And as you flex your career muscles and you practice and you learn, you will become better and stronger in your career and in the larger UX community. In making the most out of your UX career, you will be helping the people you interact with, the companies you work for, and ultimately, the users of the products you work on. And you will have made a difference.

Good luck. Stay in touch and let me know how it goes.

Cory Lebson

cory@lebsontech.com | www.lebsontech.com | @corylebson | linkedin.com/in/lebson

---

Get more online at uxcareershandbook.com/future

Index

Entries in *italics* indicate figures.